Football Supporters and the Commercialisation of Football

As football clubs have become luxury investments, their decisions increasingly mirror those of any other business organisation. Football supporters have been encouraged to express their club loyalty by 'thinking business' - acting as consumers and generating money deemed necessary for their clubs to compete at the highest levels. In critical studies, supporters have been portrayed as passive or reluctant consumers who, imprisoned by enduring club loyalties, embody a fatalistic attitude to their own exploitation. As this book aims to show, however, such expressions of loyalty are far from hegemonic and often interface haphazardly with traditional ideas about what constitutes the 'loyal fan'. While there is little doubt that professional football is experiencing commodification, the reality is that football clubs are not simply businesses, nor can they ever aspire to be organisations driven solely by expanding or protecting economic value. Rather, clubs hover uncertainly between being businesses and community assets.

Football Supporters and the Commercialisation of Football explores the implications of this uncertainty for understanding supporter resistance to, and compromise with, commodification. Every club and its supporters exist in their own unique national and local contexts. In this respect, this book offers a Euro-wide comparison of supporter reactions to commercialisation and provides unique insight into how football supporters actively mediate regional, local and national contexts, as they intersect with the universalistic presumptions of commerce.

This book was previously published as a special issue of *Soccer and Society*.

Peter Kennedy lectures in the Sociology of Sport and Health at Glasgow Caledonian University. His most recent published work is in applying sociological theories to understanding health and medicine and football supporter responses to commercialisation.

David Kennedy is Visiting Lecturer and Researcher at Glasgow Caledonian University. His most recent published work is in the area of football supporters and governance of professional football clubs.

Football Supporters and the Commercialisation of Football
Comparative Responses across Europe

Edited by
Peter Kennedy and David Kennedy

LONDON AND NEW YORK

First published 2013
by Routledge
2 Park Square, Milton Park, Abingdon, Oxon, OX14 4RN

Simultaneously published in the USA and Canada
by Routledge
711 Third Avenue, New York, NY 10017

First issued in paperback 2017

Routledge is an imprint of the Taylor & Francis Group, an informa business

© 2013 Taylor & Francis

This book is a reproduction of *Soccer and Society*, vol. 13, issue 3. The Publisher requests to those authors who may be citing this book to state, also, the bibliographical details of the special issue on which the book was based.

All rights reserved. No part of this book may be reprinted or reproduced or utilised in any form or by any electronic, mechanical, or other means, now known or hereafter invented, including photocopying and recording, or in any information storage or retrieval system, without permission in writing from the publishers.

Trademark notice: Product or corporate names may be trademarks or registered trademarks, and are used only for identification and explanation without intent to infringe.

British Library Cataloguing in Publication Data
A catalogue record for this book is available from the British Library

ISBN 13: 978-1-138-05817-0 (pbk)
ISBN 13: 978-0-415-61890-8 (hbk)

Typeset in Times New Roman
by Taylor & Francis Books

Publisher's Note
The publisher would like to make readers aware that the chapters in this book may be referred to as articles as they are identical to the articles published in the special issue. The publisher accepts responsibility for any inconsistencies that may have arisen in the course of preparing this volume for print.

Contents

Series Pages vii
Citation Information xi

1. Football supporters and the commercialisation of football: comparative responses across Europe
   Peter Kennedy and David Kennedy 1

2. Football stadium relocation and the commodification of football: the case of Everton supporters and their adoption of the language of commerce
   David Kennedy 15

3. Football fans and clubs in Germany: conflicts, crises and compromises
   Udo Merkel 33

4. Split loyalties: football is a community business
   Hans K. Hognestad 51

5. From 'socios' to 'hyper-consumers': an empirical examination of the impact of commodification on Spanish football fans
   Ramón Llopis-Goig 66

6. Supporters Direct and supporters' governance of football: a model for Europe?
   Peter Kennedy 83

7. Walking alone together the Liverpool Way: fan culture and 'clueless' Yanks
   John Williams 100

8. From community to commodity: the commodification of football in Israel
   Amir Ben Porat 117

Index 132

SPORT IN THE GLOBAL SOCIETY – CONTEMPORARY PERSPECTIVES

Series Editor: Boria Majumdar

FOOTBALL SUPPORTERS AND THE COMMERCIALISATION OF FOOTBALL

Comparative Responses across Europe

Sport in the Global Society – Contemporary Perspectives
Series Editor: Boria Majumdar

The social, cultural (including media) and political study of sport is an expanding area of scholarship and related research. While this area has been well served by the *Sport in the Global Society* series, the surge in quality scholarship over the last few years has necessitated the creation of *Sport in the Global Society: Contemporary Perspectives*. The series will publish the work of leading scholars in fields as diverse as sociology, cultural studies, media studies, gender studies, cultural geography and history, political science and political economy. If the social and cultural study of sport is to receive the scholarly attention and readership it warrants, a cross-disciplinary series dedicated to taking sport beyond the narrow confines of physical education and sport science academic domains is necessary. *Sport in the Global Society: Contemporary Perspectives* will answer this need.

Titles in the Series

Australian Sport
Antipodean Waves of Change
*Edited by Kristine Toohey and
    Tracy Taylor*

Australia's Asian Sporting Context
1920s and 1930s
Edited by Sean Brawley and Nick Guoth

'Critical Support' for Sport
Bruce Kidd

Disability in the Global Sport Arena
A Sporting Chance
Edited by Jill M. Clair

Diversity and Division – Race, Ethnicity and Sport in Australia
Christopher J. Hallinan

Documenting the Beijing Olympics
*Edited by D. P. Martinez and
    Kevin Latham*

Fan Culture in European Football and the Left
*Edited by Peter Kennedy and
    David Kennedy*

Flame Relays and the Struggle for the Olympic Movement
Bearing Light
John J. MacAloon

Football in Brazil
Edited by Martin Curi

Football Supporters and the Commercialisation of Football
Comparative Responses across Europe
*Edited by Peter Kennedy and
    David Kennedy*

Football's Relationship with Art: The Beautiful Game?
John E. Hughson

SPORT IN THE GLOBAL SOCIETY: CONTEMPORARY PERSPECTIVES

Forty Years of Sport and Social Change, 1968-2008
"To Remember is to Resist"
Edited by Russell Field and Bruce Kidd

Global Perspectives on Football in Africa
Visualising the Game
Edited by Susann Baller, Giorgio Miescher and Raffaele Poli

Global Sport Business
Community Impacts of Commercial Sport
Edited by Hans Westerbeek

Governance, Citizenship and the New European Football Championships
The European Spectacle
Edited by Wolfram Manzenreiter and Georg Spitaler

Indigenous People, Race Relations and Australian Sport
Edited by Christopher J. Hallinan and Barry Judd

Olympic Reform Ten Years Later
Edited by Heather Dichter and Bruce Kidd

Perspectives on Sport and Music
Edited by Anthony Bateman

Reflections on Process Sociology and Sport
'Walking the Line'
Joseph Maguire

Soccer in the Middle East
Edited by Issam Khalidi and Alon Raab

South Africa and the Global Game
Football, Apartheid and Beyond
Edited by Peter Alegi and Chris Bolsmann

Sport – Race, Ethnicity and Identity
Building Global Understanding
Edited by Daryl Adair

Sport and the Community
Edited by Allan Edwards and David Hassan

Sport, Culture and Identity in the State of Israel
Edited by Yair Galily and Amir Ben-Porat

Sport in Australian National Identity
Kicking Goals
Tony Ward

Sport in the City
Cultural Connections
Edited by Michael Sam and John E. Hughson

Sport, Memory and Nationhood in Japan
Remembering the Glory Days
Edited by Andreas Niehaus and Christian Tagsold

The Changing Face of Cricket
From Imperial to Global Game
Edited by Dominic Malcolm, Jon Gemmell and Nalin Mehta

The Consumption and Representation of Lifestyle Sports
Edited by Belinda Wheaton

The Containment of Soccer in Australia
Fencing Off the World Game
Edited by Christopher J. Hallinan and John E. Hughson

The History of Motor Sport
A Case Study Analysis
Edited by David Hassan

The Making of Sporting Cultures
John E. Hughson

SPORT IN THE GLOBAL SOCIETY: CONTEMPORARY PERSPECTIVES

The Olympic Movement and the Sport of Peacekeeping
Edited by Ramón Spaaij and Cindy Burleson

The Politics of Sport
Community, Mobility, Identity
Edited by Paul Gilchrist and Russell Holden

The Politics of Sport in South Asia
Edited by Subhas Ranjan Chakraborty, Shantanu Chakrabarti and Kingshuk Chatterjee

The Social Impact of Sport
Edited by Ramón Spaaij

Towards a Social Science of Drugs in Sport
Edited by Jason Mazanov

Twenty20 and the Future of Cricket
Edited by Chris Rumford

Who Owns Football?
The Governance and Management of the Club Game Worldwide
Edited by David Hassan and Sean Hamil

Why Minorities Play or Don't Play Soccer
A Global Exploration
Edited by Kausik Bandyopadhyay

Women's Football in the UK
Continuing with Gender Analyses
Edited by Jayne Caudwell

Women's Sport in Africa
Edited by John Bale and Michelle Sikes

Citation Information

The chapters in this book were originally published in the *Soccer and Society*, volume 13, issue 3 (May 2012). When citing this material, please use the original page numbering for each article, as follows:

Chapter 1
Football supporters and the commercialisation of football: comparative responses across Europe
Peter Kennedy and David Kennedy
Soccer and Society, volume 13, issue 3 (May 2012) pp. 327-340

Chapter 2
Football stadium relocation and the commodification of football: the case of Everton supporters and their adoption of the language of commerce
David Kennedy
Soccer and Society, volume 13, issue 3 (May 2012) pp. 341-358

Chapter 3
Football fans and clubs in Germany: conflicts, crises and compromises
Udo Merkel
Soccer and Society, volume 13, issue 3 (May 2012) pp. 359-376

Chapter 4
Split loyalties: football is a community business
Hans K. Hognestad
Soccer and Society, volume 13, issue 3 (May 2012) pp. 377-391

Chapter 5
From 'socios' to 'hyper-consumers': an empirical examination of the impact of commodification on Spanish football fans
Ramn Llopis-Goig
Soccer and Society, volume 13, issue 3 (May 2012) pp. 392-408

Chapter 6
Supporters Direct and supporters' governance of football: a model for Europe?
Peter Kennedy
Soccer and Society, volume 13, issue 3 (May 2012) pp. 409-425

Chapter 7
Walking alone together the Liverpool Way: fan culture and 'clueless' Yanks
John Williams
Soccer and Society, volume 13, issue 3 (May 2012) pp. 426-442

Chapter 8
From community to commodity: the commodification of football in Israel
Amir Ben Porat
Soccer and Society, volume 13, issue 3 (May 2012) pp. 443-457

Football supporters and the commercialisation of football: comparative responses across Europe

Peter Kennedy and David Kennedy

School of Business for Society, Glasgow Caledonian University, Glasgow, Scotland

> European football market finances appear to be in very good health and impervious to the current Euro-wide financial crises. Yet beneath the apparent financial buoyancy a different story emerges, one of fan exploitation, spiraling debt and the threat of bankruptcy hanging over many clubs. In this introduction to the special issue we chart what is effectively a political economy of debt underpinning the European football market and threatening to bring professional football in Europe into disrepute. Against this backdrop the paper considers the impact financial exuberance and systemic debt has had on fans' identification with clubs. It is argued that whilst football fans have borne the social and economic costs of weak governance and lack of financial regulation, which have become the hallmark of European football, they have also shown themselves to be highly resistant to the commercialisation of football and innovative in their responses to this commercialisation.

Writing in his organisation's Annual Review of Football Finance in June 2010, Dan Jones, partner in the Sports Business Group at Deloitte, commented:

> European football's continued revenue growth demonstrates an impressive resilience to the extremely challenging economic times – underlying the continued loyalty of its fans and the continued attractiveness of football to sponsors and broadcasters.[1]

With economic performance in the European Union running at a negative-to-stagnant growth rate, the continued expansion of the European football market at 8% per annum meant that Jones' boast was not without substance. The first decade of the twenty-first century has witnessed market growth from €8 billion per annum in revenue to almost €16 billion per annum, powered by the so-called 'big five' leagues in England, Germany, Spain, Italy and France (Figure 1).[2] The English Premier League, Germany's Bundesliga, Spain's La Liga, Italy's Serie A and the French Ligue 1 are five of the six most highly supported leagues in world football (only Mexico's Primera Division is able to compete with Europe's elite leagues). In terms of the whole of world sport, only the US National Football League and Indian cricket's Premier League can boast higher average attendances than the best attended European football league, the Bundesliga.[3] The big five together attracted almost €12 billion in television rights deals in their last round of negotiations with media groups. Their commercial revenue, boosted by corporate sponsorship, amounts to €2–3 billion annually,[4] and Europe's flagship tournament, the UEFA Champions League, is now

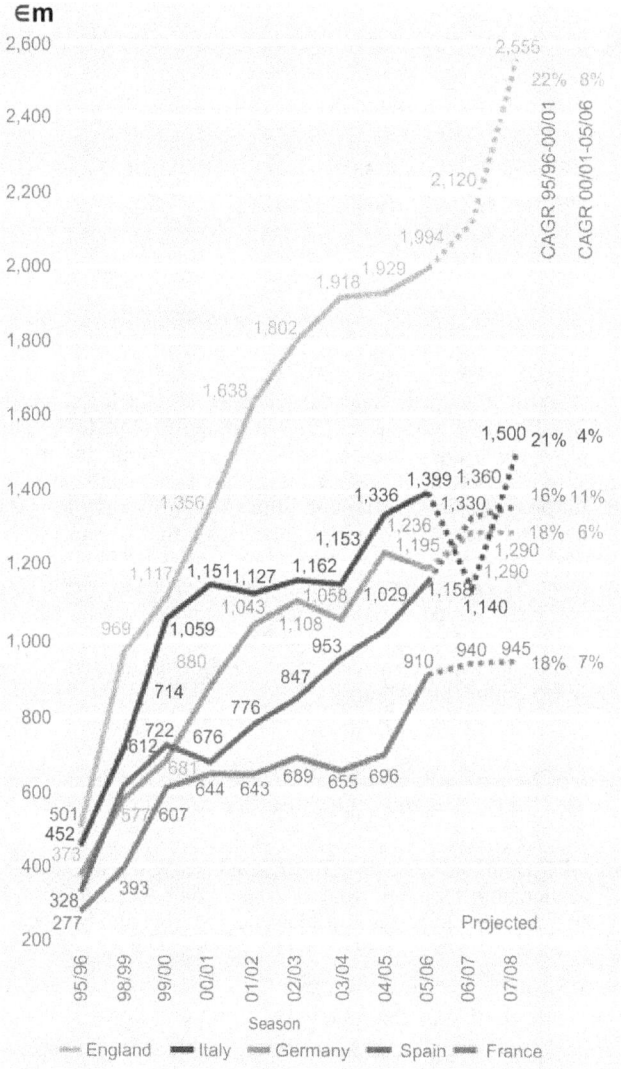

Figure 1. Revenue growth of the 'big five' European leagues – 1995/1996 to 2007/2008
Source: Deloitte Annual Review of Football Finance 2007.

confirmed as the ultimate competition in global club competition. With a worldwide audience of more than four billion viewers per season, the viewing figures for the Champions League final now surpass that of the NFL's Superbowl. The European football governing body, UEFA, receives over €500 million in broadcasting and sponsorship deals for the Champions League.[5]

While such headline figures point toward a sector in rude health, some commentators take the view that focusing on them is 'akin to complementing a man in intensive care for having a full head of hair'.[6] A more forensic examination of the state of European top-flight football reveals another, very different picture: one of debt, bankruptcy, a loss of competitive balance, and a barely concealed resentment of fan exploitation. The enormous riches pouring into European football may have produced an unrivalled spectacle of top-class players from around the globe producing football of the highest standard, played out in state-of-the-art stadiums, but this has been accompanied by instability in the game. Top-division clubs in Europe have run up bank debt and commercial loans of €5.5 billion; 32% of clubs are in negative net equity (that is, their debts are larger than their reported assets); costs consistently outstrip income; and competitive balance has been diminished both between leagues (88% of the all-important revenue generated from European-wide broadcasting goes to the big-five leagues) and within leagues (the four largest teams in each top European division have on average four times the income of their domestic opponents).[7] Though the financial spoils resulting from success are immense, the cost of failing to achieve success – realistically the only outcome for the vast majority of clubs – can be catastrophic. As one commentator puts it:

> ... the face of European football is contorted by the strain experienced by clubs attempting to remain on a financial tightrope which is constantly being yanked by their competitors. It's as simple as this. Clubs need to be successful if they are to prosper. But to be competitive they have to invest in player transfers and wages which, all too often, they are unable to afford. For all but the biggest clubs, every season represents a gamble. For those whose gambles do not pay off the result is relegation, reduced income and the prospect of severe financial difficulty. It's a kind of financial Russian roulette.[8]

Casting an eye around the various European leagues hammers the point home. In the first decade of the twenty-first century unsustainable debts drove a number of clubs to financial ruin or the brink of it. Italian clubs AC Fiorentina (2002), AC Parma (2003) and SSC Napoli (2004) were declared bankrupt, later to re-emerge under slightly different identities after spells in the lower Italian leagues. In Holland, bankrupt HFC Haarlem had their 121-year existence terminated in 2010, and BV Veendam were declared bankrupt in the same year. The case of Alkmaar Zaanstreek ('AZ') underlines the seriousness of the situation in Holland: Eredivisie Champions in season 2008/2009, the club was being run by administrators by 2009 as a result of its main sponsor, DSB Bank, being declared bankrupt.[9] The seriousness of financial woes in the Eredivisie prompted the Dutch Football Association, the KNVB, to seek a pledge from each participating Eredivisie club before the 2010/2011 season declaring that they had enough cash to reach the end of the season. In Spain, clubs in La Liga are saddled with enormous levels of debt. Between them, Barcelona and Real Madrid have debts totalling almost €1 billion (a level of debt anchored by the two clubs' ability to generate enormous commercial deals), while Valencia CF's debt is more than €600 million and Atlético Madrid has debts in excess of €300m. Traditionally, Spanish clubs' debts have been underwritten by the local state or by regional banks. When Sporting Gijón went into administration their 'brand image' was bought by the municipal authority in order to rescue the club. As one Sporting Gijon insider put it: 'The council could not let us disappear; Gijón without Sporting is not Gijón.'[10] However, this is a system coming under increasing pressure as the global recession continues to bite. More recently, RC Celta Vigo filed for voluntary insolvency, and Real Sociedad and Levante have also gone into administration. Unable to find a backer to take on its debts, RCD Mallorca went into voluntary administration in 2010, and the Spanish FA have threatened RC Deportivo La Coruña with demotion from La Liga because of their financial conduct. The English Premier League generates both the greatest amount of revenue in European football and its greatest levels of debt. The total debts of its member clubs stood at just under €4 billion in 2010, anchored by huge television broadcasting deals and the fact that – unlike in most other European leagues – clubs own their own stadiums and are able to borrow against this asset. This has not, however, prevented high-profile cases of financial failure when clubs have taken on unsustainable levels of debt in their attempt to fulfil competitive ambitions: Leeds United FC – Champions League semi-finalists in 2001 – went into voluntary administration in 2007; West Ham United FC narrowly avoided bankruptcy in 2009 when their holding company, Hansa Holdings, went into administration; and most recently Portsmouth FC filed for administration after running up €160 million in debt. The problem of debt is not confined to the continent's premier leagues. Further down the pyramid, lower league clubs, attempting to make the breakthrough into more financially lucrative divisions, are equally susceptible to insolvency. In the summer of 2010, for example, 20 Italian clubs from Serie B, Prima Divisione and Seconda Divisione were declared bankrupt and prevented from competing in their respective divisions.[11]

The loosely regulated path that football has taken has brought with it socioeconomic consequences for football fandom. The massive expansion in football finances is driven, directly and indirectly, by the commercial exploitation of a 'brand loyalty' that generates money from fan allegiance to football clubs nurtured over generations. The emphasis is upon the *consumption* of football, through expertly targeted merchandising that exploits communal identity and the adoption of an exorbitant pricing policy for watching football, both in terms of matchday tickets and of pay-per-view broadcasting. And, of course, through such participation fans help to create the spectacle that attracts commercial sponsorship. Fan allegiance is seen as elastic. If existing stadia cannot churn out the required revenue, supporters can be shunted to new locations and new stadia which *can* improve the club's finances; if a club is not considered to be viable from a commercial perspective, it can be merged with local rivals. Even in the teeth of an economic recession fan identity is a rich seam that revenue-hungry clubs are eager to mine. For instance, the traditional moderately priced ticket to watch matches in the German Bundesliga – a reasonably well regulated league in comparison with others across Europe – has come under threat from successive price hikes and the introduction of premium-game surcharges. German supporter groups fear a situation will develop in which young and lower-income fans will be squeezed out of match attendance and a process of 'gentrification' of German football, similar to the process witnessed in the English Premier League in the past years, will be set in motion.[12]

As the commercial ethic penetrates further into the game, a sense that the social value of football is beginning to be ground down by financial imperatives has caused alarm. UEFA's president, Michel Platini, has spoken of an

> explosion of sectoral and corporate interests at both league and club levels in all team sports that are played professionally. These initiatives, which often attract enormous media coverage, are designed to benefit one element, particularly if it is powerful and rich, rather than the masses. Attempts are made to reduce a discipline into a show, to demean a sport in order to convert it into a product. It is becoming more important to make a profit than to win trophies.[13]

An institutional response to this 'reductionism' – with the European Union and UEFA at the vanguard – has been forthcoming. In 2005, under the auspices of the

United Kingdom's presidency of the European Union, sports ministers from Britain, France, Germany, Italy and Spain set up a working group to provide the European Union with a sports model which enshrines in European law the principles contained in the Nice Declaration (2000), which underlines 'the social, educational and cultural functions inherent in sport'. For their part, the sports ministers concentrated attention on the issue of fair competition and, with respect to this, on professional football; this was reflected in the addition to the steering group of Sepp Blatter, the general secretary of world football's governing body, FIFA, and Lennart Johansson, then chief executive of European football's governing body, UEFA. The outcome of that meeting was the setting in motion of an Independent European Sport Review (IESR), which the ministers commissioned Portugal's former deputy prime minister, José Luis Arnaut, to carry out. In May 2006 Arnaut produced his report, *The Independent European Sports Review* (IESR). Arnuat concluded:

> Sports in general and football in particular are not in good health. Only the direct involvement of political leaders, working together with the football authorities, can put it back on the road to recovery... there is a real risk that the ownership of football clubs will pass into the wrong hands, the true values of the sport will be eroded, and the public will become increasingly disaffected with the 'beautiful game'.[14]

He presented a series of recommendations aimed at curbing and controlling the commercial excesses that have been viewed as bringing professional football in Europe into disrepute. Arnaut recommended a fit and proper persons test for all potential owners of football clubs – principally as a means to deter the use of European clubs as money-laundering operations. He also suggested the need for a *salary cap* for players as an important step toward securing a competitive balance between clubs. The Report also called for the issue of player-trafficking to be addressed, with Arnaut in favour of stricter controls on the licensing of football agents. A more even distribution of wealth generated by the game was also a key element of the report. To this end it was argued that 'central marketing' of the game (that is, national leagues collectively bargaining with TV companies over the sale of image rights to televise matches) is the most suitable vehicle through which to begin to bridge the gap in income between top clubs and others. The ultimate objective of these recommendations was to 'provide a comprehensive and robust legal framework' for football's governance which allowed UEFA the authority to take a forceful lead on these issues, free from vested commercial interests' threats of legal challenges to their efforts in the European Court.

One of the most eye-catching statements made by Arnaut with respect to football's governance is that supporters should have a greater say in the running of the clubs they support. Arnaut stated that a 'properly structured supporter involvement will help to contribute to improved governance' of football clubs.[15] The report highlighted the work carried out by Supporters Direct in Britain, an organization which aids the foundation and development of football supporters' trusts committed to the principle of mutual ownership of shares in football clubs. The report, noting the absence of a pan-European body representing the interests of supporters that UEFA could enter into structured dialogue with, advocated enquiries into the feasibility of 'rolling out' the British Supporters Direct model at a European level (while taking into consideration the different club ownership models that exist across Europe). In 2009 a joint UEFA/Supporters Direct report was published, entitled *What is the Feasibility for a Supporters Direct Europe?*[16] Most recently of all – effective from the 2013/2014 season – is UEFA's directive imposing financial fair play regulations across its member associations.[17] Seeking to curb the big spending that has been the catalyst for many bankruptcies, UEFA are now insisting on a so-called 'break-even' requirement that will compel clubs not to spend more than the income that they receive. Clubs will also have to ensure they pay liabilities promptly rather than building up vast mountains of debt.

The various new reforms are, in essence, no more than measures for sustainable spending and rational business plans which have been advocated for a long time by 'industry' experts – UEFA's requirements are an intervention on these grounds, rather than relying on often unforthcoming clubs and individual associations to self-regulate and bring about financial discipline.[18] However, this and other interventions into football governance by legislative bodies are promulgated along the lines of a plan to combat an existential threat to the game. Speaking to the European Parliament in 2008, Michel Platini commented:

> Two key aspects make the European model of sport both unique and completely fair: the financial solidarity between the different levels of European sport and the openness of competitions... Any attempt to undermine these two elements would sound the death knell of the fundamental relationship that exists between sport and society in our continent.[19]

This view is shared in much of the critical literature, where the future of football is portrayed in terms of a struggle to determine its primary role as either an economic or a community asset. The debate is usually framed in terms of the ongoing commodification of football:

> that process by which an object or social practice acquires an exchange value or market-centered meaning... involving the gradual entry of market logic to the various elements that constitute the object or social practice under consideration.[20]

Overall, the ascendant view within this literature would appear to suggest that football has become, or is in the process of becoming, a business, and that the relationship between football clubs and their supporters is becoming narrowly defined in terms of producer and consumer.[21] While there is little doubt that professional football, as with professional sports in general, is experiencing commodification, the reality is that football clubs are not simply businesses, nor can they ever aspire to be organizations driven solely by the desire to expand or protect economic value. Football's desire to be seen as a community asset based on local identities and traditions, on the one hand, and its pretensions to be a business on the other hand, contradict each other and rest on an uneasy compromise. Clubs hover between this ontological uncertainty: between being businesses and being community assets.

The collection

The aim of this collection of studies is to render the implications of this uncertainty for an understanding of football supporters' resistance to, and compromise with, commercialization. Moreover, football clubs and their supporters exist in their own unique national and local contexts, making some clubs/fans more or less prone to being drawn into the commercial pressures sweeping through professional football. In this respect, a European-wide study can offer us a comparison of the variety of reactions to commercialization and a vantage point from which to understand what is happening within the European game at this moment.

To begin, David Kennedy's contribution uses the vehicle of English Premier League club Everton FC's attempts to relocate to a new stadium as a means to examine supporters' attitudes toward commercialization and the changing nature of football communities. In December 2006 the board of directors at Everton Football Club declared their intention to explore the possibility of moving from Goodison Park, Liverpool, their home since 1892, to a new stadium in Kirkby in the nearby borough of Knowsley. The proposed move was hugely controversial for Everton supporters. During the course of the Everton stadium dispute Kennedy carried out and published research which attempted to cast light on the variety of different viewpoints concerning the club's proposed move, in an effort to draw out the complexity of the fans' opinions regarding the relocation of the club. In particular, he sought to assess the balance of forces among supporters, between those who could be described as *traditionalists* (or 'cultural conservatives') and those defined by a *market-led* attitude. Football fans' behaviour toward the commercial strategies of club owners has usually been framed in terms of either accommodation with or resistance to the commodification of professional football. However, the author rejected, on the basis of his findings, any thesis assuming either the inexorable process of commodification *or* fierce resistance to this process, suggesting instead that the reality is somewhat more complex and nuanced. Overall, the evidence presented pointed toward supporters pragmatically adapting to commercial *rhetoric*, simply to press their case: fans from both sides of the stadium relocation debate deployed the language of commercialism in order to support or undermine the business case for the move. In later research – which forms the basis for his chapter in this study – it was found that the language of commerce had become even more influential among fans, evidenced by varying degrees of willingness to fuse the needs of business with notions of football club tradition. Intrigued by the softening of attitudes toward commercialism, Kennedy sets out here to provide a theoretical understanding of this development by utilizing Jürgen Habermas' concept of a struggle between the *systems world* and the *life world* (with the former tending to colonize and corrupt the latter). By enlisting this concept, the author provides an explanation of events in terms of the attempted superseding of one 'common sense' view of football community (in which supporters accept a pragmatic accommodation to commercial pressures – though, crucially, this is mixed with an outright rejection of their identification as consumers or customers) with another 'common sense' view of that community (a new configuration of motives and ideas that advance commercialization, in which a supporter's sense of moral ownership of the club has been weakened by the diktats of concern for its competitive resources and financial health).

We continue our study with a chapter concerning football governance in Germany. Drawing on a number of interviews with fans and industry commentators, supplemented by a wide range of secondary sources, Udo Merkel provides an account of the attempted bourgeoisification of football in the *Bundesliga*, contextualizing the movement toward greater commercialization of German football by highlighting traditional football communities' stubborn resistance to the process. Deploying Antonio Gramsci's theory of hegemony, Udo argues that the struggle over the direction football has taken in Germany cannot be viewed in isolation from the wider debate about social-class relationships in that country. He concludes that, despite the shift toward a greater commodification of the game in Germany, the scope for democratic involvement of fans in the control of the game there remains strong relative to other major European leagues.

The onset and intensification of commerce within German Football were reflective of the changes occurring in the wider political economy, arising from corporate and media interests in the mid-1960s, and eventually ruptured the hegemonic hold of amateurism over football authorities clubs and their wider fan base, through which the upper and middle classes were able to retain their dominance over the direction of elite football in Germany. However, while money poured into football, rationalizing the number of clubs, making the remaining clubs into corporate-backed business entities and breaking player wage barriers, German clubs have never been the target of takeover bids from foreign capitalists with apparently unlimited supplies of money. Commercialization here was based on homegrown capital and was more susceptible to fan resistance. German football may have become increasingly commercialized, but it still remained a German affair, involving German players, fans, corporations and media. Those who had commercial interests in the club (such as corporate patrons, advertisers and media) were highly sensitive to fan loyalty. When many fans 'voted with their feet', staying away from football grounds in the early 1970s and again in the early 1980s in response to rising ticket prices and the growing social and cultural gap between fans and 'overpaid players', clubs reacted quickly by introducing corporatist measures (for example, by regulating the ticket market and encouraging a closer relationship between players and community). In the early 2000s the reliance of German football on German capital, this time in the form of the media group Kirchsport (a business entity that owned the broadcasting rights to the top two German league matches), proved again to be fragile. When the media corporation went bankrupt in 2001 clubs were forced to slow down and reverse the pace of commercialization, drawing them closer to their community of fans once more. The author describes how a second wave of fan resistance came in response to other aspects of commercialization, namely the commercially friendly environment of the new stadia that have emerged in recent decades and the resultant new middle-class fan base. Working-class fans' resistance took symbolic forms: using dress codes and national flags, and emphasizing solidarity with the traditional values of the football fan. The close relationship between clubs and communities meant that this resistance was transformed into clearly defined political stances – perhaps the most obvious example of this is to be found in the close-knit subculture of fans of FC St. Pauli of Hamburg, where wider social issues, such as opposition to racism, homophobia and fascism, have informed and fuelled resistance to the 'corporate takeover' of German football.

In his chapter, Amir Ben Porat provides an outline of the historical shift in the structure of Israeli football, from what are seen as political preoccupations among the game's governing bodies in that country to the embracing of entrepreneurial forms of governance and a greater emphasis on clubs' independence from national federation constraints. This movement, Amir argues, mirrors the development of Israeli state economic policy away from central control and toward the embrace of a free-market economy. 'The story of football's commodification in Israel', he explains, 'is understandable only in the context of the history of Israeli society'. With respect to this, he presents the evolution of football in Israel – the move away from its roots as a 'community project' toward a privatized form of sport – in the form of a series of phases of commodification.

The game's early impetus in Israel in the post-World War Two period came from the auspices of general sports federations organized around political groupings from across the political spectrum: from the Labour Camp on the left, to the right-wing Zionist parties. Football clubs in the early period of the game's history in Israel were closely associated with the political ideology of their founding members; strictly amateur affairs, they were reliant on municipal patronage for the financing of their efforts. From the 1950s, football in the country went through a series of stages in a move toward greater commercialization of its operations. The move toward the greater commodification of football in Israel begins with the disintegration of amateurism – first with the advent of semi-professionalism in the 1960s and 1970s, and later with full-blown professionalism. The breach was initially made with Israeli players turning professional with clubs outside of Israel. Gradually, the national associations became powerless to stave off the clamour for an internal market for players amongst competing domestic clubs. One of the main reasons for the incremental movement toward an accommodation with professionalism was the political nature of football in Israel. The social glue that the game provided for the new state, integrating a variety of groups – from established Israeli citizens, to new immigrants from different countries, to the local Arab population – meant that the modification of control over club/player relations was a price worth paying. Another reason was the pressures being exerted on old political allegiances by changes taking place within the economy.

Professionalism in football was encouraged and enabled by deregulation of the state economy, which reached a critical stage during the 1980s with the increased privatization of traditional areas of state activity. These changes are argued to have been responsible for the transformation of views of Israeli football, from its being seen as a community asset toward acceptance of the sport's being within the orbit of commodified social relations. This changing state of affairs was manifest in the increasing power and independence of Israeli League clubs *vis-à-vis* the sports federations that traditionally enjoyed control over them. In basic terms: the role of the public sector within the game shrank, and with it any vestige of non-commercial influence. Amir concludes his historical analysis of the growing commodification of Israeli football by assessing its impact on Israeli football fandom. More particularly, he assesses what he sees as key differences in outlook among fans created through this repositioning of the Israeli game.

Hans K. Hognestad's chapter analyses trends in football fandom in his native Norway. In Scandinavia, and more especially in Norway, football fans have for many decades developed allegiances to overseas clubs parallel to those with their local team. The huge levels of transnational support for English clubs in Norway which has gathered pace since the 1990s is of particular interest for the understanding of the globalization and commodification of football. Hans examines the extent to which fan identity has fallen victim to the type of cultural homogenization that is said to accompany the expansion of international capitalism, marked by the advent in football of *transnational networks* (that is, the rise to prominence of fan identification across borders with dominant foreign and commercially successful football leagues and their pre-eminent clubs) and, on the other hand, the ways in which fans have resisted this process through the maintenance of traditional local identities that evolved through football support. The author concludes that the contestation of identity is far more complex than is offered by these polarities, however. Although a multitude of media platforms are devoted to bringing a highly commodified global football 'product' into our lives (not least through the market dominance of the English Premier League), and although football discourse is facilitated and structured by capitalist corporations, fan experiences and practice are always charged with a particular, local content, and an ongoing tension exists between global forces and the particular or local. Hans argues that it is increasingly difficult to find convincing arguments for making a general division between the domestic (or what the author describes as 'thick solidarity') and the transnational (or 'thin solidarity') in football fan identity.

Ramon Llopis-Goig provides us with a study that looks at the changing landscape of Spanish football in the context of the process of commodification of the country's social and economic life. Traditionally, the Spanish game has been analysed in scholarly studies in terms of either the effects of crowd violence or the nationalist and regionalist implications of Spanish clubs. Latterly analysis has also stretched to include gender issues (and the process of constructing masculinity, in particular) and there has been a spate of studies dealing with racism and xenophobia, both of which have blighted the Spanish game in recent years. Little attention, however, has been given to studying the effect on fans of the rapidly expanding influence of commercialization on Spanish football. Helping to remedy the paucity of coverage in this respect, Ramon carries out an empirical study of fans of Valencia FC and Levante UD. In particular, a discourse analysis is carried out on interviews conducted with fans of the two clubs, which seeks to unpack opinions concerning club ownership and perceptions of the effects of increased commodification on football fan culture. The conclusion drawn is that by and large, the process of commodification has not affected fans' feelings of identification with their clubs. The author argues that 'hyper-consumption' *has* been generated – to a great degree via intensification of football information in the media. This has in turn led to an intensification of the 'entertainment-festive dimension' of match attendance at stadiums. However, this is accompanied by a sense of symbolic ownership of their clubs among the fans interviewed – a situation in no small part driven by paternalism, the local roots of the majority of the clubs' presidents and the strong pull of the clubs as totems of regional identity. A growing contradiction exists, therefore, between Spanish football's role as part of an entertainment industry that produces great enthusiasm among the fans, and this enthusiasm's coexistence with an uneasy feeling about the dangers of the course that has been embarked upon.

The penultimate chapter in the collection comes from Peter Kennedy, who examines the role of Supporters Direct, a football initiative set up by the British government in 2000 as a way of intervening in the unequal relationship that exists between the relatively powerless supporters of football clubs and the private shareholders who have organizational control of clubs. Primarily, the focus of Supporters Direct has been facilitating the establishment of mutual forms of ownership at football clubs by offering a helping hand in setting up supporters' trusts. Although the empirical element of the study is chiefly concerned with a critique of the performance of Supporters Direct as it has influenced British football, there is a European dimension to it in that the model has been given the backing of the European football governing body, UEFA, which is encouraging its rolling out across other European leagues. Offering a Marxist political economy of football that gives priority to the unstable commodity structure of the football business, the aim of Peter's contribution is to question the assumed progressive nature of Supporters Direct and reveal an alternative view of that organization: that it is an integral part of a social policy aimed at the preservation and extension of commodified social relations. Peter argues that there is a contradiction at the heart of the supporters' trust movement, its 'levelling' ideology being counterbalanced by a willingness to be utilized for commercial purposes by the football club hierarchies that the trusts seek to replace – a contradiction that, if one is concerned with attempts at formulating a more democratic governance for the game, ought to be considered with care before the Supporters Direct model is rolled out beyond the United Kingdom and into mainland European leagues.

The final contribution is from John Williams. The analysis of the ongoing Liverpool FC ownership struggle forms the backdrop to his contribution to the collection. In the midst of the high finance drama played out between competing billion-dollar consortiums seeking to gain control of the Merseyside club, a grass-roots movement has emerged through fan groups such as Share Liverpool and the Spirit of Shankly supporters' union. In his chapter the author seeks to highlight attempts by organized Liverpool fans to both come to terms with the commercial realities faced by a global force like Liverpool FC *and* to reinforce a moral economy by preserving what are seen as non-negotiable, traditional values underpinning and defining the organization.

Conclusion

The major purpose of this book is to describe and analyse supporters' reactions to the commercialization of football in Europe. What we discover is that the process of commercialization is uneven, as are the resulting tensions between football as both culture and business, and as both community asset and economic commodity. What the book demonstrates is how supporters contextualize and respond to these tensions within local histories, which ensures that any examination which adopts over-arching processes, such as neoliberalism, in an attempt to understand the commercialization of football must consider how they are pulled out of shape, altered and reconfigured by the embrace of local politics, social habitus and tradition. Hence we find plenty of examples where the relationship between football fans and clubs is characterized by a high degree of resilience, vitality and unpredictability – the fans' opposition has a rebellious and subversive quality and has helped to force a large number of compromises on the other side.

And yet, the volume also finds evidence that the fragile business status of the football club increasingly exposes supporters to the game's rampant commercialization. It is certainly the case that this exposure has diverse consequences for supporters. Nevertheless, as this book explores, it can drive supporters more firmly into the language of commerce, as they feel there is no way out except to support their club's fight to stay in the business and 'compete' with other clubs with much bigger 'asset bases'. There is little irony in the fact that it is often the strong sense of moral and symbolic ownership internalized by supporters that makes them just as susceptible to the promises of economic redemption and a future laced with success proffered by hostile or friendly takeovers as they may be to the guile of paternalism and the local roots of club owners.

The volume considers how on the one hand, commercialization can tend to incite supporters' interest and fascination with their club. As the club spins through an uncertain and heady cycle of change (owners, staff, players, sponsors all come and go in the search for success), the one abiding relationship remains that between fan and club. Hence the club becomes a reference point for supporter identity in a fast-changing and unstable environment. It also considers how on the other hand, supporters often react to the same commercial forces in very different ways – for example, becoming football nomads; tourists, disillusioned with their local club, lured by the consumer choices offered by the mediatization of football.

Notes

1. Deloitte: 'European football market grows to €15.7 billion'.
2. Europe's 'big-five' total league revenue (combined matchday, commercial and TV revenue) 2010:
English Premier League €2.3 billion
Bundesliga €1.6 billion
La Liga €1.5 billion
Serie A €1.5 billion
Ligue 1 €1.0 billion
The big five leagues are followed in terms of revenue generation by the Dutch Eredivisie (€422m), the Russian Premier League (€352m), the Turkish Super Lig (€342m) and the Portuguese Liga (€256m). To underline the gulf, the English Football League Championship (English football's second tier) is bigger in revenue terms than any of these leagues (€440m). See https://www.deloitte.com/view/en_RU/ru/press/029abc-deb4959210 VgnVCM100000ba42f00aRCRD.htm
3. Average attendance in 2009/2010: Bundesliga 42,000; Premier League 34,000; La Liga 30,000; Serie A 27,000 average; Ligue 1 20,000. See *European Football Statistics*. Attendances will rise in France and Italy over the coming years if the planned stadium improvements in those two nations go ahead: see fourfourtwo.com, 'New Stadiums Not a Cure for All Italians'; Ligue1, 'Stadium Development: France's Sporting Renaissance'. For the Bundesliga international comparison see EA.com., 'Bundesliga Has Third-Highest World Attendance'.
4. Leading the way is the English Premier League: the total value of the Premier League's current broadcasting rights deal, including the overseas packages – a market the English game has had particular success in compared with their largest European rivals – stands at €4.3 billion. EPL figs based on exchange rate of £1 = €1.2 as per time of writing. See 'Deloitte Annual Review of Football Finance 2010'. The current Bundesliga contract – relatively modest in comparison with the other leagues in the big five, given the attraction of the German League for fans and sponsors – is €1.65 billion. Legal restrictions on pay-per-view contracts are currently under review, however, with leading figures in the German game such as Bayern Munich president, Karl Heinz Rummenigge, pushing for greater broadcasting options that could see the Bundesliga's revenues from this quarter soar: see Goal.com, 'The more profitable Bundesliga has a brighter future than the debt-riddled Premier League, say analysts'; see also 'Rummenigge rejects Bundesliga TV idea, calls for better rights deal'. With no collective bargaining in La Liga, Real Madrid and Barcelona dominate the revenue from television agreements. Both clubs signed a deal with Grupo Mediapro in 2006 that expires in 2013. Real Madrid's contract is worth €1.1 billion and Barcelona's €1 billion: see 'Real Madrid, Barcelona Face Pressure on Television Deals'. Serie A will receive a total of more than €1 billion from the new collective TV rights: see 'Serie A Likely to be Back in Black on TV Boost'. In Ligue 1, the Ligue de Football de Professionnel reached an agreement with Canal+ and Orange over four seasons for €2.75 billion: see '"Everyone Gains" on Rights Issue'.
5. www.bbc.co.uk, 'Champions League Final Tops Superbowl for TV Market'.
6. The Telegraph, 'Deloitte's Picture of Football Shangri-La Not Enough to Fool Top Clubs'
7. 'The European Football Club Landscape', UEFA Report, February 2010. The most comprehensive financial review ever undertaken by the body, the report surveyed 732 top-division clubs across all European leagues.
8. Cuttler, 'Big Debate: Football's Finances'.
9. AZ owner Dirk Scheringa is also DSB Bank's owner. In 2006, Scheringa, who had financed the club with the bank's money and allowed a €67 million club debt to amass,

decided to change that debt into club shares. When DSB Bank went bankrupt the administrators naturally turned their attention to the club. See 'Dutch Clubs Still Facing Financial Peril'.
10. *The Guardian,* 'Domination by Barcelona and Real Madrid making Spain the new Scotland'.
11. FIFPro, 'Crisis hits hard: 20 Italian clubs dissolved'.
12. When Saturday Comes, 'German Fans Fighting Bundesliga Price Rises'; see also BBC Sport, 'German Club Fans Set for Boycott'.
13. UEFA, 'Platini Plea for Values'.
14. *Independent European Sports Review* 13–4.
15. *Independent European Sports Review,* 72–3.
16. However, sustaining the approach of Supporters Direct within the context of continental Europe is, by the organization's own admission, fraught with difficulty. Different countries have distinct sporting and legal systems, making share ownership – the cornerstone of supporter trusts – not the most logical way to deal with governance issues. It is the case also that some organized fan groups value non-involvement in club affairs, preferring to keep their independence and integrity, which could be compromised by being part of the ownership and command structure of a football club. See 'Supporters Direct Keeps the Faith in Fan Ownership Despite Setbacks'.
17. 'UEFA Club Licensing and Financial Fair Play Regulations 2010'.
18. From Deloitte's Annual Review of Football Finance 2010: '…we appear to be seeing a continuing shift from a sustainable "not for profit" model towards one with potentially calamitous consistent and significant loss making characteristics… On many occasions we have hoped that increased revenues would facilitate a move towards a more rational approach but, in a classic example of competitive game theory, clubs are continually driven to maximise wages rather than profitability.' See Deloitte, 2–3.
19. 'Platini Plea for Values'.
20. Giulianotti, 'Supporters, Followers, Fans, and Flaneurs'.
21. Nash, 'Contestation in Modern English Professional Football'; Hudson, J. 'Critically Examining the Commercialisation of English Football'; Crolley and Hand, *Football, Europe and the Press*; Giulianotti,. 'Sport Spectators and the Social Consequences of Commodification'; Robinson, 'The Business of Sport'.

References

BBC. 'The EUFA Champions League Marketing'. http://www.ekospor.com/Sports-Marketing/Sport%20Marketing%20uefa.pdf.
BBC. '*Champions League Final Tops Superbowl for TV Market*'. http://news.bbc.co.uk/sport1/hi/football/europe/8490351.stm, January, 2010
BBC Sport. 'German Club Fans Set for Boycott'. BBC Sport. http://news.bbc.co.uk/sport1/hi/football/eng_prem/8986321.stm
Bloomberg.com. 'Real Madrid, Barcelona Face Pressure on Television Deals'. Bloomberg.com. http://www.bloomberg.com/apps/news?pid=newsarchive&sid=adpXdkd1hMgk
Crolley, L., and D. Hand. *Football, Europe and the Press*. London: Routledge, 2002.
Cuttler, M. 'Big Debate: Football's Finances'. SportBusiness.com. http://m.sportbusiness.com/print-edition/big-debate/big-debate-football-finance
Deloitte. 'Real Madrid Remains Top of the Football Money League as Sterling's Slide Puts Brakes on English Clubs'. https://www.deloitte.com/view/en_RU/ru/press/029abcdeb49592 10VgnVCM100000ba42f00aRCRD.htm
Deloitte. 'Deloitte Annual Review of Football Finance'. Deloitte. http://www.deloitte.com/view/en_GB/uk/industries/sportsbusinessgroup/sports/football/0a4be867d38f8210VgnVCM200000bb42f00aRCRD.htm
EA.com. 'Bundesliga Has Third-Highest World Attendance'. EA.com. http://forums.electronicarts.co.uk/real-football/871558-bundesliga-has-third-highest-average-world-attendance.html
Earthtimes.org. 'Rummenigge Rejects Bundesliga TV Idea, Calls for Better Rights Deal'. Earthtimes.org. http://www.earthtimes.org/articles/news/340308,calls-better-rights-deal.html
European Football Statistics. http://www.european-football-statistics.co.uk/attn.htm

FIFPro. 'Crisis hits hard: 20 Italian clubs dissolved'. http://www.fifpro.org/news/pdf/366
Fourfourtwo.com. 'New Stadiums Not a Cure for All Italians'. Fourfourtwo.com. http://fourfourtwo.com/news/italy/40596/default.aspx
Giulianotti, R. 'Supporters, Followers, Fans, and Flaneurs: A Taxonomy of Spectator Identities in Football'. *Journal of Sport and Social Issues;* 26 (2002): 25–46.
Giulianotti, R. 'Sport Spectators and the Social Consequences of Commodification: Critical Perspectives From Scottish Football'. *Journal of Sports and Social Issues* 29 (2005): 386–410.
Goal.com. 'The More Profitable Bundesliga has a Brighter Future than the Debt-riddled Premier League, say Analysts'. http://www.goal.com/en-gb/news/2890/world-cup-2010/2010/06/26/1996144/the-more-profitable-bundesliga-has-a-brighter-future-than
The Guardian. 'Domination by Barcelona and Real Madrid making Spain the New Scotland'. The Guardian. http://www.guardian.co.uk/football/blog/2010/mar/28/barcelona-real-madrid-spain
Hudson, J. 'Critically Examining the Commercialisation of English Football: A case for Government Intervention?'. *Sociology of Sport Online* 4, no. 1 (2001): 181–98.
Independent European Sports Review (final version, October 2006). http://www.independent-footballreview.com/doc/Full_Report_EN.pdf
Ligue1.com. '"Everyone Gains" on Rights Issue'. Ligue1.com. http://www.ligue1.com/actualiteLFP/lireArticle.asp?idArticle=9664
Ligue1.com. 'Stadium Development: France's Sporting Renaissance'. Ligue1.com. http://www.ligue1.com/ligue1/lireArticle.asp?idArticle=16407
Robinson, L. 'The Business of Sport'. In *Sport and Society*, ed. B. Houlihan, 2nd edition London: Sage, 2008.
Reuters.com. 'Serie A Likely to be Back in Black on TV Boost'. Reuters. http://football.uk.reuters.com/leagues/seriea/news/2010/08/23/LDE67M0ED.php
Nash, R., 2000. 'Contestation in Modern English Professional Football: The Independent Supporters' Association Movement'. *International Review for the Sociology of Sport* 35: 465–86.
Soccernet. 'Dutch Clubs Still Facing Financial Peril'. ESPN. http://soccernet.espn.go.com/columns/story?id=753098&cc=5739
Supporters Direct. 'Supporters Direct Keeps the Faith in Fan Ownership Despite Setbacks' Supporter Direct. http://www.guardian.co.uk/football/blog/2009/oct/14/supporters-trust-uefa-david-conn; http://www.supporters-direct.org/downloads/pdfs/SDEurope-Full-Report.PDF
The Telegraph. 'Deloitte's Picture of Football Shangri-La Not Enough to Fool Top Clubs'. The Telegraph. http://www.telegraph.co.uk/sport/football/european/7408059/Deloittes-picture-of-footballs-financial-Shangri-La-not-enough-to-fool-top-clubs.html
UEFA. 'Platini Plea for Values'. UEFA. http://nl.uefa.com/uefa/aboutuefa/organisation/president/news/newsid=649269.html
UEFA. 'UEFA Club Licensing and Financial Fair Play Regulations 2010'. UEFA. http://en.uefa.com/MultimediaFiles/Download/uefaorg/Clublicensing/01/50/09/12/1500912_DOWNLOAD.pdf
UEFA. 'UEFA Report'. http://www.uefa.com/MultimediaFiles/Download/Publications/uefaorg/Publications/01/45/30/45/1453045_DOWNLOAD.pdf
When Saturday Comes. 'German Fans Fighting Bundesliga Price Rises'. When Saturday Comes. http://www.wsc.co.uk/content/view/5756/38/

Football stadium relocation and the commodification of football: the case of Everton supporters and their adoption of the language of commerce

David Kennedy

Glasgow Caledonian University, Glasgow, Scotland

> To what extent have supporters surrendered to the view that football is just another business to be understood in terms of the power of money? This question is posed by looking at the recent debate between supporters of Everton Football Club concerning their club's proposed ground move from Goodison Park, Liverpool to Kirkby in the neighbouring Metropolitan Borough of Knowsley in Merseyside. What comes to the fore is the tension between fans manifested in the contradictory ways supporters are now approaching the game: at once concerned with football as an emotional asset *and* mindful that, as a business, their club must place heavy emphasis on commercial strategies. We posit the point of view here that an emerging *commonsense* appears to be eroding the traditional feelings of emotional solidarity between supporters in their collective attachment to the club whilst encouraging more individualistic, instrumental and quantifiable forms of attachment. The findings are contextualized by drawing on the work of Jürgen Habermas, in particular his concept of a 'systems world' colonizing and corrupting the 'life world'.

English football clubs pride themselves on their home ground being central to their heritage and identity. Stadiums are viewed in emotional terms that one usually associates with places of religious worship. In recent years this view has had to give way, particularly in the English Premier League, to a more secular, even calculative view of stadia. Clubs are now given to viewing stadia as fundamental to generating revenue and developing the club 'brand'. New stadiums are now seen to offer a springboard for clubs to create partnerships with other 'market-players' across various industries, such as finance, leisure, entertainment and tourism. One Premier League club after another has upped sticks and decamped to a new stadium. In 2007, Deloitte estimated that '[t]otal stadia investment by English clubs since 1992/93 is now well into its third billion – with £2.2 billion spent up to the end of the 2005/06 season...', suggesting that '... stadium investment can deliver a significant element of a successful club business strategy'.[1]

The owners of Everton Football Club have taken this rationale on board in recent years and have sought to move away from Goodison Park – their home since 1892. Their most recent effort to leave the current stadium was a (heavily criticized) proposal to move to a new stadium in the town of Kirkby, on the outskirts of the City of Liverpool. We have detailed in studies elsewhere the trajectory of the club's attempt to move away from its long-time home at Goodison Park to Kirkby and have offered a detailed account of the struggle for and against this among Everton's fan base.[2] In this chapter, however, we are more centrally concerned with retracing the controversy surrounding that dispute and, in a more general sense, what the Everton stadium dispute highlighted in terms of supporter attitudes to the commercialization of English Football. In what follows, we first describe Everton supporters' reaction to an article we submitted to one of their main fan websites, with a view to tracking changes in supporter attitudes to commercialization. Our argument within that paper was that the language of commercialization is gaining ground in supporter discourse. We then sought fans' responses on this proposition via a forum debate.

Later in the chapter we seek to contextualize our findings from the forum debate by drawing on the work of Habermas – in particular, his concept of 'system' and 'life' worlds. The chapter begins, though, with an overview of the Everton board of directors' rationale for the move, and the timescale involved.

Background

In December 2006 the board of directors at Everton Football Club declared their intention to explore the possibility of moving from Goodison Park, Liverpool – their home since 1892 – to a new stadium in Kirkby, in the nearby borough of Knowsley. The club entered into an exclusivity deal with prospective partners Knowsley Borough Council (the owner of the land on which the new stadium would be erected) and Tesco PLC (the retailer providing 'enabling funds' for the scheme). In the months that followed, plans were announced to build a 50,000-seat stadium as part of a £400-million development aimed at the regeneration of Kirkby town centre. The Tesco-driven scheme would also see the building of a 24-hour Tesco Extra supermarket, 50 additional retail units, new bars, restaurants, and a hotel and leisure development.[3] Everton's project was part of a larger trend among Premiership clubs to either regenerate or build new stadiums from scratch in an attempt to 'develop the iconic brand', take advantage of multi-use facilities and construct media-friendly arenas.[4] For their part, multinational corporations like Tesco have been keen to foster links with sport as a means of constructing 'socially responsible' corporate identities and 'building brand communities' vis-à-vis local authorities and sporting institutions, to address stricter urban planning regulations.[5]

With the firming up of the proposal to relocate the club, Everton FC chairman Bill Kenwright declared himself duty-bound to offer the club's fans a ballot on the proposed move to Kirkby and stated that any decision made by the fans would be abided by. Between 6 and 23 August 2007, Everton Football Club, with the aid of the Electoral Reform Society, conducted a ballot of 38,000 season ticket holders and shareholders to gain their views on the proposed stadium move. The ballot period revealed major tensions and splits over the issue, indicated not only by the 59% to 41% majority in favour of the move, but also by the high percentage of abstentions (almost one third of those entitled to vote). In their official notification of the ballot result on Friday 24 August 2007 the Everton board of directors reflected: 'Whilst we concede that the proposed move has undoubtedly provoked a heated and sustained debate, it is reassuring to know that the majority of Evertonians do support the Club as it pursues its long-held desire to provide a world-class stadium for its world-class support'.[6]

This declaration did little to quell a fierce debate amongst Everton supporters concerning the rights and wrongs of the proposed move. The central issue was over the potential loss of identity. A grassroots organization, 'Keep Everton In Our City', became both the rallying point for dissenters to the project and the target of ire for supporters broadly favouring the board's decision to move to Kirkby. Opponents to the move in particular became highly active in lobbying public and private institutions, both local and regional, capable of influencing a rethink on the Kirkby stadium scheme, and the issue provoked national interest.[7]

Though the club remained steadfast in the face of heavy criticism, a period of uncertainty for its relocation plans was ushered in when, in August 2008, the Secretary of State for Communities and Local Government judged the proposal to fall foul of local and regional planning policy. At that point the scheme was 'called in' for inspection at a public inquiry. Over a year later, on 26 November 2009, the Secretary of State – agreeing with the planning inspector's opinion that the project breached local area planning policy and would discourage business away from nearby town and city centres – rejected the scheme; a decision the applicants declined to appeal.[8] In the immediate aftermath of the rejection Bill Kenwright conceded that the issue of moving Everton out of the city's boundaries had been controversial and divisive. The owners of the club declared that, while they were still seeking a new stadium as a solution to the ongoing financial limitations faced by the organization, any such stadium would have to be located within the City of Liverpool.[9]

The toxicity of the issue of relocating professional football clubs meant that the heated debate between supporters was almost exclusively portrayed in local and national press coverage in terms of a break along a stay/go fault line – the situation apparently being made more pointed in this case by the proposed shift taking the club outside civic boundaries. However, what the Everton stadium debate demonstrated most clearly (and something which united both sides on a more fundamental level) is the contradictory ways in which the club's supporters now approach the game: at once concerned with football as an emotional asset and mindful that, as a business, their club must place heavy emphasis on commercial strategies.

Overview of previous findings

During the course of the Everton stadium dispute we carried out and published research which attempted to cast light on the variety of different views concerning the club's proposed move. It was clear that the debate over Everton's proposed move was more nuanced than the simple division over spatial concerns generally attributed to it, with subdivisions among both supporters and opponents of relocation. Our objective was to acknowledge this complexity and also to draw some conclusions regarding the essential differences between supporters beyond their rejection or acceptance of Everton's plan to shift the club out of the City of Liverpool.

In particular, we sought to use the Everton stadium debate as a case study in order to assess the balance of forces amongst supporters: between those that could be described as *traditionalists* (or 'cultural conservatives') and those defined by a *market-led* attitude. It is widely recognized that, traditionally, football supporters share strong bonds, a common identity and a sense of 'moral ownership' of their football club. Studies on football fandom, though, indicate that supporters are increasingly aware of the financial exigencies of the club they support. The behaviour of football fans in relation to club owners' commercial strategies has been framed in terms of either an accommodation with or resistance to the commodification of professional football. On the basis of our findings, however, we rejected any thesis assuming either the inexorable process of commodification *or* fierce resistance to this process, and suggested that the reality in any given circumstance may be somewhat more complex and nuanced.

While there was some evidence to support the axis of 'accommodation and resistance' in terms of commodification, overwhelmingly our case study suggested that what united Everton supporters across the fan divide over the stadium issue was a critical and reflexive attitude toward the proposed move, forged out of an ability to deploy market rhetoric and argument to make their case. Overall, the evidence presented pointed toward supporters pragmatically adapting commercial *rhetoric* simply to press their case: fans from both sides of the stadium relocation debate deployed the language of commercialism in order to support or undermine the business case for the move. Those against the move (even those whose primary critique was based on the language of tradition and community) executed their argument over the presumed shortcomings of the club's relocation's plans in the form of a sustained critique of its *economic irrationality* (supplemented by a rigorous appraisal of possible alternative business ventures with respect to either the refurbishment of the club's Goodison Park stadium or a new stadium built within the City of Liverpool's boundaries). The central finding of our work, then, was that Everton supporters were able to deploy the language of the market both for and against the move, with a mixture of pragmaticism and scepticism at the fore.

The conclusions drawn on the stadium debate made us curious to discover whether this snapshot of Everton supporters was a balanced representation, not only of their attitude to the proposed stadium move, but also in terms of their relationship with their football club. We wondered if supporters' responses to our original findings would reinforce or contradict our earlier conclusions. With this in mind we submitted our views as an article on Toffeeweb – the longest established independent Everton website, and the premier internet source for commentary and discussion of the club's fortunes – and took part in a dialogue with supporters over the course of two days in October 2008 in order to probe further into the fans' mindset. In light of their experience of the then ongoing stadium relocation saga, we specifically attempted to gauge the extent to which supporters had surrendered to the view that football is just another business to be understood in terms of the power of money, and the extent to which they resisted this viewpoint.[10]

What we found, in part, was a gulf between on the one hand, those who advocated a more complete integration of football into the market economy (supporters who could be approximated as being more than willing to accept the 'commodification of football' thesis), and on the other hand, those who rejected any suggestion of a need to embrace commercial strategies which would colonize what was viewed as a sacrosanct cultural icon. So, for example, one supporter took this view of football's role in the world economic order and the opportunity this present state of affairs affords his football club:

> Like it or not, globalization is a fact, a part of modern day society. That facilitates corporations AND individuals being able to broadcast themselves and reach markets and other individuals across vast distances in an instance in ways previously unheard of.

> A successful strategy [corporate involvement in football clubs] in extending your client base and thus improving your income streams and projecting your image to new markets is... I prefer the club to stand or fall within a free market rather than one over-legislated.

Another supporter exhibits sentiments diametrically opposed to the above point of view in this statement:

> My blood runs cold at the thought of My Club losing its heritage and identity... Or that it becomes the plaything of some semi-interested billionaire... English football needs an example, proof that the game hasn't completely lost its soul, it needs a club that can stand toe to toe with the the clubs who have sold out. I would not be broken hearted if that club was to be Everton.

Such a chasm of difference featured in our initial published research papers. However, these points of view can be considered to be extreme outliers in the context of our later canvassing. For the greater part of the exercise we found the language of commerce had become even more influential, evidenced by varying degrees of willingness to fuse the needs of business with notions of football club tradition. A point is reached at which 'tradition' becomes *instrumental* to the increasing hegemony of commercial rationality amongst fans. This can be demonstrated by first highlighting the range of views on the proposed Kirkby stadium relocation and then broadening the analysis to establish Everton supporters' views of the more general debate regarding commerce and football.

Recent findings

One of the major talking points revolved around the importance of preserving what many supporters view Everton to be – a community asset – while coming to terms with the need to expand the club's commercial potential. This was the crux of the debate over relocation: it was not so much a geographical dispute between those advocating staying in Liverpool at all costs and those seeking a switch to Kirkby, but a debate concerning the nature of community. Both culture and economy are constituent parts of community in the formation of club and supporter identity. What is of interest in what follows is how fans respond to the tension between culture and economy in supporting arguments concerning how they identify with their club. In this respect, all supporters recognized that it was necessary to preserve community, but this was accompanied by a debate that was tempered by what was deliverable in an economic sense and the financial benefits to be accrued from moving to a new location. Indeed, as will become clear, the preservation of community appears here to be premised to variable degrees on this 'economic sense'-making in the construction of community. Initially, ideas regarding 'community' that are directly linked to tradition and an anti-market perspective could be discerned, but they had far less 'purchasing power' with respect to capturing the centre ground of discussion as the discussion progressed.

It was put to the Everton supporters that the club's role at the hub of a community was one of the defining features of the relocation debate and that fear of frittering away the stock of social capital built up by disturbing the status quo was a primary concern within the debate. Here, the pro- and anti-relocation fans found common ground. The view of one fan that 'football fans care about winning but they associate with the club for kinship, tradition, community, tribal roots and passion' was one that resonated with other participants in the discussion. Convergence on the issue was however tested by the question of just what defines 'community', and this invariably brought the issue of financial 'deliverability' into the equation. So for some, the club's home of Goodison Park was central to providing a sense of communal identity:

> [T]here is a passion and an ownership for the club in the city. That's why there is fierce debate because when a family is threatened the natural instinct is to protect and fight for the values you hold dear. Over the past 40 years we have seen the heart ripped out of the city and seen it rebuild itself but there has been constants that have been held dear, Anfield and Goodison Park to both sets of supporters have provided the community with a focal point of stability for so long.

Other supporters were not impressed that the club threatened to degrade the communal basis of the organisation. One took this theme up:

> The fact that more money was available to support a particular decision is not the only factor to be considered – in other words it should not be possible to site the Everton FC 'franchise' if it ever exists in the middle of Milton Keynes if a business model says we would make more money there.

For other supporters, a sense of community is a moveable feast that can be fostered through appropriate investment and marketing:

> Of course, both Everton and Liverpool football clubs are woven into the very fabric of the city of Liverpool AND Greater Merseyside. That is not to say that either clubs' sphere of influence or ambition should be limited to – say – a 50 mile radius of the city. Good investment and marketing CAN consolidate the existing family, rather than break it up. More… it can EXTEND the family and embrace even greater numbers across the entire globe. I do not think that DILUTES the club's relationship with its fans, or the fans affiliation to the club. Rather, it consolidates and builds on it… Under the governance of 'big business' [community] does not have to be limited to Liverpool postcodes.

After coming under fire from some for his boldly pro-corporate language, the same correspondent sought to clarify his position in order to allay the criticism, though he continued to underline what he believed to be a pragmatic commercial approach to the relocation issue in an attempt to outflank detractors.

> Yes the physical move isn't what anyone wants but in our situation we have no right to expect to be able to afford that massive stadium – and this is a way we can. If our financial situation changes then that imperative changes too… We take pride in our history – but that history is studded with times when our forefathers took risks… So – lets take the good parts of the Man U business model and the good parts of being a community club and try to put them together in Everton football club – that is what the current regime are trying to do.

This elaboration found favour amongst other contributors, who – while conceding to the supporters perceived to be arguing from an outmoded parochial notion of the football community that chasing revenue growth should not be the only consideration in relocation – counterposed a future of treading water in a competitive sense with the chance that a new stadium might offer to push for on-field success:

> The community has changed and all that is happening now is that the stadium might be moving slightly to offer us a far more comfortable stadium. The move is not an ideal situation, but in my view is tolerable. This move is not just about following money, it is about improving what the club offers its community – its whole community.

> I think there is only one consistent desire in all of us fans – the desire to win... I want us to take every course of action within our power to achieve that success again ... for me risk is all part of the game and indeed part of life itself. For some this club is a sort of family, and they project the same protective feelings towards it as they would their biological family. For me it exists to win trophies and little more, it lives and dies trying to do that.

Overall, the dominant view that appeared to unite supporters was acceptance of the need for a 'viable' (a word that was used often by contributors) stadium plan that could see the club better commercially geared for the future, in an effort to increase on-field competitiveness.

Given that the argument for relocation put forward by the club's owners primarily rested on the need for a financially 'deliverable' stadium, and that even the supporters of that line in our discussion group conceded it was a risky strategy, it was suggested that another approach to the club's stadium issue might be to explore the possibility of the club remaining at Goodison Park or within its immediate environs. The global financial downturn left a question mark hanging over the private sector-led Kirkby stadium plan. The existing proposals relied heavily on cheaply available debt finance and the consumer spending spree necessary for the envisaged retail and leisure scheme required by the club's enabling partners. Supporters were asked whether, under these circumstances, an alternative solution involving local government (in this case Liverpool City Council), supporters and club could offer a realistic way forward. Not unlike the situation at some clubs in Europe which are organized on a mutual partnership basis, this would involve local government taking responsibility for building a new stadium, sharing revenue with the club and, perhaps, working toward a situation whereby supporter representatives and other community representatives had a say in the club's affairs. However, such an approach was unwelcome on both practical and ideological grounds. One typical reaction was the suggestion that a municipal/mutual stadium solution had its own pitfalls:

> That strikes me as being way too interventionist and, potentially, even more destabilising to the club with such a hotch-potch of interested parties governing it.

In a similar vein, another fan stated that, though not opposed in principle to such a model, he was

> doubtful of its viability for Everton FC. Whilst supporters occasionally make a lot of noise in this context, when it comes to action they generally start looking at the ground and start shuffling their feet. Similarly, given their track record until now, I don't have much confidence in the ability of Liverpool City Council to be competent partners in such a package.

Talk of ownership and governance prompted a broadening of the discussion to address whether there was a danger of Everton's total capitulation, as an organization, to the sort of hard-nosed business ethic increasingly adopted by English Premier League clubs. This turn in the discussion was also stimulated by a statement made on the club's official website by Everton chief executive Robert Elstone. Although Elstone's intervention was made in relation to the general trends within the English Premier League concerning business models, his thoughts must be seen in relation to the Everton situation in particular, in which severe questioning and criticism of the club's own business plan for the Kirkby stadium scheme and its failure to address outstanding issues raised by supporters regarding the move continued to dog the Goodison hierarchy. In a revealing passage, the Everton CEO argued that:

> Football's never been short of people telling it how to run itself. ... the fan-ownership model has been put forward on many occasions as the mechanism to 'give back the Club to the fans'. Besides the small matter of raising funds, and, as we know hundreds of millions of 'funds', whether we like it or not, fan or customer ownership, as far as the UK goes, is an alien business model. [L]ike it or not, football is a business, commanding huge revenues, employing household names and embracing significant economic and social responsibilities. In my view, we (fans) cannot accept the cash to build stadia and invest in players and then turn around and dictate how the business is run. We cannot have our cake and eat it. The best way to run such businesses – football businesses, is the same way it is done in any other business – the long-established and rigorously tested corporate model...[11]

The supporters involved in our discussion were asked whether this robust defence of football's place in the market economy, the insistence on corporate governance of football clubs and the perceived role of supporters as offering only their custom by way of influence, was reflective of their own thinking. On the issue of governance, there was an almost universal acceptance that supporters were not appropriate owners or decision makers for a professional football club. As one contributor put it:

> [A] committee of supporters running Everton amounts to, and is fraught with, difficulties. The company articles and terms of engagement in the day to day running of the club would need to be very, very clearly scripted for such a union to even begin to function effectively. That's even before we get to the contentious issue of just who is nominated to represent the different groups you propose, how they are elected into (and out of) office, how their roles are defined in the set up, what executive and veto powers they have, and what constitutes the different parties percentage of voting power in the overall scheme of things. That's just off the top of my head.

Others took up this theme concerning what were believed to be the insurmountable practicalities of the supporter ownership governance model:

> ... you cannot choose to ignore the considerable finances involved in the running of a professional sports club and view it as somehow prostituting the club, selling out its fans, history and 'soul'. I fully appreciate the emotive pull allegiance to a football club has for its followers. But important decisions cannot be taken on emotion alone. A degree of pragmatism has to be taken, too.

This opposition along financial, logistical and legal grounds to a more democratic model of club organization was underscored by an ideological affirmation of running clubs along business lines, with businessmen owning and controlling the organisation. This was evident when the discussion turned toward the Everton

CEO's belief that football is a business and that Everton should be run as other companies are run. A supporter challenged the discussion group

> to propose an alternative to Everton FC being run as a money making business, because I can't see any other way to achieve success. It is all very well bemoaning the loss of some sort of 'true spirit' of the game but unless you want us to stand alone against the tide of cash this is little more than a narrative of changes within the game ultimately caused by professionalism.

Picking up this theme, another supporter was at pains to underscore the essential corporate nature of the club:

> We are NOT a Sunday League football club. Our brand is a registered company, competing in the most lucrative professional league of the world's most popular sport. That simply cannot be ignored.

This issue of 'branding' was then taken up, with the discussion group being asked whether the use of such language in relation to their club was itself a reflection of the dominance of the business ethic ushered in by the acceleration of football's commercialization in recent years. One contributor disagreed strongly:

> The fact is we ARE a registered brand... The business ethic and money has ALWAYS dominated professional football. To believe otherwise would be naïve. I doubt if there has ever been a golden age of professional football when there was a perfect balance between the governance of the club, its supporters and its playing staff... Because of the riches that are now coming in (AND flowing out of the game...) at the highest level of professional football, the issue has come into sharper focus than ever before... Like it or not – Everton Football Club is a professional sports team, competing in the most lucrative league in the world. The word 'competing' is key here. Because we are not only competing on the playing field we are competing in the market place. And if we have serious ambitions – as supporters, never mind the club management – then we have to accept that to improve as a club, we need to chase the bucks too...

While other supporters did not concur with the analysis that football has historically embraced the business ethic and that this has always dominated the rationale of football clubs, there was widespread (and reluctant) acceptance that its pro-business sentiment was now the only realistic one to hold:

> Tradition has brand value. Tradition dictates why we love our club but there is a realisation that life changes, the game has changed and so must we. Do we adopt commercialism to the point of Chelsea and now Man City? Or do we forge our own values and say this is what we as a club stand for and where we belong... Can we afford to join the race or can we afford it if we don't?

> To be or not to be, that is the question. Do we run the Football Club as a business... or are we in the Football Club business? How far do we push each is the only question.

Reflections on recent findings

The above offers a small but representative sample of a more extensive discussion, which demonstrates our earlier point that business rationality takes centre stage among fans. While there was some evidence to support the axis of 'accommodation and resistance' to commodification, the evidence of this case study suggests that what unites supporters is their willingness to deploy market rhetoric in their argument to make their case, without necessarily succumbing to commodification; a reluctant acceptance of a business model rather than a wholesale buying into that model and viewing their relationship with the club as that of a customer or consumer. Significantly, there were only a few clear examples of resistance to the language and practice of commerce. These supporters' comments, while intimating a degree of cynicism towards corporate involvement, nevertheless showed an air of market realism with respect to the financial future of the club and the necessity of securing that future through corporate strategy – albeit one that meets resistance when that strategy imposes what is perceived to be an existential threat to identity (as underlined by the proposed relocation of Everton's home outside the civic boundaries). What we witnessed overall, then, was a more pronounced *conservatism* than was found in our earlier papers. This outcome was slightly unexpected. By the time of our discussion with the group of supporters, expectations that the club's proposed relocation would come to fruition had been greatly reduced by the government's decision to 'call in' the stadium development scheme for inspection. Under these circumstances one might, by and large, have expected supporter appetite for Everton's turn toward greater commercial involvement to have been blunted rather than, as appears to have been the case, remaining healthy. This brings the argument back to our earlier point: initially, ideas regarding 'community' directly linked to 'tradition' and an anti-market perspective can be discerned, but they became far less prominent and had far less purchase with respect to capturing the centre ground as the discussion progressed.

How can this be explained? The discussion between supporters would appear to indicate that ideas surrounding 'community' are being colonized by language associated with the market as opposed to language associated with tradition and locality.[12] In this respect, the market (or business ethic) is gaining a strong hold, becoming hegemonic in defining the common-sense language of community. If one views community as symbolizing and embodying the tension between culture and economy, then the common sense influencing supporters is one in which the economy takes priority over culture in constructing arguments about the nature of community and how best to sustain it.[13] The debate amongst Everton supporters suggests that culture as symbolic of cooperation, tradition and sense of place is losing ground to the language of the economy (winning, competition, efficiency, business acumen) as a means of defining community, due to commercial pressures gaining an ever-increasing foothold within the game.

One can say that one form of shared *commonsense*[14] is being dislodged – if not replaced – by another. In this case, the dislodged commonsense is grounded in and through traditional images of football for its own sake, expressed in terms of mythical ideals of a golden age of football 'for itself'. Here, players and management are part of the community (playing/managing solely for the love of the game), where supporters accept a pragmatic accommodation to commercial pressures, mixed with an outright rejection of their identification as consumers or customers. Dislodging this view is an emergent commonsense which would appear to include elements of the old, subordinated within a new configuration of motives and ideas that advance commercialization by reinforcing an environment in which a supporter's sense of moral ownership of their club is weakened by the diktats of concern for club resources and financial health. The emerging commonsense appears to be eroding the status of those holding traditional feelings of emotional solidarity between supporters in their collective attachment to the club and encouraging more individualistic, instrumental and quantifiable forms of attachment. Habermas[15] might well sum this point up by suggesting this is one more piece of evidence of a much larger process in which the 'systems world' is colonizing and so corrupting the 'life world'. Indeed, we feel it is worth pursuing the 'system' and 'life world' concepts, because they help to place the changing dynamics of fans' orientations to football clubs in a wider context.

Theoretical reflections on changing supporter discourse

Both 'system' and 'life worlds' intersect as *tendencies* in the one world of late modern capitalism, which, for heuristic purposes, can be separated to allow a clearer grasp of the meaning and consequences of each. Habermas (1971) refers to the *life world* as ideas and practices that are communicated through culture and mediated through myths, symbols and rituals. It is social life weaved from inter-subjective understanding and communication between people, treated as ends in themselves rather than means to an end.[16] As Brown and Goodman (2001) reflect:

> [f]rom the viewpoint of the participating subject, the life world is a resource of implicit assumptions, pre-interpreted knowledge and traditional practices. As such, the life world provides the necessarily assumed context for individual actions that are often in conflict with the actions of others.[17]

While the life world in modern capitalism cannot escape rationalization (abstract relations) in the sphere of cultural, social and personal relations, rationalization remains embedded in and subject to a more critical and reflective approach to culture, the development of formal legal institutions in society and personal skills, attitudes and motivations.[18] Therefore, rationalization may complement collective tradition and inter-subject coordination when it is tempered by the concurrent development of reflexive communication, negotiation and democratic dialogue.[19] To put it another way, more abstract general means of control, such as bureaucracy, the market and professional expert systems of knowledge, remain subordinate to tradition, custom and hence inter-subjective human control.[20]

In terms of football and our discussion of Everton supporters above, then, the life world has definite affinities with the traditional commonsense mentioned above, where supporter identity is constructed around notions of locality and tradition and in which Goodison Park is more than the sum of its parts – effectively a conduit for the lived experience and heritage of spectators. Indeed, one might situate those supporters keen to argue for maintaining ties with a revitalized Goodison Park within this imperative. Or, to revisit one fan's comment:

> The fact that more money was available to support a particular decision is not the only factor to be considered – in other words it should not be possible to site the Everton FC 'franchise' if it ever exists in the middle of Milton Keynes if a business model says we would make more money there.

In contrast, the counter-tendency to create social interaction by means of the *systems world* manifests in the development of abstract social structures that steer society and constrain, shape and dominate inter-subjective understanding. The structures in question include money and economic markets (and the related language of economic science), as well as rational bureaucracy, with its abstract rules across industry and government.²¹ When the systems world dominates inter-subjective understanding, debate and discussion are steered by 'money talk' and management-technical-speak borrowed from 'expert knowledge' systems (economics, accountancy, political science, and so on). It is this kind of language that reverberates around the new commonsense among Everton supporters mentioned earlier, which places emphasis on economic rationality in defining community in ways that treat the proposed ground move as 'good business sense' and the ground as simply bricks and mortar. Indeed, the orientation towards the common sense of 'money talk' and management-technical-speak borrowed from 'expert knowledge' systems is captured time and again in the quotes raised earlier and is never better epitomized than in the quote revisited here:

> The fact is we ARE a registered brand... The business ethic and money has ALWAYS dominated professional football. To believe otherwise would be naïve. I doubt if there has ever been a golden age of professional football when there was a perfect balance between the governance of the club, its supporters and its playing staff...

This line of thinking is conducive with the prevailing wider environment, in which the steering structures of the systems world now dominate more than ever before and so are not isolated. The steering structures of the systems world emerge for two positive reasons: first, to manage and moderate unintended consequences – which, by definition, fall outside of communicative discourse – and so steer them towards particular intended ends based on democratic dialogue (inherent to the life world); second, as a way of coordinating means-ends without recourse to constant communication, argument and negotiation. However, once system imperatives dominate to the point of corroding the life world, the means-ends dialogue become governed by economics and finance.²² We see this clearly in supporter dialogue, whereby arguments about the 'Goodison tradition' and alternatives to the Kirkby move are increasingly thwarted and nullified by the mantra of 'lack of money in a commercialized environment', and so treated with incredulity.

It is suggested that the more dominant the systems world, the more likely it is that the sense we make of our interactions with others will be justified in terms of the prevailing structures and rules governing the economy (money, science, bureaucratic organization, and so on). ²³Individuals will tend to treat other individuals, or the meaning and purpose of groups and organizations, according to the imperatives of the abstract system and less as ends in themselves.²⁴ Hence, supporters arguing for the move to Kirkby or a new stadium within the City of Liverpool gain a greater hearing than those who wish to remain at Goodison, because they are working with the imperatives of the systems world as currently structured. As Habermas reflects, 'to the degree that the economic system' dominates, the 'motives of performance and competition gain the force to shape behaviour. The communicative practice of everyday life is one-sidedly rationalised'.²⁵

Despite the tendency for the systems world to dominate life worlds, the dominance is permeated by resistance.²⁶ This is clearly evident in the case of football supporters and websites: the internet offers greater scope for official discourses from football clubs and institutions to colonize fan forums and steer discussion towards system imperatives, yet the same communicative capacity can provide an alternative collective voice for supporters which they can build on and develop into a potentially rivalling anti-systemic discourse. Yet much of the information fans access is produced within the football media and related business industries: one example is fans' use of surveys and research produced by football industry accountants Deloitte, which gravitates analysis towards market realism. This is a source of colonization we observed at play in the case of Everton supporters, who drew knowledgeably on the business and financial literature related to football.

This *dialectic* between the systems and life world can aid understanding of supporters' attitudes. For example, it was initially noted, with respect to Everton supporter dialogue, that during its most heated moments the debate conjured up a polarization of attitudes: for example, one fan declared that they would 'prefer the club to stand or fall within a free market rather than one over-legislated...', while another deplored the prospect of their 'club losing its heritage and identity, by moving to a second-rate stadium in the middle of nowhere, just to enable a few people to profit...' The polarization within the terms of reference of systems and life worlds would appear to suggest that uncoupling had occurred, rather than the former having dominance over the latter. However, it was also noted that this polar opposition quickly faded in favour of of an attitude consistent with a systems-world mentality. It would seem that, despite there being a polarity, those who declare that they would 'prefer the club to stand or fall within a free market rather than one over-legislated...' are increasingly more representative than are ardent 'traditionalists'. Habermas' conceptual framework would seem to offer help in understanding why opinion is weighted toward this viewpoint even if it is, of necessity, sometimes modified in terms amenable to 'traditionalists'.

However, it needs to be stressed once more that systems-world dominance is never complete. According to Habermas, no matter how dominant the systems world threatens to become, practice and language are invariably compromised because the lifeworld perspectives are always present. Firstly, individuals have an interest in understanding and empathizing with others and developing a grasp of shared meanings; developing hermeneutic knowledge about our place in culture and within systems of shared meaning. Secondly, we have an inbuilt interest in emancipatory knowledge, which is knowledge aimed at critical reflection on what is right and wrong, moral or unethical – what is the good life. Habermas expresses concern, however, that if left unmanaged the systems world will continue to have a negative influence on the life world. On the one hand, there is hope for a more progressive fusion between system and life worlds (the unfinished business of modernity); on the other, recognition that systemic dominance and colonization remains the (albeit attenuated) reality.[27]

Indeed, it is this *attenuated* dominance and colonization which can be seen most clearly in the tone and substance of the attitudes described earlier as 'market realist' and summed up rather well in the quote '[t]radition has brand value. Tradition dictates why we love our club but there is a realisation that life changes, the game has changed and so must we'. The tone is also one characterized by a cost benefit analysis that errs toward rational calculation where choices about the direction the club ought to take are concerned; by, for example, what is best for the fan vis-à-vis other fans of the club, and what is best for the club vis-à-vis other clubs: 'I think there is only one consistent desire in all of us fans – the desire to win... I want us to take every course of action within our power to achieve that success again...' On both calculations, the question of what is best for Everton Football Club as a community asset with wider implications for stakeholder ownership is marginalized.

Moreover, as we have seen, moral dilemmas about the direction the club ought to take are governed more by the kind of instrumental rationality found in business schools and far less by enduring cultural concerns about the place of football in society and how football ought to conduct itself with regard to supporters and the wider community within which clubs operate. As noted earlier with respect to supporter attitudes, wider issues concerning who should own and control clubs and what their role in the community ought to be are ruled 'out of court' or derided as out of touch with 'the times', or are opposed along financial, logistical and legal grounds. What is left standing is an altogether different 'ought': a more democratic model of club organization, underscored by the ideological affirmation of running clubs along business lines.

In this respect, Morgan's[28] reflection is apt: underpinning Habermas' concerns about the over-weaning dominance of the systems world is the inevitable and culturally corroding 'seepage of instrumental reasoning into moral reasoning, and the social/moral decline it sets in motion, is no where more apparent than in the case of contemporary sports…' The seepage in this case study, it can be argued, is top-down, from the corporate structure of the football industry as a whole, through Everton PLC to its fans. It is a seepage which can be identified, for example, in the rational calculation of the means and ends to achieve maximum revenues through attracting global media contracts, building the brand, gaining corporate endorsements, expanding the real and virtual fan-base, and by intervening in the moral deliberations amongst fans ('turning moral deliberation into a species of instrumental reason').[29] It can be argued that the corporate owners of Everton FC are drawn only to 'rounding the edges off' of their embrace of the systems-world language of economic calculus by situating this embrace as a reluctant duty they must carry out to facilitate the club's survival and progression into the future; a position that those club supporters uttering 'market realist' sentiment seem only too willing to echo.

The concepts of systems and life worlds provide useful insights into the dichotomies and contradictions of the football industry and help to frame an understanding of how supporters are responding to commercialization. However, every conceptual framework has its limits, and concepts can never hope to capture the complexities of social life; at most they can provide a useful map for situating the particular within general social patterns and power relations. One can rightly argue that the level of abstraction of 'systems world' is such that it cannot take account of the specificities of industries and therefore the stability and dominance of their commodity structure: for example, the football industry does not have the same security of commodity structure as, say, the fast food industry, and therefore there are limits to the practical deployment of concepts such as the 'systems world' across all social institutions. Nevertheless, the concepts of *systems* and *life world*, and perhaps more crucially their application as dialectically related, can – as we have shown in the case of the discussion and debate between Everton supporters – provide valuable insights into particular conflicts and their relation to wider systemic changes in society at large. To recall one supporter's comment:

> To be or not to be, that is the question. Do we run the Football Club as a business… or are we in the Football Club business? How far do we push each is the only question.

Conclusion

We began this chapter by recognizing that Everton Football Club's bid to move to a new stadium was part of a trend amongst elite clubs in England. Indeed, new stadiums are closely related to the political economy of debt financing that has engulfed the English Premier League. When giving evidence to the Culture, Media and Sport Select Committee recently, Greg Clarke, the chairman of the Football League, remarked: '[If I] had to list the ten things about football that keep me awake at night, it would be debt one to ten'.[30] A report conducted by UEFA in 2010 outlining the scale of debt across European football calculates the combined debts of the twenty Premier League clubs at 'just under €4bn (£3.5bn) – around four times the figure for the next most indebted top division, Spain's La Liga'; or, put another way, 56 per cent of European club football's debt.[31]

The problem of debt is, in turn, internal to the modes of governance prevalent in the English Premiership. Clubs oscillate between taking on an Anglo-Saxon model of ownership fuelled by debt, or becoming a multimillion-pound plaything of the rich and famous.[32] In between these options are clubs like Everton, mired in a 'portfolio of debt' that is increasingly difficult to service and lacking the necessary asset base that the current owners of Manchester United can 'sweat' in order to churn service debt endlessly. They are also without a billionaire suitor willing to wave their debt away. Whatever the predicament elite clubs find themselves in, in all cases the political economy of debt ensures that monetary concerns rule the English Premier League when it comes to footballing matters. English Premier League football is becoming a vehicle for attracting – and, just as quickly, consuming – money, as more of it circulates inward from advertising income, bank loans, ticket price hikes, mega TV deals and outward again in the form of spiralling wage costs, payments to agents, and/or interest payments to banks.

It is in this context that new stadiums take on strategic economic importance to elite clubs. Therefore, the clamour for new stadiums is only partly driven by the requirement of football as spectacle and is mostly driven by money motives – perhaps not so much driven by the propensity to *make* money (this would be merely the icing on the cake), but more by the belief (however unfounded) that a new stadium will add enough extra revenue to help close the gap between what pours into football and the pace at which it is consumed from within and without the game. Yet this is not the only motivation for pursuing new stadiums. A new stadium may also be attractive for club owners facing stagnation on and off the field; that is, owners with little prospect of winning major trophies, unwilling or unable to hand over the reins to an oil-rich tycoon, but intent on bridging the gap between money pouring in and money pouring out of the club and/or lessening the general aura of disenchantment among fans concerned with their club's middling status or its prospect of stagnation.

The failed attempt by the current owners of Everton Football Club to secure a move away from Goodison Park and build a new stadium in Kirkby should be judged in this latter context. Firstly, monetary considerations drove the move: as the fan protest group Keep Everton In Our City note,

> In the years that Everton have managed to publish annual accounts it is noticeable that since the formation of the Premier League the club's total debt has steadily increased from less than four million to approaching £80m whilst the club's assets have measurably declined.[33]

However, the attempt to depart Goodison for pastures new was driven by more than the necessity of closing the debt gap mentioned above, crucial though this task was (and remains). Another motivating factor was the attempt to generate an *aura of progress* in a situation of stagnating ambitions (a strategy to enchant and animate supporters amid the reality of season-long disenchantment). The motives behind stadium moves are complex, and never more so than in the case of Everton Football Club. Notwithstanding the belief that a ground move was in the interests of football, a new stadium was a monetary strategy: a new asset to sweat; a new bargaining chip to secure a higher share price if and when the club were to be sold on. Even before this option began to split at the seams an air of desperation had surfaced within the club, percolating through into the *life worlds* of supporters active on websites. Indeed, the KEIOC campaign witnessed a perceptible shift in the balance of argument, from the traditionalist solution of remaining at Goodison toward alternative stadium sites that are guaranteed to add more value to Everton's coffers.

In summary, the debate between Everton supporters signifies a situation in which Everton Football Club's fragile business status is increasingly exposed by the rampant commercialization of the game. But this exposure drives supporters more firmly into the language of commerce, as there is no way out except to fight to stay in the business and 'compete' with other clubs with much bigger 'asset bases' – to use Habermas' language, the life-world is threatened with colonization by the systems-world. As community assets and aspiring commercial entities, football clubs are by their very nature always going to be on the edge of viability. This edge exposes the tensions we have noted in the discourse between Everton supporters.

Notes

1. Deloitte, 'Football Money League: The Reign in Spain'.
2. D. Kennedy and P. Kennedy. '"It's the Little Details that Make Up Our Identity": Everton Supporters and Their Stadium Ballot Debate'.
3. M. Hickman, 'New Everton Stadium Plan'. As chairman of Everton FC Bill Kenwright reflected in 'Everton FC's Kirkby Move is dead "But We Need More Investment"', 'I would love to stay at my blue and white palace forever but there is not enough capacity, there are too many restrictive seats and even health and safety regulations is an issue'.
4. Aritua et al., 'Managing the Delivery of Iconic Football Stadiums in England', 55–60.
5. Balmer, J.M.T. 'Corporate Brand Cultures and Communities'.
6. For details of the vote see http://stadium.evertonfc.com/news/ballot-result.php The ballot question simply stated: 'Are you in favour of relocating Everton Football Club to Kirkby? Yes or No'.
7. KEIOC, 'Our Position Explained'.
8. CLG 'Communities and Local Government final decision on Destination Kirkby scheme'.
9. Kenwright, B. 'Everton FC's Kirkby Move'.
10. Toffeeweb, 'The Kirkby Stadium Debate'.
11. EFC Ecclestone.
12. Larry et al.,.*Culture and the Economy After the Cultural Turn*, 4.
13. Gudeman, *The Anthropology of Economy*.
14. The concept of commonsense relates back to the work of Gramsci and draws attention to how ideological hegemony is never secure and relies on ruling ideas becoming accepted and taken for granted in everyday life and identity amongst the masses. In relation to football supporters, Giulianotti provides a good account of how the structures of hyper-commodification facilitate a number of competing fan-types of behaviour and attitude, which are the carriers themselves of common sense attitudes to football and being a fan. See Giulianotti, 'Supporters, Followers, Fans and Flaneurs'.
15. Habermas, 'Lifeworld and System'.
16. Habermas, . 'Lifeworld and System'.
17. Brown and Goodman, 'Jürgen Habermas' Theory of Communicative Action'.
18. Habermas, 'Lifeworld and System'.

19. Baxter, 'The Systems World and Life World in Habermas's Theory of Communicative Action', 54.
20. Baxter, 'The Systems World', 39-86.
21. Howe, *Critical Theory*.
22. Baxter, 'The Systems World'.
23. Habermas, 'Lifeworld and System', 390; Habermas, 'Learning by Disaster', 307–20.
24. Sayer, 'For A Critical Cultural Political Economy', 700.
25. Habermas, 'Lifeworld and System', 325.
26. Habermas, 'Learning by Disaster', 1998.
27. Habermas, 'Learning by Disaster', 1998.
28. Morgan, 'Habermas and Sport', 176.
29. Morgan, 'Habermas and Sport, 176.
30. Crooks, 'Outside Edge'.
31. Conn, 'Premier League Clubs owe 56% of Europe's Debt'.
32. Football Economy.com. 'League Supremo warns of Debt Precipice'.
33. KEIOC, 'The Sound of One Hand Clapping'.

References

Aritua, B., D. Bower, and M. Turner. 'Managing the Delivery of Iconic Football Stadiums in England'. *Proceedings of the Institution of Civil Engineers Management, Procurement and Law* 161, 2 (2008): 55–60. http://eprints.whiterose.ac.uk/8531/1/mpal_2008_161_2.pdf

Balmer, J.M.T. 'Corporate Brand Cultures and Communities'. In *Brand Culture*, ed. J.E Schroeder, et al.. Abingdon: Routledge, 2006.

Baxter, H. 'The Systems World and Life World in Habermas's Theory of Communicative Action'. *Theory and Society* 16, no. 1 (1987): 39–86.

Brown, R. H., and G. Goodman. 'Jürgen Habermas' Theory of Communicative Action: An Incomplete Project'. In *Handbook of Social Theory*, ed. G. Ritzer and B. Smart. London: Sage, 2001.

CLG. 'Communities and Local Government final decision on Destination Kirkby scheme'. http://www.scribd.com/doc/23184405/09-11-25-Final-DL-Everton-Tesco-1203375

Conn, D. 'Premier League Clubs Owe 56% of Europe's Debt'. *The Guardian*. http://www.guardian.co.uk/football/2010/feb/23/premier-league-clubs-europe-debt

Crooks, E. 'Outside Edge: Take Sides in the Game of Capitalism'. *Financial Times*. http://www.ft.com/cms/s/0/097c42e6-07a5-11df-915f-00144feabdc0.html#ixzz1GPLQXYEJ.

Deloitte. 'Football Money League: The Reign in Spain'. Deloitte. http://s.ucpf.fr/ucpf/file/200702/DeloitteFootballMoneyLeague2007.pdf

Everton Football Club. http://www.evertonfc.com/home/

FootballEconomy.com. 'League Supremo warns of Debt Precipice'. http://www.footballeconomy.com/

Giulianotti, R. 'Supporters, Followers, Fans and Flaneurs'. *Journal of Sport and Social Issues* 26, no. 1 (2002): 25–46.

Gudeman, S. *The Anthropology of Economy*. Oxford: Blackwell Publishers, 2001.

Habermas, J., 1987. 'Lifeworld and System: A Critique of Functionalist Reason'. In *Volume 2 of The Theory of Communicative Action*, English translation by Thomas McCarthy. Boston: Beacon Press.

Habermas, J. 'Learning By Disaster'. *Constellations* 5, no. 3 (1998): 307–20.

Hickman. M. 'New Everton Stadium Plan'. MUST. http://www.joinmust.org/forum/showthread.php?t=28009

Howe, A. *Critical Theory*. London: Sage, 2003.

KEIOC. 'Our Position Explained'. Keeping Everton in our City. http://www.keioc.net/index.php?page=our-position-explained.

KEIOC. (2011) 'The Sound of One Hand Clapping'. Keeping Everton in our City. http://www.keioc.net/

Kennedy, D., and P. Kennedy. '"It's the Little Details that Make Up our Identity": Everton Supporters and their Stadium Ballot Debate'. *Soccer and Society* 15, no. 5 (2010): 553–72.

Kenwright, B. 'Everton FC's Kirkby Move is dead "But We Need More Investment"'. *Liverpool Echo*.http://www.liverpoolecho.co.uk/everton-fc/everton-fc-new-stadium/2009/11/27/bill-kenwright-everton-fc-s-kirkby-move-is-dead-but-we-need-investment-1002522526-4685/

Larry, J., R. Ray, and A. Sayer. *Culture and the Economy After the Cultural Turn*. London: Sage, 1999.

Morgan, W.J. 'Habermas and Sport: Social Theory from a Moral Perspective'. In *Sport and Modern Social Theorists*, ed. R. Giulianotti. London: Palgrave MacMillan, 2004.

Ritzer, G., and B. Smart. *Handbook of Social Theory*. London: Sage, 2001.

Sayer, A. 'For A Critical Cultural Political Economy'. *Antipode* 33, no. 4 (2001): 687–708.

Toffeeweb. 'The Kirkby Stadium Debate: Everton Supporters and the Commercialisation of the Game'. Toffeeweb. http://www.toffeeweb.com/season/08-09/comment/fan/article.asp?submissionID=9697

Football fans and clubs in Germany: conflicts, crises and compromises

Udo Merkel

School of Service Management, University of Brighton, Eastbourne, United Kingdom

> In 2005, the economic value of the football industry in Germany was estimated at around €5 billion. At the end of the 2009/2010 season, the 18 Bundesliga clubs registered a combined turnover of just over €2 billion. As in many other countries, the largest proportion of the clubs' income derives from sponsors, fans, the sale of TV rights and merchandising. This chapter provides a short overview of the relatively late formation of the commercial axis of professional football in Germany, focusing on the commodification, commercialization, and eventually bourgeoisification of this popular sport. This process has been accompanied by a number of conflicts and tensions, as the game's traditional fans have often been treated as 'poor relatives'. The growing wealth of players, the greed of many football directors, the lack of respect for the local community and the blatant commercialism of the industry has not gone down well with fans, as their colourful and systematic resistance to the so-called 'modernization' of the game clearly shows. I will argue that the rather fan-friendly attitudes and structures of the German Bundesliga, which provides more opportunities for fans' democratic involvement than any other professional football league, is the outcome of constant hegemonic struggles.

Introduction

Germany has won the Football World Cup three times (1954, 1974 and 1990) and has hosted this prestigious global sports spectacle twice, first in 1974 and most recently in 2006. The 2006 World Cup was full of surprises both on and off the pitch. As widely expected, the organization was smooth, efficient and flawless. What few have predicted, however, was the team's creative and attractive attacking style of play under Jürgen Klinsmann, the inexperienced but enthusiastic manager of the German national side. In the end, Germany came third. However, this World Cup will be remembered for other, more significant reasons.

There was little doubt that this World Cup was one of the best ever – a view expressed by participating teams, travelling fans, sport officials and journalists, as well as high-profile politicians such as Kofi Annan and Tony Blair.[1] This overwhelmingly positive and enthusiastic feedback from around the world had several dimensions. First, the Germans had confirmed that they could throw a decent party, with the World Cup showing the fun-loving and hedonistic side of the German people. Over one month, the country had revelled in its biggest and most enjoyable party since the Berlin Wall came down in 1989. Second, Germany presented itself as a confident, creative and multicultural host where visiting fans were not segregated but instead were encouraged to mingle. Fans without tickets were not treated suspiciously but were given a warm reception. They were invited to watch matches on giant screens, which had been put up in almost every city and town centre in the country, for free: 'Germany 2006 was the most "fan"-oriented event in the tournament's 76-year history.'[2] Third, Germans appeared to forget the country's economic problems, at least for a short period of time, as the World Cup transformed its internal mood. Most people appeared to revel in their role as generous hosts, gracious losers and optimists. Fourth, Germany's often uninspired, dull and calculating football victories in the past used to be a mirror image of the country's self-image and its desperate attempts not to put a foot wrong.[3] The new, more attractive and fairly successful playing style clearly reflected wider changes, in particular the discovery of a healthy, confident and non-threatening patriotism.[4] Millions of Germans publicly embraced the national flag and attached it to windows, balconies, cars, bicycles and prams. Germany wigs were as popular as flags painted on young people's faces. In the past this spontaneous wave of national feeling and patriotism would have caused a media-orchestrated public wave of indignation and anger, reminding the Germans of their Nazi history. On this occasion, however, British, Dutch and even Israeli media accounts were surprisingly positive and. It is gratifying to imagine tabloid executives finally shedding the old *Fawlty Towers* clichés presenting Germans as Sauerkraut-eating, goose-stepping Nazis.[5]

Germany's top football division, the Bundesliga, is often praised for its reasonable ticket prices, the preservation of a passionate terrace culture and the high standards of its stadia. However, this is not due to benevolence on the part of football clubs and their directors; rather, it is the outcome of struggles, tensions and contradictions that have been articulated most clearly through the country's various football subcultures. It is fair to say that Germany's highest division is more inclusive and allows for a certain degree of participatory democracy. These principles provide the basis for a relatively close and harmonious relationship between clubs and their fans, which the latter have been steadily fighting for ever since the introduction of professional football.

The theoretical framework of this chapter derives from Antonio Gramsci's concept of hegemony, as this critical approach to the study of sport in society has made some very important and influential contributions to a better understanding of the political economy of modern sport. One seminal text in this regard is Richard Gruenau's critical analysis of Canadian sport culture.[6] While John Hargreaves subsequently employed Gramsci's concept successfully in his systematic study of the triangular relationship of sport, power and culture in Britain,[7] George Sage has clearly demonstrated that sport has also been deeply involved in the struggle for hegemony in American society,[8] and John Sugden and Alan Bairner's study of the contested nature of sport in Northern Ireland[9] shows convincingly that Gramsci's distinction between political and civil society is a helpful analytical tool. However, this differentiation cannot be absolute, since 'the public and private spheres of society are increasingly intertwined'.[10]

Gramsci's concept of hegemony acknowledges the dynamic nature of class struggles and rejects simple notions of economically determined class domination, the traditional Marxist base-superstructure model and theorizations that blame the seductive manipulative powers of ideologies leading to a false consciousness.[11] The sociological focus of this paper is therefore on 'collective human agency in terms of "relational" features of social class, which refer to the relative capacity of social groups to deploy rules, resources and traditions in ways that further their particular interests'[12] Swingewood also suggests that 'hegemony implied a democratic relation between ruled and ruler, the existence of institutions which enable the subordinate groups to articulate their own interests and defend them, to build their own distinctive culture'.[13] Football, as an element of popular culture with mass appeal, is an integral and prominent part of the struggle for hegemony in German society. As such, this paper intends to make a contribution to wider debates about the class relationships and interrelationships that are at the heart of both hegemony theory and questions of social change. My argument is that the current organizational structuring of the German Bundesliga does indeed allow these fans more opportunities for engagement with their local clubs than many other European leagues. However, that 'privilege' is well deserved, as it is the outcome of a protracted and concerted battle which fans have been involved in for the past few decades.

This paper is informed by several empirical studies, the collection of local, national and international media accounts, attendance at a large number of football matches, (semi-structured) interviews with fans, sport administrators and journalists, and (participant) observation of various sport scenes and events in Germany over the past ten years.

In the next section I will provide a detailed account of the emergence of the commercial axis in German football. Subsequent sections then critically evaluate the various fan responses to this development. Fans are understood as those young, primarily male spectators who have a keen interest in football, are committed to one club and team, publicly display their loyalty through various symbols, consider the attendance of all home fixtures a 'must', and regularly engage in forms of collective behaviour on the terraces.[14]

Context: the gradual emergence of the commercial football axis

In comparison to other European countries, for example England and Italy, the commodification and commercialization of football in Germany happened very late and rather reluctantly. For most of the twentieth century, the German Football Association (DFB) perceived itself to be the guardian of the old Victorian amateur ideal. Football's governing body argued that the involvement of money in sport was a modern disease. As a competitive amateur game it was considered to be a continuation of genuine German physical culture, distinctly different from the English game and played in the pure and holistic spirit of physical and mental improvement of the German nation.[15]

I have shown elsewhere that middle and upper-class men's control of football's organizational structures in Germany provided the dominant classes with access in the area of popular culture to those proletarian communities whose consent they were seeking.[16] They succeeded in disciplining the working class into conformity with bourgeois norms of respectability. Consequently, workers adopted the club as their organizational model. It had a long tradition in German middle and upper-class history, was regulated by the state and formed the basis for an organizationally fairly standardized civil society.

It was only in the 1960s that the DFB abandoned its dogmatic ideological position on amateurism and the processes of commodification, commercialization and professionalization took off. The most significant date in this period of rapid change is obviously the creation of one national league, the Bundesliga, in 1963. By the end of that decade football had undergone the most dramatic and far-reaching changes seen in the sport since its arrival as a kind of by product of the engineering, mining and textile know-how of the British, who helped to industrialize the German Empire in the late nineteenth century.[17] These developments had a major impact on the organizational and cultural landscape of football and football clubs. Very quickly, the largest German towns and cities brought forth one outstanding club in a monopolistic position; the majority of small suburban clubs perished, and with them the symbolic focus of many small local communities.[18] The gradual loss of close geographical and socio-economic ties between clubs and their supporters was an inevitable consequence.

In 1972 the last barrier fell, with the removal of upper limits on players' salaries.[19] Once local heroes, the players now became national (and, in a few cases, international) stars; the supporters became fans; the clubs introduced businesses principles and practices. The modern era increasingly required synthetic symbols, such as flags, kits, badges or scarves, to bridge the growing distance between team and fans. However, these were artificial props which could not counterbalance the loss of the intense traditional relationship between local community and team. An important opportunity for individuals to locate themselves socially and culturally gradually disappeared.[20]

Critical voices had always warned that the commodification and commercialization of the game could have disastrous consequences. In the summer of 1971 their worst fears came true, when evidence emerged that 18 of the previous season's matches (1970/1971) had been manipulated in exchange for a total of more than one million Deutschmark.[21] The DFB punished two clubs, two managers, five administrators and 52 players from seven teams. Offenbach and Bielefeld lost their licences, whilst Berlin, Braunschweig and Schalke suffered severely because of their top players being banned.[22] But most importantly, the reputation of German football and the comparatively young Bundesliga had been tarnished badly.

One of the above mentioned clubs, Braunschweig, struggled as a result of this, as its best player had been banned. The club therefore decided to attract more high-quality – but expensive – players, and stretched itself financially to do this. In order to avoid looming bankruptcy, the club's president joined forces with Günther Mast's company, which had produced the herb-flavoured liqueur Jägermeister in the neighbouring town of Wolfenbüttel since 1935. In 1972, Mast provided Braunschweig with a cash injection of 160,000 Deutschmark. In return the club agreed to replace the lion in its emblem with a deer, the well-known corporate logo of Jägermeister. The DFB agreed to this modification of Braunschweig's emblem. However, once the moral authorities of German football realized that Braunschweig players were displaying the Jägermeister deer on their chests, a protracted legal battle ensued. This offered even more media exposure for Mast and his company. Despite the legal problems, Jägermeister and Braunschweig had opened a new chapter in German sport history; other teams followed swiftly in their wake, and the DFB gave up its resistance. Six of the 18 *Bundesliga* clubs turned their players into running billboards in the 1974/1975 season: Hamburg (Campari), Munich (Adidas), Düsseldorf (Allkauf), Frankfurt (Remington), Duisburg (Brian Scott) and, of course, Braunschweig (Jägermeister) together earned about 1.5 million Deutschmark for this *Werbung am Mann* ('advertising on the man').[23]

By the 1980/1981 season, all Bundesliga teams were decorated with the logo and/or name of their respective sponsors. In total they received 7.5 million

Deutschmark. By the start of the twenty-first century, sponsorship was contributing more than 150 million Deutschmark to the financing of the 18 Bundesliga teams. In the 2004/2005 campaign, funds made available by the sponsors of the first division's teams reached a historical high of more than 330 million euro (for comparative purposes, this equates to 670 million Deutschmark). By this time, Bayern Munich had become the Bundesliga's top earner, receiving €120 million from German Telecom for an eight-year deal.[24]

During the first half of the 1960s there was a widespread belief that TV coverage of football matches would have a negative impact on attendance figures. Therefore the *Sportschau*, a national TV programme covering all aspects of sport on Saturday evenings, was only allowed to report on three matches. Live coverage of Bundesliga games was strictly forbidden and fans were even left in the dark about which European midweek matches were to be shown on TV until a few hours before broadcast. In the second half of that decade the *Sportschau* increased its football coverage as well as its popularity, and for almost 20 years the 6–7pm *Sportschau* slot remained an undisputed and unrivalled institution in German media.

In 1988, four years after private television channels came into existence, the DFB sold the rights to cover Bundesliga football for three years to UFA, an agency that was part of the Bertelsmann media empire, for 135 million Deutschmark. Subsequently *RTL plus*, a new commercial TV channel, presented an innovative concept – a two-and-a-half hour show called Kick-Off (*Anpfiff*), consisting of plenty of commercial breaks and lots of rather dull match reports. However, as *RTL plus* could only be received via a satellite dish, only a small number of people had to suffer this boring embarrassment. Between 1992 and 1997 the DFB tripled its income from the sale of TV rights. The ISPR agency, which bought this privilege for the price of 140 million Deutschmark per year, was part of the Kirch media conglomerate, which also owned commercial TV station Sat.1. From then onwards Sat.1 offered a much more attractive and popular programme, which celebrated every match as an emotional climax. Due to the enormous funds Sat.1 had to generate to repay the initial investment, the traditional Saturday evening of football expanded considerably – commencing on Friday evening and finishing on Sunday evening, with three programmes on offer. Consequently, there was more space and time for advertising and commercial breaks.[25]

By the mid/late 1980s, then, an unholy alliance of ambitious football directors, a greedy DFB, an army of keen sponsors and commercial TV channels had been formed. Football's commodification in Germany had quickly gathered pace.[26] The appropriation of market logic and principles by the Bundesliga clubs was certainly completed very rapidly: the development of Bayern Munich from a small, provincial club to a football superpower and brand clearly mirrors this process.

> FC Bayern Munich mobilized not only a dislike which was rooted in regional-cultural views of Bavarians outside Bavaria, it also upset 'the man in the street' who sensed in this economically successful club a classic example of sporting high finance, a club whose victories were made possible only by the power of money.[27]

However, the commodification of German football appears to have hit a ceiling. Borussia Dortmund's attempt to generate additional revenue through floating the club on the stock market in 2000 had disastrous consequences for the club;[28] it is also worth noting that there are no Roman Abramovich, Silvio Berlusconi or

Glazer-brother figures on the German football landscape. Nevertheless, there is little doubt that the new political economy of football in Germany has caused some fundamental changes to the social and cultural relations between clubs and their supporters.

Resistance I: fans voting with their feet

One of the most convincing indicators of football's popularity is matches' attendance figures. Fans often react promptly and unequivocally to changes. In the early 1970s, for the two years immediately after the match-fixing scandal in 1971, almost all Bundesliga matches experienced a considerable decline in crowd numbers. During the 1972/1973 campaign less than five million people – a historical low – watched matches in Germany's highest league. This is an average of only 16,000 per game. Although there is no empirical evidence that identifies a causal relation, there is little doubt that the Bundesliga suffered a severe blow and lost much of its credibility. It was lucky for the German football industry that the national team won the 1974 World Cup and reconciled the nation with its most popular pastime.

Ten years later, the next crisis occurred. In the 1985/86 season only 5.5 million people, an average of 18,000 per match, could be bothered to make their way to the local Bundesliga stadiums. There appears to be a complex set of interrelated reasons for the dramatic decline in attendance figures. First, against the context of growing unemployment and a stagnating economy in Germany, many ordinary people were put off by the rising salaries of football's top earners. Players changed clubs for the sake of higher wages and earned millions of Deutschmark while many Germans were worried about keeping their jobs. In 1977, Kevin Keegan joined Hamburg for 2.2 million Deutschmark. Five years later, Karl-Heinz Rummenigge was the first German player to be rewarded with about one million Deutschmark for his services to the advertising industry.

Second, many club directors were so busy counting the income generated through sponsorship deals and TV money that they forgot to look after their 'bread and butter', the fans. Instead of appreciating their loyalty they started to consider them as another source of income. In Hamburg, club officials introduced a system which forced fans to buy two tickets at the same time – the most desirable tickets for top matches could only be purchased together with tickets for a less attractive game. Fans' angry reactions led to the scheme being quickly withdrawn.

Third, the behaviour of some players caused serious consternation among fans. Players publicly displaying their new-found wealth through status symbols, such as expensive cars, in combination with the arrogance and immaturity shown by many, undermined the common illusion that there was some sort of link between supporters and their team. Newspaper reports revealed the gambling obsessions of some players, the outrageous life styles and excessive alcohol consumption of others. A series of unacceptable events on the pitch contributed to the further dramatic deterioration of many German players' reputations.[29] Consequently, the growing socio-economic and cultural distance between football stars and their local communities became an increasingly divisive issue.[30]

The measures that clubs took to regain the confidence and support of their local communities were fairly simple. Many clubs – Bayern Munich was one example – offered concessions to the unemployed. Others, such as Borussia Dortmund, lowered their ticket prices and did not raise them for several years. Both Bayern

Munich and Schalke made their players attend their respective fan clubs' Christmas parties. A trip down a local coal mine was a compulsory and educational excursion for the whole Schalke squad. Furthermore, many Bundesliga clubs started to employ fan-liaison officers, who were tasked with building bridges between the clubs and their traditional supporter base and local communities.

But it was not only the clubs who experienced first-hand the effects of fans voting with their feet: the aforementioned TV channel Sat.1 also felt fans' wrath when it dared to abandon the 6–7 pm TV slot that had been dedicated to the coverage of sports, in particular football, since the early 1960s. In 2001, Sat.1 changed the time of its Bundesliga coverage to start at 8.15 pm. This arrangement was driven by the desire for more people to subscribe to Premiere, a pay-TV sister station of Sat.1. Not even the pleas of leading German politicians from all political parties could convince Sat.1 to abandon this plan. The fans simply did not watch the programme; instead of the usual five million viewers, only about two million people tuned in, thus forcing Sat.1 to return the football coverage to its earlier slot after only three weeks.

A much more serious crisis threatening the basic existence of many teams in both the Bundesliga and the second division occurred in the final stages of the 2001/02 season when KirchSport, owner of both leagues' TV rights, went bankrupt. The Kirch group's plight threatened the survival of several German football clubs due to their dependence on Kirch's regular payments for TV rights. Smaller clubs were worst affected – television money made up more than half of their income. This financial crisis was so serious that the German government even considered bailing out the country's top football clubs with a €200 million emergency fund.[31]

In the aftermath of the KirchSport bankruptcy, all professional football clubs had to lower their expenditure dramatically and immediately. This affected the existing squads as well as the clubs' transfer-market activities. Many clubs reduced their squad size – some even halved them – as, rather than the €460 million expected, the German Football League received only €290 million.[32] In 2003, approximately 200 professional football players were unemployed. Those who did continue to play saw reductions in their salaries. Furthermore, after years of generous spending on stadia and staff, football directors had to be much more frugal. Fans immediately rewarded the emergence of this new modesty and the return of many clubs to solid financial ground. The subsequent season (2003/2004) saw almost 11 million people watching live Bundesliga matches and season ticket sales soaring to such an extent that some clubs decided to cap their numbers.

Resistance II: symbolic rebellions and cultures of defiance

While 'in the mid-1980s the English game was synonymous in the global public imagination with spectator violence and an entrenched infrastructural decline',[33] German clubs started to repackage and rebrand the 'football match' product in order to attract wealthier spectators. The event was increasingly sold as a respectable family experience, an exciting spectacle and an entertaining leisure activity. The new but slowly growing breed of bourgeois football spectators were able to enjoy the comforts of many relatively new and modern stadia as well as the carnivalesque and colourful performances of the more traditional football fans. It is against this context of the bourgeoisification of the game that the existence and development of very distinctive fan subcultures must be understood.

The provocative symbolism of fans waving Deutschmark notes at players does not require any explanation – the message could not be more unambiguous. Other activities, however – in particular the subcultural style of football fans[34] – are very often not that easy to decipher. The subcultural performance of predominantly male, young fans which emerged in the mid-1980s is deeply rooted in traditional working-class culture and celebrates proletarian values. It demonstrates and asserts an unequivocal allegiance to a specific team, attempts to symbolically bridge the growing gap between team and fans, and is intended as a challenge to the more affluent spectators.

These fans' fairly uniform outward appearance, themed by the colours of their respective teams, not only provides a clear expression of their identity but also contributes to a sense of belonging and solidarity.[35] Wearing football shirts, jumpers, and hats is not only a public demonstration of loyalty and identification: these polyester symbols of belonging also challenge other spectators. The question raised is: who are the 'true' and 'genuine' fans? At the same time the use of provocative symbols, such as the swastika and/or badges of the Red Army Faction, a well known left-wing terrorist organization, is widespread. Flags are used to stand out of the masses and to gain the attention of television crews, who often include pictures from colourful terraces in their reports. That, in turn, gives fans the opportunity to experience themselves through the televisual media. Given their marginal status, this exposure is very likely to produce a significant sense of power. There is, nowadays, a distinctly 1970s/early 1980s feel to many of these fans' expressions of commitment and passion, with an array of patches and pin badges attached to their sleeveless denim jackets and scarves wrapped around their wrists.

The way many contemporary fans orchestrate their appearance still 'signals a body perception whose dominant principles are physical strength and aggressive masculinity'.[36] Although the celebration of masculine norms and values such as power, strength, toughness and stamina offers a fairly romanticized view of traditional working class culture, it also stresses and challenges the differences between the new, more affluent, middle class spectators and traditional supporters. The regularly occurring chants and songs focus on similar issues. They demonstrate a close or even symbiotic relationship between supporters and their team, reiterate the identity of fans and reveal an omnipotent self-perception. Provocations and insults directed at the opposing fans are also integral to the fans' ritualized behaviour.

Although the subcultural style of these fans shows a high degree of continuity, there have also been both subtle and major changes in German football stadia. Whille traditionally many fans carried small, industrially produced copies of the club's flag, nowadays their flags are often hand-made, more imaginative and much larger. The dominant feature is naturally the colour combination of the fan's team and its official emblem. Many fans have, however, added the flags of foreign players' native countries; others have sewn the name of their group and/or home town onto the fabric, and some banners highlight the club's achievements. In some stadiums an official parade of the largest and most imaginative flags prior to kick-off has become a key feature of proceedings.[37]

The behaviour and subcultural style of these young people might best be conceptualized as a culture of defiance. These fans are defiant in their attempts to assert their sense of difference to the new breed of football spectators. Such defiance brings with it a nostalgic and idealized re-reading of football's history and cultural roots. Although such manifestations of nostalgia do not necessarily point to the wish to turn the clock back, they do, nevertheless, question the direction of football's contemporary development and express a widespread dissatisfaction with the way the game is currently run.

The fans of Hamburg's less glamorous Bundesliga team, FC St Pauli, are not only defiant, but also politically very aware and pro-active. In order to understand the close relationship between politics and fandom, one needs to recognize the interconnectedness and interdependence of club and working-class suburb. In the case of FC St Pauli, the area is well known for its red-light district, squats and a buoyant alternative youth scene. Since the mid-1980s the terraces of the Millerntor Stadium have been famous for broadcasting political messages that highlight the conflict between fan culture and commerce more explicitly than those of any other fan group. But it was not only the explicit rejection of the increasing commercialization of football that caught the public's attention: fans also raised banners addressing wider political issues such as racism, sexism, homophobia, militarism, and the re-emergence of neo-fascist groups in Germany. St Pauli fans organized a number of political rallies criticizing local right-wing politicians, budget cuts, police suppression and the opening of a shop selling Nazi memorabilia. It is this combination of political activism and football fandom that has made this small club well known outside Hamburg. Interestingly, on many occasions a small number of players have actively supported the fans' activities, through both signing petitions and lending their presence on demonstrations.

At the annual general meeting in November 2007, a vast majority of attendees urged the board of directors to ensure that 'the name Millerntor-Stadium cannot be sold, modified or changed for the purpose of advertising, sponsoring or as a reward for any financial contributions to the club'. Although there was a short discussion about whether this was a legally binding decision or a moral recommendation, two weeks later the board of directors abandoned their plan to rename the ground in order to finance its expansion and modernization.[38] However, that was only one of the many battles these fans have fought in the wider war against the commercialization of their club. Most recently, in December 2010, an influential fan group called the Social Romantics published a petition that demanded a more restrained and considerate approach to the club's commercial activities. Although St Pauli's president, Stefan Orth, has repeatedly stressed that he has no intention to offer Disneyland-like experiences in the Millerntor-Stadium, many fans do not seem to trust these kinds of sweeping proclamations. One of their banners suggests that 'Good intentions are no substitute for good deeds'. The Social Romantics' petition criticizes the installation of 200 business seats and VIP boxes, one of which has been bought by Susis Showbar, a strip club from the neighbouring *Reeperbahn*: 'Women were pole-dancing during matches and stripping when St Pauli scored. Following protests, Susis agreed to desist during games and to tell its employees to put more clothes on, but the fans want the showbar's people to get out altogether.'[39] Although the Social Romantics have been invited to join a working party that evaluates the club's commercial activities, they want more concessions and have even threatened a stadium boycott. Perhaps they remember that the original symbol of St Pauli's first wave of organized resistance, the skull and crossbones, has become the club's most successful merchandising motive and an officially registered trademark. Although it has become increasingly difficult over the past two decades to differentiate between myths and reality, the multi-faceted political activities and resistance of St Pauli's fans have certainly been innovative, and the fans themselves have become role models for many others.

Drawing on props, slogans and action from political protest movements and combining these with the attempts to preserve a meaningful football fan culture is uncommon, but is typical of a very different subculture – the Ultras, who have emerged over the past 15 years. When a large number of top German players moved to the wealthy Italian Serie A league, the German media began to report on foreign matches. Although English matches and teams were generally far more popular, the fireworks, banners and large-scale choreographies of the Italian Ultras caught the attention of many German fans. Inspired by these the Madboyzs, a group of Leverkusen fans, featured prominently in the headlines in 1994, surprising the football world with some impressive pyrotechnics at one of their team's UEFA Cup matches. However, the Ultras' sense of aesthetics and appearance is not the only thing that differentiates this group. Their political explicitness also came as a surprise to many. In sharp contrast with their Italian counterparts, Geman Ultras take a left-wing stance that tries to preserve an old-fashioned, romantic and idealized version of football. A huge banner that became part of the inventory of the Allianz Arena in Munich in 2008 sums up their main cause: *Gegen den modernen Fußball* (Against Modern Football).

Many clubs initially reacted positively to the Ultras, as their aesthetically pleasing performances enriched the stadium atmosphere. However, this changed quickly when club directors realized that these were a rather critical and outspoken species of fan often displaying a left-wing political position. Ultras strongly oppose the commercialization of the game, are very unpredictable, often create their own props rather than purchasing merchandise and are not afraid of clashing with clubs' directors.

The Ultras' political agenda has gradually become more complex and differentiated. In October 2010, almost 5000 Ultras marched through the centre of Berlin in one of the most colourful demonstrations the German capital has seen for a long time. Despite the very broad motto of this rally, *Erhalt der Fankultur* (preservation of fan culture), the key concerns were very clear. Banners and chants focused on the affordability of ticket prices, the increasing fragmentation of match days, the renaming of stadia, and police surveillance and repression.[40]

The Ultras aspire to be critical, provocative and influential. Their commitment to the subculture goes far beyond football matches and affects their everyday lives. The preparation of their choreographies and the production of large banners and flags is not only time consuming but also expensive. Rehearsals often happen in disused hangars and under motorway bridges and it can take weeks for a performance to be deemed ready. Despite the Ultras' persistent attempts to offer a rebellious and creative alternative, recent studies have revealed that their normative system is rather traditional and has a number of similarities with the early football subcultures discussed above. Key elements of their value system are the confirmation and public celebration of masculinity (defined as a combination of courage, strength, stamina and lack of fear), solidarity (focusing on commitment to the group as well as loyalty to the club), impressive performances (of rehearsed choreographies, chants and songs; this also refers to the fans' visual appearance) and territorial sovereignty over the terraces that have been symbolically appropriated.[41] Equally traditional is the way Ultras are organized. Generally, these groups have hierarchical structures, with boards of directors and special responsibilities, such as for marketing, finance and PR, being allocated to individuals. Some even have written statutes.[42]

There are, however, also a number of significant differences between Ultras and other fan groups. They do not only communicate important messages through written banners, sophisticated choreographies and chants, but also rely heavily on the internet. Most of them operate colourful and very professional websites that provide a virtual stage for their subcultural practice and performances. More fundamentally, for Ultras the club is more important than individual players. Consequently, they do not wear replica shirts sporting the names and/or numbers of specific players. Furthermore, their dislike and rejection of the official club merchandise has meant that they produce their own props, symbols and outfits representing their allegiances. Some groups even sell these products via their websites. They also reject the hyper-commercialization of international football matches and tournaments – this stance has led to a conspicuous absence from these events. Ultras consider themselves to be at the forefront, as a kind of avant-garde, of the struggle to maintain a traditional fan culture; they wish to offer alternatives to the established patterns of fan behaviour and football consumption.[43] Their main concern is that DFB and Bundesliga clubs are pursuing a policy that marginalizes genuine fans and gives priority to more affluent spectators. At the same time, Ultras are keen to preserve (selected) traditions, such as the original names of stadia and clubs, the colour combinations of their teams and the terrace culture. Even if they could not and cannot always prevent changes, their patience and persistence in ignoring such modifications and continuing to use the old names of stadiums (Franken- instead of easycredit-stadium in Nuremberg, for example) or teams' established colours (such as green and white instead of green-white-orange in Bremen) is impressive.

Some other fans are not overly impressed by the Ultras, despite their visually impressive performances and explicit political agenda. The group has been criticized for appearing to have become less interested in supporting their team and more concerned about their own appearance and reputation. Their constant and relentless chanting over 90 minutes can be stupefying rather than exhilarating. Furthermore, their often cliquish and self-centred behaviour hardly leaves any scope for creative influence from other fan groups and their obsession with planning, preparing and executing their performances undermines the spontaneity of football crowds.

Furthermore, there appears to be an uneasy relationship between Ultras and the more organized fan groups. This applies particularly to the so-called Fan Projects that perform a number of roles. In the first instance, these Fan Projects are organizations for supporters, addressing a wide variety of fan issues and concerns. They also cooperate with social workers and educational institutions, and liaise with their respective football clubs. Although most of them are funded by the DFB and clubs, as well as through grants from the city and the state, they remain fairly independent – which requires a difficult balancing act. Ultras are very wary of these Fan Projects, questioning their independence and considering them to be merely repositories of club jerseys which attempt to co-opt and appropriate unofficial and grassroots fan clubs.

Despite these animosities between the different fan groups, there is little doubt that the commercialization and bourgeoisification of football in Germany has produced some emotional, innovative and imaginative responses. Most of these fan groups are defined by their loyalty to a club, but they are also driven by their resistance to these developments, and engage in unconventional and creative forms of protest and provocation. So far, the Ultras appear to be the most challenging and threatening of these subcultures, and this has led to considerable overreaction on the part of a few clubs. In 2007, the board of directors of Bayern Munich used a violent encounter between Bayern and Nuremberg fans as the pretext for unsuccessfully trying to ban more than 600 supporters from the Allianz Arena. The fans were perceived to be part of the outspoken Ultra organization *Schickeria*.

These subcultures are, however, a vital ingredient of football matches and add (commercial) value to the spectacle and commodity of the events. They even feature prominently in the marketing strategies of some football clubs. Therefore, the attempt to please all sections of the modern football audience has become a delicate balancing act for those managing the game.

The outcome: a model for other leagues?

The German football industry as a whole is at least worth an estimated €5 billion. At the end of the 2009/2010 season, the 18 Bundesliga clubs registered a combined turnover of just over €2 billion.[44] Although there is little doubt that German football, at its highest level, is a fully fledged commercial activity, the country nevertheless has one of the most fan-friendly football cultures in Europe, which is reflected in a variety of ways.

The Bundesliga has the lowest ticket prices and the highest average attendance figures in Europe. In Dortmund, the Signal-Iduna Stadium has a total capacity of 80,720.[45] On average, more than 78,000 people attended the 2010/2011 season's matches – only Barcelona attracted larger crowds. Dortmund has a giant stand, the *Südtribüne*, which is famous for its colourful and vibrant atmosphere.[46] It is regularly sold out, has a capacity of 24,454, and tickets cost €14.50: in other words, about 30% of all tickets sold in Dortmund are sold for approximately £13. Concessions (€10 and €9, respectively) are available for unemployed and disabled fans. Tickets for children under the age of six are free, although their parents are expected to make a donation of €1, and children between the ages of seven and 14 pay €6. These tickets include free use of the regional public transport system (including trains, trams, underground and buses) on match days: 'Train travel to away games costs a fraction of the normal fare, because clubs and the nationalised rail service have a very good relationship.'[47] Car parks adjacent to the ground have a capacity of around 10,000. Season tickets range from €176.50 for all 17 Bundesliga matches (on the *Südtribüne*) to €847 (although only a few hundred such tickets are available). Due to the enormous popularity of season tickets, most clubs have capped their numbers to ensure access for everyone. The visiting team is always entitled to 10% of the stadium's capacity.

In many stadiums, stewards act more like ushers. They are polite and helpful, and only very rarely face tricky situations. Consumption of alcohol inside the stadiums before, during and after matches is allowed. Even the cleanliness of the terraces is no longer a big issue – punters pay a small deposit, usually €2, on the plastic beer 'glasses' (obviously displaying the emblem and the colours of the home team), which they can then choose to either return or take home. The large video screens in almost all *Bundesliga* grounds not only keep fans up to date with scores from other matches, but also publish train times for fans' return journeys and travel arrangements for the next away game.

The scheduling of *Bundesliga* matches is far less fragmented than that of other European countries' premier divisions. It follows a simple pattern: one match only takes place on Friday evening at 8.30pm – occasionally matches will start slightly later, as referees tend to make sure that all fans have arrived before they blow the whistle; at least six matches take place on Saturday afternoon, almost all of which kick off at 3.30pm; and two are played in the late afternoon/early evening on Sunday.[48] This structure is determined not only by TV interest, but also by infrastructural considerations, such as avoiding traffic congestion in the Ruhr area, which hosts several Bundesliga clubs. In the domestic Cup competition, teams from lower divisions always play at home when drawn against opponents from the top league. Many teams agree to pre-season friendlies against local clubs without demanding a fee.

For Reinhard Rauball, president of the German Football League (DFL) – a branch of the DFB which looks after the professional teams – the three cornerstones of the Bundesliga's mission statement are stability, continuity and closeness to fans.[49] Of all the Bundesliga's statutes, the '50+1 rule' appears to be one of the most significant legal parameters, due to its massive implications. This states that members of a club must always retain at least 51% ownership: therefore, no 'outsider' can own more than 49% of a German club's shares, preventing a single entity taking control. Naturally, this deters the kind of takeover experienced by a large number of English clubs. In November 2009 the rule was challenged by Hannover's president, who proposed abandoning this principle. A meeting of all 36 first and second-division clubs rejected the proposal decisively. The presidents of 35 clubs voted in favour of the status quo,[50] ensuring that speculators and oligarchs will take no interest in Bundesliga clubs.[51]

There are two exceptions to the 50+1 rule. Leverkusen and Wolfsburg are entirely owned by the chemical giant Bayer and the car maker VW, respectively. This anomaly has a convincing justification: both companies have been supporting their local teams for several decades, have proven that they take their involvement seriously and have acted in the best interests of the club, team and local community. Therefore they have been permitted to acquire the majority of shares. These are also the only two clubs whose names clearly identify their main sponsor, and other clubs are not allowed to follow this example. There are no plans to change the names of the Bundesliga and German Cup competitions to reflect any sponsorship.

Since both companies, as well as the vast majority of members of the other clubs, are German, there is a sense that all of them also care about the performance of the national team. Consequently, there is a more balanced relationship between clubs, the German Football Association and the German Football League. Instead of persistent infighting there appears to be a sense of unity and common purpose. This is clearly reflected in the €500 million investment into total restructuring of the youth development system in 2002, two years after the German side was knocked out of the Euro 2000 at the group stage. The revamped, centrally controlled scheme forces all 36 clubs in the two Bundesliga divisions to operate youth academies. If they fail to comply they are not given the licence that allows them to play in these leagues. At any one time approximately 5000 players are going through the system. Boys are taken on from the age of 12. Furthermore, these academies have to make sure that at least 12 boys from the annual intake must be eligible to play for Germany. The new system has had impressive results: at the 2010 South Africa World Cup, Germany fielded one of the youngest sides, with an average age of 24.7. All 23 members of the German squad had come through the new youth academies. The annual investment of €80 million into the scheme also had an impact on the composition of the Bundesliga, with almost two thirds of its players eligible to play for the national team:

> There is no shortage of good players to supply the national team, no embarrassing over-reliance on imported talent on the field or in the dug-out, and while Germany may no longer be automatic favourites to reach the final of any forthcoming tournament their ranking of fifth in the world puts them deservedly ahead of England and France.[52]

At first sight, less logical but even more astonishing is the German Football League's decision against selling broadcasting rights to the highest bidder, thus losing a considerable amount of revenue. Some experts estimate that this policy has cost the DFL in the region of €150 million. Instead, all matches are freely available via the state-run terrestrial TV stations. The commercial rationale for this is fairly straightforward: its extensive TV presence keeps the game popular and provides access to a large internal market; it is therefore very attractive to sponsors and advertisers, whose payments compensate for the loss of revenue from selling the TV rights at a higher price.

On the one hand, this set-up appears to have a clear disadvantage. German football teams have been unsuccessful in European competitions in the past ten years. Since Dortmund and Munich won the Champions League in 1997 and 2001, respectively, only a couple of German teams have reached the finals of the competition, only to leave empty-handed. Furthermore, Bundesliga clubs do not have the financial power to lure international megastars to play for them, and the number of TV viewers worldwide who watch Bundesliga matches is negligible. On the other, Bundesliga seasons are competitive, exciting and unpredictable. Although Munich and Dortmund are outstanding clubs which field high-quality teams, the outcome of the league is rarely a foregone conclusion. Three separate clubs have won the Cup in the past three seasons, and there have been three different *Bundesliga* champions – often only decided on the last day of the season.

Conclusion

'A time to make friends' was the official slogan of the 2006 World Cup in Germany. The 'no-nonsense' approach of this mega-event's organizers was clearly reflected in the opening ceremony, which was low-key, charming and, most importantly, short. Too often, such occasions are memorable for their extensive length, ridiculous self-indulgence and outrageous pomposities. On this occasion, the hosts understood that the hundreds of millions of TV viewers on six continents had not tuned in for national posturing, grand political messages or sophisticated dance routines, but for one thing only: the football.

The 2006 World Cup turned out to be not only a high-quality international competition but also the most fan-centred event of this kind to have been seen for a long time. For many this did not come as a surprise, as the Bundesliga looks after its largest stakeholder better than many other European leagues. This is not due to the altruism, generosity and compassion of the football establishment in Germany, but is largely a result of the fans' opposition, which has a rebellious and subversive quality and has led to a large number of compromises. The effectiveness of the fans' resistance is facilitated by a legal framework that forces clubs to provide opportunities for democratic involvement and allows fans to engage in decision-making processes.

In order to succinctly describe the outcome of such opposition it might be useful to draw on the concept of hybridity, a term used to explain the merging of cultural artefacts with very different roots. Football culture in Germany at the highest level, that is in the Bundesliga, is constructed both by commercial interests and by the defiant and rebellious reaction to them. In other words, while the pitch hosts players worth millions, the terraces do not simply provide a colourful backdrop: they are an integral part of the multifaceted and commodified spectacle, despite their resistance and opposition to some of these developments.[53]

The relationship between football fans and those driving the commodification and commercialization of the game is characterized by a high degree of resilience, vitality and unpredictability that is typical of the hegemonic process of class interaction. It clearly shows that 'the dominant class cannot prevent the underclasses from establishing their own social enclaves of meaning and their own renegade cultural forms'.[54]

Franz Beckenbauer, football's ultimate moral authority in Germany, has repeatedly stressed that this game has the power to create a better world and to bring tribes together.[55] Beckenbauer's assessment might well apply to the short-lived and often harmless manifestations of soft nationalism in the context of international events. However, there are doubts that the tribes of fans will ever be united with the game's commercial forces. In Germany, they respect each other, but continue to carefully monitor each other's moves.

Notes

1. Harding, 'How to Win at Football'.
2. Frew and McGillivray, *Exploring Hyper-experiences*, 187.
3. Merkel, 'Football Made in Germany', 101.
4. Biermann, 'Trains Running Late'.
5. Harding, 'The War is Over'. For a more detailed account of the football rivalry between England and Germany, see Ramsden, *Don't Mention the War*, 325–62.
6. Gruneau, *Class, Sports and Social Development*.
7. Hargreaves, *Sport, Power and Culture*.
8. Sage, *Power and Ideology*.
9. Sugden and Bairner, *Sport, Sectarianism and Society*.
10. Outhwaite and Bottomore, *Social Thought*, 255. See also Giulianotti, *Sport – a Critical Sociology*, 43–61 for a detailed discussion of the strengths and weaknesses of Gramsci's concept of hegemony.
11. Merkel, 'Sport, Power and the State in Weimar Germany', 141–8.
12. Morgan, *Leftist Theories of Sport*, 69.
13. Swingewood, *A Short History of Sociological Thought*, 209.
14. Heitmeier and Peter, *Jugendliche Fußballfans*, 56–63. Although more sophisticated and differentiated, Gulianotti's typology (2002) is not necessarily applicable to the German context.
15. Merkel, 'The Hidden History of the DFB', 167.
16. Merkel, 'Sport, Power and the State in Weimar Germany', 148–60.
17. Heinrich, *Der Deutsche Fußballbund*, 192.
18. Merkel, 'Football Made in Germany', 99–103.
19. Heinrich, *Der Deutsche Fußballbund*, 189.
20. Lindner and Breuer, *Fußball als Show*, 162–70.
21. Hesse-Lichtenberger, *Tor!*, 155–59.
22. Beck, 'Wir haben den Sumpf trocken gelegt', 433–5.
23. Franzke, 'Spiele, Medien und Moneten', 400.
24. Schmeh, *Titel, Tore, Transaktionen*, 37–44.
25. Schmeh, *Titel, Tore, Transaktionen*, 78–97.

26. Giulianotti, *Football – A Sociology of the Global Game*.
27. Pyta, *German Football: A Cultural History*, 16.
28. Schulze-Marmeling, *Borussia Dortmund*, 336.
29. For example, the intentional and brutal collision between Toni Schumacher, Germany's goalkeeper, and Patrick Battiston in the semi-finals of the 1982 World Cup in Spain, which left the French defender seriously injured.
30. Schulze-Marmeling, *Der gezähmte Fußball*, 152–79.
31. Gibson, 'Germany to Rescue Clubs'.
32. Mikos, 'German Football', 151.
33. Giulianotti, 'Supporters, Followers, Fans and Flaneurs', 25.
34. Brake, *Comparative Youth Culture*, 12.
35. Merkel, 'Football Identity and Youth Culture in Germany', 52–66
36. Becker, 'Haut'se, Haut'se in'ne Schnauze', 80.
37. Merkel, 'Milestones in the History of Football Fandom in Germany', 221–39.
38. Hasenbein, 'Eine andere Fußballwelt ist möglich', 78–9.
39. Honigstein, 'Trying Times at St Pauli'.
40. Honigstein, 'Are German Fans Really Turning Against the Beautiful Game?'.
41. Utz and Benke, 'Hools, Kutten, Novizen und Veteranen', 103–4; Pilz, *Wandlungen des Zuschauerverhaltens*, 104–5.
42. Sommerey, *Die Jugendkultur der Ultras*, 81.
43. Schwier, 'Die Welt der Ultras', 23
44. For comparison, the Premier League's income from TV was almost €2 billion in the same year.
45. Dortmund's spectacular ground was previously – and remains better – known as the Wesfalenstadion.
46. The terracing in many German stadiums can be quickly transformed into seating areas for European club games and other international matches.
47. Oliver et al., *World Cup 2006 - Special Report*, 23.
48. In the very final stages of an annual campaign all matches take place at the same time on Saturday afternoon.
49. Wilson, 'Doing the Right Thing'
50. To be precise, 32 voted against this proposal and three abstained; only Hannover themselves were in favour.
51. Wilson, 'Doing the Right Thing'.
52. Wilson, 'Doing the Right Thing'.
53. Gabler, *Die Ultras*, 120.
54. Morgan, *Leftist Theories of Sport*, 71.
55. Crowley, 'The Cup that Rules the World'.

References

Beck, O. 'Wir haben den Sumpf trocken gelegt'. In *100 Jahre DFB – Die Geschichte des Deutschen Fußball-Bundes (100 years DFB – The history of the German Football Association)*, ed. Deutscher Fußball-Bund, 433–5. Berlin: Sportverlag Berlin, 1999.

Becker, P. 'Haut'se in'ne Schnauze" – Das Fußballstadium als Ort der Reproduktion sozialer Strukturen". In *Sport und Körperliche Gewalt*, ed. Günther Pilz, 72–84. Reinbek: Rowohlt Verlag, 1982.

Biermann, C. 'Trains Running Late and Football with Flair – We'll do Anything to Fit'. *The Guardian*, June 25, 2006.

Brake, M. *Comparative Youth Culture – The Sociology of Youth Culture and Youth Subcultures in America, Britain and Canada*. London: Routledge, 1980.

Crowley, J. 'The Cup that Rules the World'. *The Observer*, June 11, 2006.

Franzke, R. 'Spiele, Medien und Moneten' (Matches, media and money). In *100 Jahre DFB – Die Geschichte des Deutschen Fußball-Bundes (100 years DFB – The history of the German Football Association)*, ed. Deutscher Fußball-Bund, 400. Berlin: Sportverlag Berlin, 1999.

Frew, M., and D. McGillivray. 'Exploring Hyper-experiences: Performing the Fan at Germany 2006'. *Journal of Sport and Tourism* 13, no. 3 (2008): 181–98.

Gabler, J. *Die Ultras – Fußballfans und Fußballkulturen in Deutschland. (The Ultras – Football Fans and Football Cultures in Germany)*. Koeln: PapyRossa Verlag, 2010.
Gibson, O. 'Germany to Rescue Clubs if Kirch Folds'. *The Guardian*, April 4, 2002.
Gruneau, R. *Class, Sports and Social Development*. Amherst: University of Massachusetts, 1983.
Giulianotti, R. *Football – A Sociology of the Global Game*. Cambridge: Polity, 1999.
Giulianotti, R. 'Supporters, Followers, Fans and Flaneurs – A Taxonomy of Spectator Idenities in Football'. *Journal of Sport and Social Issues* 26, no. 1 (2002): 25–46.
Giulianotti, R. *Sport – A Critical Sociology*. Cambridge: Polity, 2005.
Harding, L. 'How to Win at Football'. *The Guardian*, July 10, 2006.
Harding, L. 'The War is Over'. *The Guardian*, December 26, 2006.
Hargreaves, J. *Sport, Power and Culture*. Cambridge: Polity, 1987.
Hasenbein, R. "Eine andere Fußballwelt ist möglich: Möglichkeiten und Strategien gegen eine völlige Enteignung der Fans am Beispiel des FC St. Pauli' (A different football world is possible: Possibilities and strategies to avoid the total alienation of fans drawing on the example of FC St. Pauli)'. In *Teil-Nehmen und Teil-Haben - Fußball aus der Sicht kritischer Fans und Gesellschaftswissenschaftler* (Participating and partaking: Football viewed by critical fans and social scientists), ed. Bernd Lederer, 78–9. Göttingen: Verlag Die Werkstatt, 2010.
Heinrich, A. *Tooor! Toor! Tor! 40 Jahre 3:2*. (Goal! Goal! Goal! 40 years after the 3:2). Nördlingen: Rotbuch Verlag, 1994.
Heinrich, A. *Der Deutsche Fußballbund - Eine politische Geschichte* (The German Football Association – a political history). Köln: PapyRossa, 2000.
Heitmeier, W., and J.I. Peter. *Jugendliche Fußballfans* (Young football fans). Munich: Juventa Verlag, 1988.
Hesse-Lichtenberger, U. *Tor! - The Story of German Football*. London: WSC Books, 2003.
Honigstein, R. 'Are German fans really Turning Against the Beautiful Game?' *The Guardian*, April 7, 2008.
Honigstein, R. 'Trying Times at St Pauli as Fans' Faction Fights to Maintain Values'. *The Guardian*, January 31, 2011.
Lindner, R., and T. Breuer. "Fußball als Show – Kommerzialisierung, Oligolisierung und Professionalisierung des Fußballsports' (Football as entertainment – the commercialisation, making of oligopolies and professionalisation of football as a sport)'. In *Fußball – Soziologie und Sozialgeschichte einer populären Sportart.* (Football – Sociology and social history of a popular sport), ed. Wilhelm Hopf, 162–70. Bensheim: Päd Extra, 1979.
Merkel, U. 'Football Made in Germany: Solid, Reliable and Undramatic but Successful'. In *Hosts and Champions - Football Cultures, National Identities and the World Cup in the USA*, ed. John Sugden and Alan Tomlinson, 93–118. Avebury: Gower Press, 1994.
Merkel, U. 'Football Identity and Youth Culture in Germany'. In *Football Cultures and Identities*, ed. Gary Armstrong and Richard Giulianotti, 52–66. London: Macmillan, 1999.
Merkel, U. 'The Hidden History of the German Football Association (DFB): 1900–1950', *Football and Society* 1, 2 (2000): 167–86.
Merkel, U. 'Sport, Power and the State in Weimar Germany'. In *Power Games – Theory and Method for a Critical Sociology of Sport*, ed. John Sugden and Alan Tomlinson, 141–60. London: Routledge, 2002.
Merkel, U. *'Milestones in the Development of Football Fandom in Germany: Global Impacts on Local Contests'*. *Soccer and Society* 8, no. 2/3 (2007): 221–39.
Mikos, L. 'Football – A Media-economic Survey: the Impact of the KirchMedia Company on Football and Television in Germany". In *German Football: History, Culture, Society*, ed. Alan Tomlinson and Christopher Young, 143–54. London: Routledge, 2006.
Morgan, W.J. *Leftist Theories of Sport – A Critique and Reconstruction*. Urbana, Ill: University of Illinois Press, 1994.
Brian, O., Luke Harding, Amy Lawrence, Jamie Jackson, Anna Kessel and Nadja Korinth, 'World Cup 2006 – Special Report'. *The Observer*, December 11, 2005.
Outhwaite, T., and W. Bottomore. *The Blackwell Dictionary of Social Thought*. Oxford: Blackwell, 1995.

Pilz, G., S. Behn, A. Klose, V. Schwenzer, W. Steffan, and F. Wölki. *Wandlungen des Zuschauerverhaltens im Profifußball* (Changes in the spectator behaviour in professional football). Bonn: Hofmann Verlag, 2006.

Pyta, W. 'German Football: A Cultural History'. In *German Football: History, Culture, Society*, ed. Alan Tomlinson and Christopher Young, 1–22. London: Routledge, 2006.

Ramsden, J. *Don't Mention the War – The British and the Germans since 1890*. London: Abacus, 2007.

Sage, G.H. *Power and Ideology in American Sport*. Urbana, IL: Human Kinetics, 1998.

Schmeh, K. *Titel, Tore, Transaktionen (Titles, Goals and Transactions)*. Heidelberg: Redline Wirtschaft, 2005.

Schulze-Marmeling, D. *Der gezähmte Fußball – Zur Geschichte einer subversiven Sportart (Tamed football – the history of a subversive sport)*. Göttingen: Verlag Die Werkstatt, 1992.

Schulze-Marmeling, D. *Der Ruhm, der Traum und das Geld – Die Geschichte von Borussia Dortmund* (Fame, dreams and money – The history of Borussia Dortmund). Göttingen: Verlag Die Werkstatt, 2005.

Schwier, J. 'Die Welt der Ultras. Eine neue Generation von Fußballfans' (The world of Ultras – a new generation of football fans), *Sport und Gesellschaft* 1 (2005): 21–38.

Sommerey, M. *Die Jugendkultur der Ultras – Zur Entstehung einer neuen Generation von Fußballfans*. (The youth culture of Ultras – The emergence of a new generation of football fans). Stuttgart: ibidem Verlag, 2010.

Sugden, J., and A. Bairner. *Sport, Sectarianism and Society in a Divided Ireland*. Leicester: Leicester University Press, 1995.

Swingewood, A. *A Short History of Sociological Thought*. London: MacMillan, 1991.

Utz, R., and M. Benke. "Hools, Kutten, Novizen und Veteranen' (Hooligans, fans, novices and veterans)'. In *Kursbuch Jugend Kultur (Youth and Culture)*, ed. SpoKK, 102–15. Mannheim: Bollmann Verlag, 1997.

Wilson, P. 'Doing the Right Thing is German Football's Forte'. *The Guardian*, November 22, 2009.

Split loyalties: football is a community business

Hans K. Hognestad

Department of Sport and Outdoor Life Studies, Telemark University College, BØ, Norway

> This chapter discusses changes and continuities in football support, drawing primarily on studies in Norway and Britain. Examples of resistance to hypercommodification are analysed in relation to the game's growing appeal as a source of social capital, delving into how this has affected the sociality of supporter communities. While football fan culture is intertwined with the current commodification of the game, this can by no means be seen as a one-dimensional, chronological process. The politics of football identities continue to be carved out through conflict and rivalry in football, but also increasingly through bonds of mutuality and transnational networks. While the incredible increase in television coverage has altered football fandom during the past decades, evidence of a striking continuity is still to be found in the sociality of matchday rituals in many places. The polygamous way in which European football fans relate to several clubs should be understood not only as a media phenomenon, but as a result of physical explorations and social networking between football communities.

Introduction

Football has functioned as a confirmation of belonging and symbol of citizenship since the late nineteenth century.[1] However it was not until the 1990s, and especially after the publication of Nick Hornby's autobiographical novel *Fever Pitch*,[2] that football fandom developed into a sign of cultural sophistication, legitimacy and cultural capital for the 'educated classes' in many societies. Simultaneously the game has gone through a dramatic commodification in societies structured around global capitalism. This is evident in the sale of television rights for matches in the most popular leagues and star players' dramatically rocketing salaries. The same period has witnessed a widening of the gap between large and smaller clubs, in terms of both financial muscle and sporting success, in many national leagues. These processes have altered the footballing habitus for a lot of fans over a relatively short period of time. It is possible to view the development of football during the past 20 years as a transformation from a subculture to a global cultural reference point and mega-business, involving media and transnational corporate ownership structures.[3] Richard Giulianotti has labelled these processes in football as a kind of *hypercommodification*.[4] In his pioneering analysis of football spectators, issues of resistance, consumerism and identity are viewed through four ideal-type football spectators: supporter, follower, fan and flaneur. These categories will guide some of the discussion in this chapter.

It is often argued that football has moved from its working-class cultural heritage toward a more commercial culture, evident also in new stadium designs, matchday events and crowd practices. It is not controversial to agree with the assertions made by John Hargreaves two and a half decades ago that – particularly in Britain – from the early twentieth century, terrace culture had been flavoured by a dominant working class, often exclusively male, culture.[5] However, these assertions need more nuanced scrutiny. From certain historical perspectives, football is a game which has changed remarkably little over the past 150 years. Historian Dave Russell pointed to a significant explanation for the game's popularity in arguing that 'rough' and 'respectable' cultures mingled in the football ground, challenging the widespread notion that the recent processes of commodification have seen middle-class spectators replacing traditional working-class supporters. Russell also argued, in contrast with preceding sociological analysis of terrace culture and football hooliganism in Britain in the 1970s, that the stands at football grounds have always had a substantial middle-class representation.[6] Yet it is possible to argue that recent processes supersede such discourses on traditional class divides in the game. In this article I shall delve into some examples of how football fan cultures have changed during the past couple of decades, drawing primarily on studies in Norway and Britain and highlighting questions of autonomy and resistance toward the prime examples of commodification which are widely perceived as threats to the sociality of footballing communities. A key argument in this chapter is that while football has indeed entered a state of hypercommodification and fan culture is intertwined with the commodification of the game, fans still act as *auteurs* in many respects, from local political resistance to transnational networking.

Activists, hooligans or just fans?

The Marxist-inspired sociological analyses of football carried out in the 1970s by Ian Taylor and Chas Critcher viewed the game as a political battlefield for working-class resistance against bourgeois control.[7] As Giulianotti highlights, both can be regarded as pioneers in the analysis of the commodification of football.[8] Taylor identified corporate processes in the game as early as the 1960s, concluding that they worked to alienate the old working-class supporters and focused on local teams, masculinity and a participatory subculture in which the most important thing was to get behind the teams and encourage them to win games. Taylor viewed the introduction of family sections in the ground and a stronger focus on skill, spectacle and the game being 'a day out' for the whole family as clear indications of attempts to shift the game to better suit the tastes and needs of middle-class consumption.[9] This, Taylor argued, contributed to changes in the relationship between club and spectator which, in effect, gave rise to the hooligan culture that arose in the 1960s. Hooliganism thus interpreted may be seen as an expression of cultural alienation and resistance – an argument found also in some of Hargreaves' arguments.[10]

While Taylor's Marxist understanding of football fandom may be seen as outdated by many, some of his analysis is prophetic with regard to supporter mobilizations, politics and practices which never really took off until two decades later. The rise in fanzines in Britain from the late 1980s, and the establishment of independent supporters' clubs, grew out of the crisis caused by disasters such as the Bradford and Heysel tragedies in 1985 and, especially, the Hillsborough disaster in 1989. More recently a number of supporter-based initiatives and mobilizations of either a local or a transnational character have appeared, acting as resistance movements against what David and Peter Kennedy label 'commodity fetishism' within the modern game.[11] When the owners' proposal for Wimbledon FC to move to a stadium in Milton Keynes, 56 miles north of their old home in London, was sanctioned by the English Football Association in June 2002, it took just a few days for a group of supporters to found new club AFC Wimbledon, following a season marked by effective protests and boycotts of the club they had once supported. AFC Wimbledon started at level nine of the English league system in 2002. After five promotions in nine years, it is now a professional club, controlled by its supporters, and has risen to the fourth highest tier of English football. Similarly, after American businessman Malcolm Glazer's takeover of Manchester United in 2005, dissatisfied United fans founded a new club, FC United of Manchester. The club has had one of the highest average attendances for non-league games, and attracted a 7000-strong crowd to its first-round FA Cup match against local team Rochdale in November 2010. Should such movements be seen as examples of a naïve local heroism, as argued by Andrews and Ritzer,[12] or should we see them as genuine, influential responses to the commodification of the game?

Supporters or consumers?

With a greater focus on analysing the complex interconnections between local and global communities, Giulianotti introduced Robertson's term, 'glocalization', to football studies after a period in which both the culture and the business of football had undergone dramatic structural changes.[13] With a stronger focus on how fan practices are structured by an overwhelming capitalism, Andrews and Ritzer moved the focus on fandom further away from particularized studies, criticizing research on football fans and hegemonic virtues within football fandom as corrupted by a focus on local heroism in the face of globalization. By adopting the concept of 'grobalization' to the study of football, they question the authenticity of identities presumed to be locally rooted.[14]

This critique must be viewed in light of a 'grobal' process in football which can partly be located in the establishment of the English Premier League in 1992, when the media corporation BSkyB purchased exclusive rights to screen live matches and also, to some extent, to dictate the timing of fixtures. This marked the beginning of a new era as many other leagues in Europe followed suit and adopted similar marketing and media strategies. It could be argued that commercialism hit football long before 1992, yet the incredible increase in turnover for the big leagues and big clubs in Europe did not take place until the 1990s.[15] The past two decades have seen a distinct increase in governance by high capitalist principles, evident in clubs' multinational ownership structures, new and modern all-seater stadiums, higher ticket prices and options to watch an almost endless amount of pay-per-view live games on TV or streamed via the internet – from all over the world. The recent global recession has hit many football clubs and fans badly, but the financial muscle of the global clubs in the biggest leagues seems only to increase, widening the economic gaps in a sport and business governed by a wealthy footballing minority.

How have these global processes changed the lives of fans? From the traditional idea of true fandom consisting of providing loyal and unconditional support to one's team – in contrast to assumed 'fair-weather fans' who only turned up for glamorous games in the sun – from the early 1990s the notion of supporting one's team became just as enmeshed with the purchase of the latest replica top or other items from the new football fashion industry. Richard Giulianotti's taxonomy of football spectators evolving between two basic binary oppositions – traditional-consumer and hot-cool – framed within a conceptualization of thin and thick solidarity appear apt conceptual tools for understanding the shifting characteristics of the allegiances between club communities and various types of spectators.

Hot and cold spectatorship

In this taxonomy, inspired by theorists such as Baudrillard and McLuhan, 'the supporter' is presented as a 'hot', traditional spectator who has a long-term emotional relationship with a football club. He (sometimes she) might offer more than just vocal support during games by buying shares in the club and expensive gear from the club shop. The supporter is usually a season-ticket holder, travels to away games and spends a considerable amount of his income supporting the team. This attitude can be seen as the basis from which football clubs have generated, and sometimes exaggerated, their status as symbolic icons for a local community or ethnic group for generations. The latter position, is for a supporter, far more important than issues of financial instability. A supporter defines him or herself as part of a 'we' marked by what Giulianotti calls 'a thick solidarity', in which children are socialized into the club through primary relations to parents and siblings. While players and managers may be adored and cherished, the supporter understands that they generally come and go on a professional basis. Therefore supporters generally see themselves as the most stable part of the club community and the most important emotional stakeholder. Hence, the supporters constitute a subcultural community of commitment, loyalty and solidarity, with the stadium standing out as a symbolic representation of the club community, often drenched in topophilic sentiment.[16]

The other traditional spectator described is 'the follower' – someone with a strong interest in football, who is implicitly aware of particular identities and communities relating to specific clubs. The follower is less personally involved with specific clubs or teams and may instead opt to develop relations across club boundaries to a variety of footballing communities and institutions. Relationships to clubs located in other leagues may have certain ideological attractions, such as the ethnopolitical characters of clubs like Celtic or Barcelona, the politically left radicalism of Italian side Livorno or St Pauli of Hamburg, or in some cases the fascist subcultures of a variety of clubs in Italy and Spain. The follower may develop ties of thick solidarity with these clubs by establishing bonds and developing friendships despite club rivalries, forming part of a transnational network. On a collective level, subcultural groups of fans in Scotland and England are known to have formed informal transnational networks and friendships with various Ultras in Italy. Obviously, the follower can also develop a series of links to other clubs and institutions marked more by a thin solidarity caused by having watched specific games, players or managers, usually on TV or other media. This is described by Giulianotti as 'cool' spectatorship.[17] In this model, a follower would usually define himself against more consumerist values and ways of support by declaring traditional motives in order to make his status appear more authentic, for example by following clubs with no obvious history (or future) of success. The follower is knowledgeable enough not to develop links to clubs which are locally rooted as mutually exclusive rivals, such as declaring an allegiance to *both* Celtic and Rangers, Roma and Lazio or Barcelona and Real Madrid, but does not harbour the same sense of place and belonging or knowledge about a club and its surrounding community as the supporter does. Typically, it could be argued that spectators at a national team's match will be mostly followers, as commitment and participation may be active during a matchday ritual, but will not be grounded in a local community. From such a perspective it is possible to claim that active spectators at games between national teams are followers, not supporters or fans, while the more passive spectators at mega-events like the World Cup, through the gaze of a tourist, resemble the flaneur.[18]

Giulianotti goes on to define the fan as a 'hot consumer spectator'. The fan is passionately involved with their club and may develop intimate ties with players, coaches and managers. Such relationships are more distant and less reciprocal than those developed by supporters. The hypercommodification of the game has to a large extent dislocated players and club officials from supporters, leaving the fan to experience their club and its traditions mostly through the purchase of replica tops and a variety of other club merchandise, alongside subscriptions to commercial TV channels and websites streaming live games with their club. A fan is more likely to accept the rules of a free market by realizing that the club depends on financial contributions in order to exist at a desired level of professionalism and generate sufficient cash to purchase good players. Giulianotti argues that by imposing upon spectators consumer-oriented fan identities, clubs run the risk of seeing fans drift away to other markets, should their market strategies fail. This leads Giulianotti to position the football fan in a category comparable to that of fans of musicians, actors and other celebrities in its unidirectional nature and lack of reciprocal bonds between admirer and admired. This is evident in the way that current star footballers have fully become a part of celebrity culture and how football's new markets, particularly in Asia, have seen a rise in fans of individual players, like Cristiano Ronaldo, rather than clubs and their adherent communities. Although much the same could be said about the celebrity status of George Best in Britain in the 1960s, Giulianotti concludes that the fan identity is increasingly under pressure from the flaneur, or 'cool consumer'.[19]

The flaneur is presented as a direct opposite to the supporter in this taxonomy, although both categories to a certain extent depend on each other and, as binary opposites, feed the other category with meaning. The category is originally drawn from mid-nineteenth century literature, in which Baudelaire described an urban male from a bourgois background who would seek a variety of sensations and experiences of a fleeting nature, preferring to lead a hedonistic life in cafés and other public spaces rather than, for instance, commiting to family life and routinized work life. In a modern setting the flaneur represents a less gender-specific but more middle-class kind of spectator, as he or she needs both economic, educational and cultural capital in order to maintain a more cosmopolitan interest in the game. In this sense the flaneur is presented as a 'cool' customer spectator, entering and experiencing football predominantly through a series of virtual, depersonalized relationships such as through television or the internet. The flaneur gazes on collected, chosen events and is not involved in the participant cultures, grounded identities and partisan rivalries of the supporters. His or her involvement is cosmopolitan and non-tribal in nature. The spending power of the flaneur makes him/her interesting as a customer of various footballing products. In that sense the flaneur is embraced by many local supporters of bigger clubs as they realize that in a neoliberal financial environment, the club needs income – which can be generated by attracting wealthy cosmopolitan flaneurs and their penchant for spending money on cultural events that are considered sufficiently important and glamorous. The contemporary tendency for football clubs to flirt with flaneurs is evident in the case of CF Barcelona, widely considered the best team in the world at the moment. Tourists wishing to view symbols of Catalan ethno-political identity consider guided visits to Barcelona's home ground, Camp Nou, just as relevant as visits to iconic buildings designed by Catalan architect Antoni Gaudi, such as Sagrada Familia or Casa Mila. Hence the flaneur can also stand out as a symbol of football's recent move from being widely considered a more exclusive working-class cultural activity, to a source generating cultural capital for a much broader population.

Resisting or embracing hypercommodification?

This author's first experience of studying football supporters came in 1992 when, as part of my thesis in social anthropology, I travelled to Edinburgh to conduct a study among supporters of Heart of Midlothian. The English Premier League had just been established, alongside Sky Sports, the broadcasting company which became a driving force in the moneyspinning era that football was about to enter, but football in general was at a threshold at this time in Europe. Three years after the Hillsborough disaster and the following Taylor Report on ground redevelopment, British clubs were faced with the necessity for substantial and financially demanding modernization.[20] In the case of Hearts, then-chairman Wallace Mercer had proposed a takeover of local rivals Hibs and relocation of the new 'Edinburgh United' outside the city centre. This stirred strong sentiment among both sets of supporters, whose united protests eventually led to all such plans being put to rest. These two traditional rivals from the Scottish capital are among the oldest clubs in the world, founded in 1874 and 1878 respectively, and both had decided to modernize their old stadiums, located in the townships of Leith (Hibs) and Gorgie (Hearts), after a series of attempts to relocate the inner-city stadiums to sites outside Edinburgh. For my study of Hearts fans I was looking for supporters who showed their commitment by regular match attendance and active participation in the social rituals of a matchday routine. Back then it would probably have been hard to understand the definition of a football flaneur, but spectators who followed only the most successful teams were often described as 'glory hunters'. In Edinburgh this term was often used to describe locals who travelled to Glasgow to follow the big teams, Celtic or Rangers, rather than support one of the local teams, Hibs or Hearts.[21]

The political and moral aspects of support were expressed at the time through various protests and demonstrations against the owners and the numerous fanzines that had started to appear in club communities across Britain. These fanzines were written and produced in a punk-inspired 'do-it-yourself' style at a low cost, with the aid of a photocopier.[22] Some of these fanzines were aware of clubs' attempts to attract new and more wealthy spectators, to which the fanzines expressed considerable resistance. Hearts' chairman at the time, the late Wallace Mercer, was known to be a local representative of the Conservative Party. The aforementioned attempted takeover of local rivals Hibs, and plans for relocation away from their home in the Gorgie part of Edinburgh, where they had played since 1882, were met with fierce protest from Hearts supporters. A defeat at home to Airdrie in December

1992 triggered around 1000 supporters to line up outside the boardroom at Tynecastle Park to show their dissent at the way the club was run. For an outsider, the protests must have resembled a socialist workers' strike, as chants of 'You're just a fat Tory bastard' and 'You stole our money' were aimed toward the bar of the boardroom where Mercer and his wife were trying to enjoy a spot of post-match socializing.

The co-editor of Hearts fanzine *Dead Ball* described the proposals for a multipurpose stadium outside the city centre as a 'post-modern nightmare', referring to the multitude of 'leisure activities' the stadium would be engaged with. After environmentalist groups also voiced their protests against a relocation to a green-belt site outside the city, Hearts finally announced in December 1992 that they were in fact planning to redevelop Tynecastle into a smaller, all-seater stadium. Since 1993 Hearts have knocked down three stands of the old stadium and replaced them with new, modern all-seater stands. There are further plans to redevelop the old main stand, built in 1914 and designed by the legendary architect Archibald Leith,[23] in order to expand the current capacity of 17,500. While a new ground, in certain ways, inevitably means altered matchday experiences from those of the days of predominantly standing terraces, it is also possible to locate striking similarities in the sociality taking place before, during and after games. A visit to Tynecastle Park for the New Year derby match on 1 January 2011 revealed an atmosphere and level of noise which could in no way be seen as any less partisan and intense than that witnessed in the ground in the early 1990s. Normal matchday routines were still evident in the number of crowded pubs and social clubs around the stadium, as supporters revelled in the extended social rituals of an important game. I had agreed to meet a friend and former research subject in a pub called The Diggers after the game. As I entered I found my friend with the same co-drinkers and fellow supporters I had known back in 1993, standing more or less in the same spot, about three yards from the exit door. They were all 18 years older and one had brought his son along as he was now old enough to enter licensed premises, showing lines of continuity and heritage in support. That apart, time had stood still. The bar staff served the same mostly locally brewed ales, the walls were adorned with the same photographs, all illustrating the history of Hearts FC, and the interior colours still matched the maroon and white of the Hearts strip. So, in the age of hypercommodification, there are still oasises of status quo to be found in the world of football. During my first field trip to Edinburgh I was shown a Hearts supporter's cherished collectors' item, a booklet containing a fixture list from the 1895/1896 season. At the end of the booklet there were several advertisements. One of them was for the 'Midlothian Arms', which he told me was the old name of the Tynecastle Arms, the pub located just outside the Hearts ground. The ad read: 'Before and after games, enjoy our fine selection of wines, spirits and ales'.[24] Hence it seems reasonable to assert that male participation in extended social rituals before and after games has been passed down through generations and taken place for as long as the game has existed as a spectator sport. However, in Britain the Taylor Report meant that a number of clubs did decide to relocate to more suburban locations, which has in turn altered the social practices around games, as stadiums outside city centres generally have poorer social and physical infrastructures.

While the two Edinburgh rivals decided to stay at their old stadiums, moving forward to 2010 it was not difficult to find examples of new stadiums which are well attuned to the vision outlined above. Arsenal FC's ground in London, while relocated remarkably close to their old ground at Highbury, can be read as something of a symbol of the new era, with a cool, state-of-the-art design and facilities tailored to facilitate comfortable consumption on match days, whether inside the ground or in the adjacent 'Arsenal World', a shopping centre suited to cater for all tastes in footballing fashion and expressions of Arsenal allegiance. Named after a major sponsor, the Arab airline company Emirates, one could easily argue that Arsenal's new stadium, along with most new football stadiums built in recent decades, resembles French anthropologist Marc Auge's depiction of a 'non-place' – a term introduced by Auge to describe the lack of culture-specific significance attached to transient physical spaces like airports, supermarkets, hotel rooms and motorways.[25]

This alignment of new football stadiums is thought-provoking and relevant, yet we need to contextualize their global impact on spectator practices. Examples of 'localism' and culture-specific dialogues in chants and crowd practices still prevail in many places. In August 2010 I travelled to London to watch two pre-season friendly matches: Millwall v Hearts on one day and Arsenal v Celtic the next. This was like moving between the old world and the new. The games took place in the same city at almost the same time, yet in terms of atmosphere and as social dramas, the games were very different. The first game took place at the New Den, Millwall FC's home ground in South Bermondsey, deep in south-east London. Around 2000 of the 10,000-strong crowd were visiting Hearts fans. The hosts had obviously not expected such a turn-out at a pre-season friendly and had only opened one window of the ticket office, leading to long queues and hundreds of fans entering well after the game had kicked off. The banter inside the intimate ground was marked by dialogical singing between the opposing supporters, with Millwall fans typically chanting 'In-ger-land, In-ger-land, In-ger-land' at their Scottish counterparts, who responded by chanting the name of Germany in reference to England's 4–1 loss to the latter country's team in the recent World Cup in South Africa. The dubious attractions and stereotypical reputation of Millwall supporters, analysed brilliantly by Garry Robson a decade ago,[26] were confirmed after the game. I happened to be in a crowd of Hearts supporters looking for a drink after the game. A group of Millwall supporters walked into the pub we had found along the River Thames in the London Bridge area, making no secret of their intention to have a fight. After realizing the type of pub we were in, however, one fan stated: 'No, it's a family pub'. Instead of fighting, he chose to socialize with his rival fans.

The following day, I travelled to Arsenal's stadium with a group of friends to take in one of two afternoon games in their annual pre-season tournament, the Emirates Cup. The home side welcomed Celtic, from Glasgow. Even though a crowd of 45,000 had tickets to the game, we were inside the stadium within a couple of minutes. Food and drinks could be purchased from one of the countless sales outlets under the stands with great efficiency and with hardly any queuing time. As we found our seats we could hear the travelling Celtic supporters chanting, but the noise was distant and largely drowned out due to the spacious design of this state-of-the-art modern stadium and the cacophony of often repeated electric noise over the stadium's loud speakers. As the game was played during what is typically the high season for holiday makers all over Europe (early August), we could hear Dutch, Spanish, Norwegian and Italian being spoken in our immediate vicinity. While the odd spectator in a replica Aresenal shirt could be seen, there was little singing or common ground found by the spectators in order to indulge in active match participation. Eventually a Mexican wave was started at one side of the ground. A local Arsenal supporter who sat next to us restricted himself to showing his middle finger, demonstrating his contempt at this universal crowd ritual which indeed could fit into the rituals of a non-place: the Mexican wave is often seen as a bland and meaningless act, unsuitable to carry the messages of specific club support. While the latter example may serve to support arguments suggesting that top-level football is currently designed to suit the needs and the wallets of 'cold and consumerist' flaneurs, the former example illustrates how there is a parallel world within lower-level professional football, in which the 'hot traditional' supporter continues to dominate.

Shouting at the TV: virtual sociality in the pub

Outside Britain, the hedonistic rituals of drinking in connection with football games are a rather new phenomenon. In Norway, it is possible to locate the dawn of drinking rituals around regular club games with the commodification of the game which evolved in the 1990s, especially in the mediated fandom of long-distance supporters of English football clubs. In Scandinavia, and especially in Norway, football fans have for decades developed parallel allegiances with one local Norwegian team and one English team. The historical background for the mediated fandom and huge transnational support of English clubs in Norway is of particular interest in the understanding of the globalization and commodification of football. While television and the internet allow many fans to indulge in virtual consumption of football,[27] the more recent business of specialized football pubs has opened up a greater number of collective ways to experience and consume football. These, along with the dawn of budget airline companies and new media technologies, have to a significant degree altered accessibility to other football leagues since the early 1990s and, as a consequence, the sociality of fan practices.

The passion for English football in Norway is not a recent phenomenon.[28] Media reports from English football matches can be dated back to 1902, the same year the Norwegian FA was founded While pictures of footballers included in cigarette boxes during the 1930s and betting on English games from the late 1940s contributed to the popularization of English football, it was the introduction of the live televised matches in 1969 which colonized football imaginations in Norway, securing a near-cult position among youngsters by the early 1970s.[29] During the 1970s and 1980s a variety of supporters' clubs for English football teams were founded; today these have been united into a common supporters' union for British football.[30] As of January 2011, this organization had a total membership of 98,978, with support spread over a total of 45 different clubs. While nearly 80% support global clubs Manchester United and Liverpool, more subcultural statements of identity are evident in the number of supporters of lower-division teams such as Macclesfield, Scarborough and Woking – teams which have never appeared on Norwegian television. Many of these fans regularly travel to watch games and indulge in the local cultures of the clubs they support. This parallel support is a sign of the times in European football, as low-cost airlines allow supporters to develop relationships with teams and supporters in other leagues. During my research among Hearts supporters, I found a lot of them had developed relationships with club communities elsewhere, obtained either from holidays or from following European games with their local Scottish club. Supporters from a variety of cities in Europe travelled to follow Hearts on a more or less regular basis. Such relationships can be categorized as more shallow than the support for their local team, marked more by what Giulianotti defines as the behaviour of a follower. This is also evident in Norway, where a number of Premiership clubs can boast a modest foreign contingent of supporters. The practice of groundhopping, which entails collecting and listing visited grounds in various fora, adds to the flow and level of transnational contact between supporter communities.[31]

The lifting of restrictions on screening live English games during the 1990s and into the new millennium saw the dawn of a new and more public way of viewing, in the shape of pubs showing live English games for enthused fans with a taste for the combination of beer and football. It paved the way for a whole new business, as pubs literally started to make a living from a combination of selling beer and showing televised football. The Scandinavian branch of Liverpool's supporters' club has a pub guide on their website listing more than 300 pubs in Norway recommended specifically for Liverpool supporters. The guide also recommends dozens of pubs and bars overseas, based on recommendations from travelling supporters, from the Faroe Islands via the Philippines to Peru![32] Hence this is part of a global phenomenon in which the brewing industry has expanded its traditional business of serving pre- and post-match drinks for football revellers attending games in a stadium, toward exploiting a market of supporters watching games on TV in pubs.

Supporters of various teams arrive in such pubs, most of whom will be wearing replica tops and other symbols of specific club allegiance. Games are announced on the internet and, on busy days in the busiest pubs, where four or five games are screened simultaneously, you can even get information on the corner of the bar that will be showing the game of your choice during the next week or so.[33] I once took my partner along to such a pub in Oslo. Not interested in football, she felt she was entering the privacy of a supersized boys' room, with the walls and even the ceiling completely covered with nostalgic pictures of football teams and players – mostly taken from football magazines from the 1970s and 1980s – reflecting the childhood heroes of the pub's current manager, who is in his late 40s. Any square inch not covered by a picture displayed club paraphernalia from across the world, and male beer drinkers completely dominated the scene. Unlike other cafes and pubs, where people talk to each other, my partner found that here people were not talking, but shouting – at the television. The pub in question was Bohemen; founded in 1998, it is located in Oslo city centre and partly owned by *Klanen* (The Clan), the official supporters' club for Norwegian Premier League club Vålerenga.

Football pubs provide opportunities for a far more public and community-based kind of long-distance support as fans turn up supporting their teams with or without club colours, creating a collective, social basis for support. The originally individual, idiosyncratic orientation around support for English teams has given way to more collective rituals akin to those of supporting a local club, central to which is a licensed premises and shared consumption of beer. Typically, the pub discussed here is frequented by local fans of Vålerenga before and after games in the domestic league, yet it holds an inclusive profile with regard to fans of foreign teams. Oslo-based fans of a variety of English clubs use this pub as a social meeting point to watch games, while the transnational following of the politically leftist orientated German club St Pauli is evident as around a dozen Vålerenga fans gather regularly to watch and support the German team during televised games from the Bundesliga. The pub is known for its multicultural profile, and games from the Italian and Spanish leagues also attract a substantial number of customers/fans. Hence this pub is a place where supporters of the local club mingle with a variety of other fans, of which Norwegian fans of English clubs dominate. In February 2011, on a very busy night in the Bohemen, the weekly Wednesday-evening sports quiz took place as a local derby from Hamburg kicked off on the screens, followed by around 20 St Pauli fans – all regulars, all Norwegian and all supporters of Vålerenga. However, the main event of the evening was the Champions League game between Arsenal and Barcelona. As it turned out, Arsenal's own TV channel, Arsenal TV, had turned up with a crew to film and interview some of the 100 or so Arsenal fans who were there to see their team transform a 1–0 deficit into a 2–1 win, causing wild celebrations, with cheerful Arsenal fans and a happy TV crew leaving the bar.

Gospels about the local hero

There has also been an evident rise in the number of proactive supporters of local Norwegian teams defining themselves in opposition to what is widely seen as the 'anglophile' group of supporters, especially since the turn of the new millennium. Such symbolic acts have especially evolved around games between Norwegian and English teams where a clear majority of attending fans are usually Norwegian. The latest example of this was when Norwegian Premier League side Stabæk played a friendly against Manchester United's reserve team in January 2010. Unknowingly, the Norwegian United fans gathered behind a banner visible to everyone in the stadium but themselves, which simply read: 'Anglophile losers'. The banner had been put there by fans of a team widely known as Norway's *nouveau riche* club, with a history of top-flight football dating back only to the mid-1990s. Similar expressions of a nation-centred morality have been seen at European matches elsewhere in Norway, notably in the game between Brann and Everton in the last 32 of the UEFA cup in February 2008 and the Champions League game between Rosenborg and Arsenal in Trondheim in September 2004.[34] Antagonism toward long-distance supporters of English clubs from the more recently created supporter cultures of local Norwegian clubs are coloured by calls for monogamy and thick solidarity, rooted in local communities. In this sense, 'anglophiles' are ridiculed by some for their superficial involvement in the media-dependent glamour of the English Premier League. However, as I have shown in this chapter, the culture of support for English clubs in Norway precedes the era of hypercommodification and has a longer history than support for Norwegian teams. Hence moral definitions of the 'real' fan raise more complex issues than the question of birthplace or which passport one holds. Such conflicts point to interesting contestations about notions of good and bad support and issues related to hegemonic fan moralities.

Current discourses on football and globalization in the Norwegian public take various shapes and positions. In Norway the influence of supporter movements has moved from negligible to substantial in the past 20 years. Most Norwegian teams' supporters' clubs have a voice in boardrooms and have in the past decade proved influential in anything from ownership issues to the fight against 'eventification', which was evident in the ways matchday organizers at a number of football grounds tended to marginalize voices from the stands via electronic noise from the tannoys. The dawn of a number of cultural supporter practices in Norway since the early 1990s also shows how inspiration and impulses are no longer drawn solely from English terrace culture. Inspiration drawn from Italian fan practices is evident in the number of choreographed displays of support at Norwegian football ground, in the shape of huge home-made banners referred to as *tifos*.[35] While this shows how local Norwegian football support has adopted a strengthened belief in self-made ways of expressing support, it also shows how inspirations and impulses move across borders. Another sign of resistance to globalization is the way that newspapers generally regard the inflated number of foreign players in the professional league as a threat. In an article entitled 'Here are the statistics on [player] imports which pleases Football-Norway' the national newspaper *VG* showed how the number of foreign players in the league was declining, while espousing the view that players in the Norwegian league should carry a Norwegian passport,[36]. In the past couple of years, some local papers have even listed the number of local players on the pitch as part of their coverage of football teams in their region.[37] This could be interpreted as a retreat to a localized sense of belonging. Which appears to be out of tune with the greater awareness and even search for transnational networking, which may even include political resistance. While dominant virtues of 'local heroism' continue to guide hegemonic notions of good and bad football support, there are many reasons to question the authenticity of retreat to a universally valid local monogamy. For football fans, cheap flights are one of the benefits of neoliberal capitalism, providing them with unprecedented opportunities to travel and explore footballing communities elsewhere. It is currently commonplace for club supporters across Europe to adopt relations with club communities located in other leagues and nations. These networks may generally induce a sense of belonging which appears to be best suited to the category of a 'follower' – a connoisseur of the game and the club in question, but one without the locally rooted sense of belonging reserved for Giulianotti's definition of the 'supporter'.

Thin cosmopolitans? A story from the eternal city

I happened to watch the 2009 Champions League final in a bar in Rome, which appeared to be a gathering spot for an amazing international breadth of AS Roma fans. Fans from Glasgow, Southampton, Manchester (City), Ljubljana (Slovenia), Bergen (Norway), Moscow, Lierse (Belgium) and Christchurch (New Zealand) gathered in the days leading up to the last league round of Serie A. Of the travellers from Glasgow, eight were Celtic fans and some had set up what they called a Celtic-Roma brigade, giving the outsider cause to speculate that Catholic pilgrimage to the Pope's home city might be an aspect of their allegiance with AS Roma. Catholicism may have played a structuring role in the Celtic-Roma connection, but attempts to find proof of this among the Glaswegians proved futile. A Glasgow-born Celtic and Roma fan with Iranian parents argued that sectarianism played no part in the connection – an argument supported by the presence of the Manchester City fan who also supported Celtic's major Glaswegian enemy, Rangers. For the Roma fans from Slovenia, their support was explained more through cross-border hostilities toward the northern Italian cities of Milano and Torino, hence attaching themselves to the north-south divide evident in Italian football. Not one of the foreign Roma fans seemed to have any interest in visiting the Vatican. The only holy site that all seemed to visit during their days in Rome was the mural of Fransesco Totti, the near-sanctified Roma striker, which was located 50 metres from the bar they were drinking in. A trip to the mural appeared to be a compulsory and indeed a pilgrimic gesture.

Most fans were already in Rome during the Champions League final between Barcelona and Manchester United. Not one seemed to be cheering for United – possibly indicative of a global contempt for the current international dominance of that club, but as far as local Roma fans were concerned, also indicative of the old and more general Latin v Northern Europe divide. Nonetheless, one local Roma fan pointed out to me that had the final been between Roma's city rival Lazio and Manchester United they would of course have rooted for United, underlining the locally rooted arch-rival logic as the universally privileged ethos in football support. Similarly, contempt for the Italian national side was also evident, based on much the same ethos; for them it makes little sense to support a team with players from your fiercest local rival.

Concluding remarks

While the tradition of support – or mono-support – for an English club has been challenged in recent times by supporters of Norwegian teams, calls for a 'local monogamy' are in many ways at odds with a footballing world structured by globalization. Televised football and commodification have altered football fandom during the last decades, although I have also given examples of continuity in the sociality of match day rituals in different locations. The polygamy evident in European football fans' relating to several clubs should be understood not only as a media phenomenon, but also as a result of physical explorations and social networking between football communities. Such explorations are more in accordance with Giulianotti's definition of a follower, rather than that of a fan or a supporter, although in cases where transnational visits to footballing communities are lacking in social and cultural connectedness they may be more easily adapted to the 'thin transnationalism' or 'banal cosmopolitanism' explored elsewhere by Giulianotti and Robertson.[38] I have here shown how the definitions of supporter, fan, follower and flaneur may be applied to various contexts in ways I have found fruitful. Nevertheless, the ideal differences between a fan and a supporter will often be blurred in a practical context. Spectators with a 'hot' involvement are likely to use these labels synonymously, be it as spectators, customers, hooligans or political activists against hypercommodification. The walls between the categories will soften if adapted to different social practices, and we are likely to find a flow between the categories, even in individual spectators: it is possible to imagine the same football spectator calling him or herself a supporter during a domestic league match, a fan of a club mostly watched on TV, a follower of the national team and a flaneur during glamorous mega-events such as the World Cup. While nationality retains an important structuring role in the game, it is increasingly difficult to find convincing arguments for making a general division between domestic 'thick solidarity' and transnational 'thin solidarity'. Further, it is entirely possible to imagine a development in which declining neoliberal market strategies may buckle under the pressures of community-based cultures of mutuality, as predicted by Kennedy and Kennedy.[39] Within the current cluster of subjective orientations and objective structures in football, flexible models that are open to influence from ideological resistance and cultural complexities are required in order to fully grasp the contestations of moralities and identities within supporter practices in football.

Notes

1. Russell, *Football and the English*, 64; Holt, *Sport and the British*, 172.
2. Hornby, *Fever Pitch*.

3. Rowe, *Sport, Culture and the Media*; Boyle and Haines, *Football in the New Media Age*.
4. Giulianotti, 'Supporters, Followers, Fans and Flaneurs', 29.
5. Hargreaves, *Sport, Power and Culture*, 67.
6. Russell, *Football and the English*.
7. Taylor, 'Football Mad'; Critcher, 'Football Since the War'.
8. Giulianotti, 'Supporters, Followers, Fans and Flaneurs', 27.
9. Taylor, 'Football Mad', 364.
10. Hargreaves, *Sport, Power and Culture*.
11. Kennedy and Kennedy, 'Towards a Marxist Political Economy of Football Supporters'.
12. Andrews and Ritzer, 'The Grobal in the Sporting Glocal'.
13. Giulianotti and Robertson, *Globalization and Sport*.
14. Andrews and Ritzer, 'The Grobal in the Sporting Glocal', 40–1.
15. Solberg and Gratton, *The Economics of Sports Broadcasting*.
16. See Bale, 'Playing at Home: British Football and a Sense of Place'.
17. Giulianotti, 'Supporters, Followers, Fans and Flaneurs', 35.
18. See Urry, *The Tourist Gaze*.
19. Giulianotti, 'Supporters, Followers, Fans and Flaneurs', 37.
20. Taylor, *The Hillsborough Stadium Disaster: Final Report*.
21. Hognestad, *The Jambo Experience*.
22. See Haynes, 1995, for an early account of the football fanzine cultures in Britain.
23. Archibald Leith was responsible for the design of a number of football grounds in Scotland and England in late nineteenth and early twentieth centuries. Many of these grounds are currently listed buildings, notably Ibrox Stadium in Glasgow and Arsenal's former ground, Highbury. See Inglis, 1987.
24. Heart of Midlothian Football Club – 1895/96 fixture booklet.
25. Auge, *Non-places*.
26. Robson, '*No One Like Us, We Don't Care*'
27. See Hjelseth, *Mellom børs, katedral og karneval*.
28. For early historical accounts of how this 'English sport' spread and developed in Norway see Goksøyr and Olstad, 2002.
29. While FA Cup finals were broadcast live from 1963, a league game between Sunderland and Wolves in November 1969 marked the beginning of regular screening of English football over the national broadcasting monopoly, NRK. For more detailed analysis of how the introduction of live TV coverage of English football affected football support in Norway see Hognestad, 2003, 2006 and 2009.
30. See http://www.supporterunionen.no.
31. A forthcoming article co-authored by this author and Gary Armstrong and currently being considered for publishing delves into the practice of groundhopping among Norwegian supporters (Giulianotti, 2002: 34-6).
32. See http://www.liverpool.no (figures from March 2011).
33. See for instance http://www.bohemen.no
34. See Hognestad, 2009, 365.
35. *Tifo* is the Italian word for supporting a team.
36. *VG*, 18 March (translation by the author).
37. C.f. *Jærbladet* in their coverage of 1st Division team Bryne F.K. during the 2009 and 2010 season.
38. Giulianotti and Robertson, *Globalization and Sport*.
39. Kennedy and Kennedy, 'Towards a Marxist Political Economy of Football Supporters', 196.

References

Andrews, D.L., and G. Ritzer. 'The grobal in the sporting glocal'. *Global Networks* 7, no. 2 (2007): 135–53.
Auge, Marc. *Non-places: Introduction to an Anthropology of Supermodernity*. London: Verso, 1995.

Bale, J. 'Playing at Home: British Football and a Sense of Place'. In *British Football and Social Change*, ed. J. Williams and S. Wagg, 130–45. Leicester: Leicester University Press, 1991.

Boyle, R., and R. Haynes. *Football in the new Media Age*. London: Routledge, 2004.

Critcher, C. "Football Since the War". In *Working Class Culture – Studies in History and Theory*, ed. J. Clarke, C. Critcher, and R. Johnson, 161–84. London: Hutchinson, 1979.

Giulianotti, R. 'Supporters, Followers, Fans and Flaneurs: a Taxonomy of Spectator Identities in Football'. *Journal of Sport and Social Issues* 26, no. 1 (2002): 25–46.

Giulianotti, R., and R. Robertson. *Globalization and Sport*. Malden, MA: Blackwell, 2007.

Goksøyr, M., and F. Olstad. *Football!*. Oslo: NFF, 2002.

Hargreaves, J. *Sport, Power and Culture: A Social and Historical Analysis of Popular Sports in Britain*. Cambridge: Polity Press, 1986.

Haynes, R. *The Football Imagination – a Study of Football Fanzine Culture*. Aldershot: Ashgate Publishing, 1995.

Hjelseth, A. 'Mellom børs, katedral og karneval: norske supporteres forhandlinger om kommersialisering av football' ['Between stock exchange, cathedral and carnival: Negotiations on the commercialization of football among Norwegian supporters']. Unpublished PhD thesis, University of Bergen, 2006.

Hognestad, H. 'The Jambo Experience – Identity, Social Practice and Meaning among Supporters of Heart of Midlothian Football Club. Unpublished PhD thesis, University of Oslo, 1995.

Hognestad, H. 'Long-Distance Football Support and Liminal Identities among Norwegian Fans'. In *Dance and Embodied Identities*, ed. E. Archetti and N. DyckSport, 97–115. Oxford: Berg, 2003.

Hognestad, H. 'Transnational Passions – a Statistical Study of Norwegian Football Fans'. *Soccer and Society* 7, no. 4 (2006): 439–62.

Hognestad, H. 'Transglobal Scandinavian – Globalisation and the Contestation of Identities in Football'. *Soccer and Society* 10, no. 3-4 (2009): 358–73.

Holt, R. *Sport and the British*. Oxford: Clarendon Press, 1992.

Hornby, N. *Fever Pitch*. London: Gollancz, 1992.

Inglis, S. *The Football Grounds of Great Britain*. London: Willow Books, 1987.

Kennedy, D., and P. Kennedy. "Towards a Marxist Economy of Football Supporters". *Capital & Class* 34, no. 2 (2010): 181–98.

Rowe, D. *Sport, Culture and the Media – the Unruly Trinity*. Buckingham: Open University Press, 1993.

Russell, D. *Football and the English*. Preston: Carnegie Publishing, 1997.

Solberg, H. A., and C. Gratton. *The Economics of Sports Broadcasting*. London: Routledge, 2007.

Supporterunionen For Britisk Fotball. http://www.supporterunionen.no

Taylor, I. "'Football Mad' – A Speculative Sociology of Soccer Hooliganism'. In *The Sociology of Sport: a Selection of Readings*, ed. E. Dunning, 352–77. London: Cass, 1971.

Taylor, Lord Justice. *The Hillsborough Stadium Disaster: Final Report*. London: HMSO (CM962), 1990.

Urry, J. *The Tourist Gaze*. London: Sage, 2002.

Other sources:

http://www.bohemen.no.
http://www.liverpool.no.
http://www.supporterunionen.no.
Heart of Midlothian F.C. 1895-96 season, fixture booklet.
Always the Bridesmaid, Hearts-fanzine, no. 9 (1992).

From 'socios' to 'hyper-consumers': an empirical examination of the impact of commodification on Spanish football fans

Ramón Llopis-Goig

Department of Sociology and Social Anthropology, University of Valencia, Spain

> Traditionally, the Spanish game has been analysed in scholarly studies in terms of the effect of crowd violence or the nationalist and regionalist implications of the Spanish clubs. Latterly analysis has also extended to include gender issues (and the process of constructing masculinity, in particular) and a spate of studies dealing with racism and xenophobia, both of which have blighted the Spanish game in recent years. Little attention, however, has been given over to the study of the effects on fans of the rapidly expanding influence of commercialization on football in Spain. With this gap in mind, this study sets out to examine, from an empirical perspective, the social consequences of the commodification processes of football in the discourse of the sport's fans.

Introduction

In the past twenty years, Spanish football has undergone intensive changes that have dramatically transformed some of its main structural characteristics. This process is directly related to the commodification tendencies that have also affected other aspects of social and economic life and has had a strong influence on the recent evolution of football, determining aspects as varied as the greater professionalization and global migration of players, the corporatization of clubs, the proliferation of merchandising, rule changes to draw in new customers, and a general redefinition of the competitive structures and ethos of the sport.[1]

The impact of these commodification trends on football fans, especially in relation to the cost of attending matches or watching them on subscription television stations, has been a matter of concern in the United Kingdom, where the impact of commodification on spectator identities has been explored in both theoretical and empirical terms.[2] In Spain, however, research about the effects of football commodification on fans is non-existent. The social sciences have paid little attention to football, a circumstance that may be related to the fact that for many years this sport was considered an instrument of the extension of domination and ignorance. Since the 1990s, diverse studies and papers have been published on Spanish football, but always dealing with questions related to violence in stadiums[3] or the nationalist and regionalist implications of the Spanish clubs,[4] a topic closely linked to the multicultural composition of Spanish society.

In the past five years, however, the range of issues related to football that have been studied from a social sciences perspective has increased considerably. Spanish football has been examined in relation to other elements of social structure, such as gender and the process of constructing masculinity,[5] football's relations with news media,[6] and racist and xenophobic displays.[7] However, this research has not focused on football *fans*, and even less consideration has been given to the impact of commodification on Spanish football fans.

With this gap in mind, the purpose of this study is to examine, from an empirical perspective, the social consequences of football's commodification processes in the discourse of the sport's fans. To this end, between October 2010 and February 2011, 19 fans, six sport journalists and three sport managers were interviewed. In the case of the fans, the observations on which this paper is based were made by fans of Valencia FC and Levante UD – two clubs with quite different characteristics, which makes it possible to discover a broad range of experiences, expectations and opinions about the consequences of Spanish football's commodification. The fans included members of football *peñas* (fan communities), season-ticket holders, and regularly-attending followers of the teams. The majority of the sport journalists and managers were linked to television channels, newspapers and sporting organizations at the national level.

Although research has dealt with many questions related to the social consequences of Spanish football's transformation in the past two decades, the present study takes an in-depth look at three specific thematic areas. First, the changes in relations between fans and their football clubs in recent years are analysed. Second, the fans' opinions on football clubs' ownership and governance are examined. Third, and finally, fans' perceptions of the mercantilization process, as well as the reactions and changes this process has produced in football culture, are studied. Before delving into these questions, some data and considerations are presented in order to contextualize the study, especially for readers who may be less familiar with Spanish football.

Context of the study

Football is a topic of enormous interest in Spanish society. A survey carried out in May 2007 by the Centre for Sociological Research (CIS) showed that a little more than half of the population over 18 years of age (54%) claimed to be interested in the sport.[8] This is a 10% increase on the number obtained in a 1974 Gallup poll. Surprisingly, the CIS survey pointed out that the proportion of Spaniards who say they follow one particular football team (66.8%) is greater than the percentage who claim to be interested in the sport – a clear example of the way that identification with a team goes beyond mere interest in football as a sport. The two teams with the greatest social support were Real Madrid and Barcelona FC, with 32.8% and 25.7%, respectively, of respondents identifying themselves as fans. This was followed at a great distance by Valencia FC, with 5.3%.[9] The percentage of interviewees who stated that they were followers of Levante UD was 0.2%.

Founded in 1909, Valencia FC has a 57,000-capacity stadium, and its budget for the 2010/2011 season was €131 million. It is the fifth most successful Spanish club in terms of national titles – following Real Madrid, Barcelona FC, Athletic de Bilbao and Athletic de Madrid – having won five UEFA Cups, six Spanish Leagues and seven King's Cups. Levante UD is a more modest club. Also located in the city of Valencia and founded in 1909, it currently competes in the League and has a budget of €20 million. It has only played in the League in six seasons, including the current one, and its stadium holds 25,534 fans. The average attendance at Levante's local games is around 10,000, a number quite inferior to that of Valencia FC, which attracts an average of 38,263 fans to its stadium in Mestalla.

Alongside the social significance of football in Spain, its importance can also be seen in its economic dimension. It generates approximately €4 billion, almost 0.9% of GDP (and 1.2% of the GDP of the services sector). If other indirect effects, such as employee wages and gross operating profit, are added the aggregated figure corresponding to football's total impact on the Spanish economy rises to €8.066 billion, approximately 1.7% of GDP and 2.5% of the services sector's GDP.[10] In the 2008/2009 season, Real Madrid was considered the club with the highest income in the world, at €401 million.[11] Of this income, 29% comes from tickets, quotas paid by members and exploitation of the stadium's services. Television provides 36% of the income, marketing brings in 31%, and friendly matches, together with prizes won in competitions, yield 4%. In the case of Barcelona FC, second in income with €366 million yearly, tickets make up 14%, television provides 36%, and marketing brings in 31%, although this team earns somewhat more than Real Madrid from friendly matches and prizes won in competitions.

The financial reality of the Spanish football clubs is, however, much gloomier than the aforementioned numbers might lead one to think. The study *Football and Finances: The Economy of the League of Stars* points out that during the 2007/2008 season, the Spanish League lost about €300 million; its net patrimony was €340 million.[12] According to this report, the majority of the Spanish clubs face serious economic problems related to the large volume of their debts. In 2007, the total debt of the clubs in the League was €2.7795 billion; one year later it reached €3.4438 billion. The highest debt was that of Real Madrid, at €562.8 million, followed by Athletic de Madrid and Valencia FC, with €510.8 and €502.3 million of debt respectively. The team with the next highest debt is Barcelona FC, which owes €437.8 million, followed at a distance by Deportivo de la Coruña (€292.3 million) and Villarreal (€239.9 million). Four other teams had debt of more than €100 million in the 2007/2008 season: RCD Espanyol (151.5), Racing de Santander (136.9), Real Zaragoza (111.5) and Sevilla FC (109.9). The ten remaining teams' debt was under €100 million each. These social and economic data provide the context in which the following study is situated.

The relationships between fans and their football clubs

The data referred to in the first paragraph of the previous section show how strongly Spanish fans continue to identify with Spanish football teams, with 66.8% of the adult population claiming to be a follower of some football team. But how has the merchandizing tendency of football affected relations between fans and their clubs? Have the fans' feelings of identification with their clubs been modified in relation to previous eras? How has the merchandizing process affected fans' behaviour? These questions will be addressed in this section.

Analysis of the information obtained in the interviews with fans, journalists and sport managers leaves no doubt about the evolution of relations between fans and their clubs in the past twenty years. On the one hand, the interviewees state that their feelings of identification have not varied in basic ways, while on the other they point out that there have been substantial changes in fans' behaviour.

> '... in basic things it hasn't affected anything; that is, the fans' identification with the club is the same...'

Two arguments clarify why feelings of identification with clubs continue to be important in Spanish society. The first has to do with the structure of the initiation to football consumption that has characterized Spanish football in the past few decades. This process began in early childhood in the family sphere, and acted according to a model of generational transmission that maintained its coherence and solidity throughout the lifetime of the fan. Thus, at a very young age a type of socialization occurred that largely explains the later fidelity to the colours of the club. This emotional component of identification with a club continues to be strong among football fans, and has not been essentially affected by the changes in Spanish football in recent years.

> ... people still think Valencia FC is their club for life, their grandparent's, their parent's, and in every city, all the fans think the same thing...

> ... someone who has gone to the stadium from the time he was little to see Levante UD play, it's difficult for him not to follow the team as an adult. It stays in you forever, at least in the case of Levante...

It is not likely that this mechanism will continue to function in the same way, as there have already been signs that the structure of identification with football is becoming more plural and diverse. This change could give rise to an 'identitary map' based less on generational transmission than on the influence of news media, the Internet and football superstars.

The second argument concerns the way football clubs act as symbolic representatives of the different regions in Spain. Although historically this identitary symbolism was especially developed in the Basque country and Cataluña, with the transition to democracy that took place after the death of the dictator Francisco Franco in 1975 and the subsequent creation of the State of Autonomic Regions, regionalist expressions extended to other regions like the Valencian Community, Galicia and Andalucía, whose main football teams were to become symbolic representatives of the region.[13] The interviewees point out that today this regional–identitary dimension of the clubs has weakened and does not have the force it had in the 1980s, but it continues to be important and present to the degree that it is impossible to understand fans' feelings of identification with their clubs without mentioning this component.

> ... it's not that there is a permanent conflict between territories here, but it does channel the expressions of affirmation and disagreement of many ...

Although feelings of identification with clubs have remained, there has been a substantial change in the repertoire of behaviours that fans develop in relation to their enthusiasm and sympathy toward a football team. The aforementioned CIS survey offers some empirical evidence of this change in revealing that among the followers of any football team, 72.8% watch their team's matches on television whenever they can, 42% have flags, shields and other team objects at home, and 36.9% usually attend their team's matches at the stadium. Other high-percentage behaviours correspond to the purchase of team clothing or personal objects (like watches, wallets and so on) and paying to see games on television, with an incidence of 24.2% and 21%, respectively. Finally, 15.3% and 2.6% of fans, respectively, say they travel to other cities or countries to watch games played by their team.[14] All of this shows the growing importance of consumption as a dimension that articulates the relationship between Spanish fans and their football clubs.

The interviews with fans, journalists and sport managers show that consumption has become a core dimension in relations between fans and football clubs, which has produced a profound transformation in the behavioural repertoire of the typical fan. In general terms, this has produced a broadening and intensification of the consumption of football, which, paraphrasing Gilles Lipovetsky, could be defined as *hyper-consumption of football*.[15] This means that the behavioural repertoire of the fan is not limited to attending the league game that his or her team plays in its own stadium once every fifteen days, or to watching games broadcast free of charge on television every week, regardless of which teams are playing. These would be two of the most typical behaviours from what we could define as the previous era, but in the age of hyper-consumption, others have arisen and intensified.

Two comments are needed to characterize this hyper-consumption of football. First, it has involved an extraordinary development in the presence of information and football in the media, especially on television. Fans now have available to them a communicative system that has increased the number of days, the timetable and the number of games televised, as well as the number of programmes and news items related to football in one way or another.[16]

> … it has changed formally as far as your relation with the team is not limited exclusively to going to the stadium every fifteen days, but instead the media have created a lot of other things…

The media have developed a broad offering that allows fans to be completely informed about developments regarding their team and watch all the games played without having to leave their homes. These advances have made it possible for fans to consume more information about their clubs on a much more regular basis.

Second, it is important to note that this increase in the news offering has been developed around each club, so that the football consumption of each fan is related more and more to the club with which he or she identifies. This would be, then, the second characteristic of the hyper-consumption of football in the present moment: it is a *personalized consumption*, or, to be more exact, it is more personalized than in previous eras:

> … in the past, if you didn't go to the stadium, you would watch the football game they televised every Sunday, and at the end of a year you might have seen four or five of Valencia's matches. Now you can see all the League games on television, paying, of course …

What has been characterized as hyper-consumption presents some additional issues that make it possible to further examine the way relations between fans and their football clubs have evolved in the past few years. These characteristics are not necessarily completely novel – to a certain degree, they were already present before the dramatic changes in Spanish football – but in the current context they have been strengthened extraordinarily.

The first aspect that has been strengthened by the current set-up of Spanish football is its facet as a pleasurable experience. Football consumption, whether in the form of attendance at the stadium or viewing televised broadcasts, is an activity whose recreational gratification component is progressively reinforced, to the detriment of any other type of social and political connotations. The experience of watching a football match is, above all, a festive and fun activity.

> ... Football is a place of enjoyment, of passion, of having a good time, of living an intense experience, because sometimes there is suffering, but it's an experience that is, most of all, fun...

A second aspect strengthened by the situation of hyper-consumption that characterizes relations between fans and their clubs is the reinforcement of football's condition as entertainment. In relation to this statement, one of the results of the aforementioned CIS survey is that 79.7% of the Spanish population consider professional football to be more of a show than a sport, while 12.2% state the opposite, and 8.1% are not sure which of the two options is most applicable.[17]

The statements of the fans and sport journalists interviewed completely confirm the consideration that fans view football as entertainment, but they clarify the meaning of this statement. When they say that it is a show, the emphasis is on its appearance as a play or performance whose status would be closer to an artistic production than to a sport competition:

> ... I think more and more it is less a question of being a great fan and more a question of enjoying a play, a performance, entertainment; I think the fans go to watch football like one goes to a show...

These are, then, the characteristics that define the relationship between the fans and their clubs in present-day Spanish football: a relationship that has been defined by the term hyper-consumption, which is characterized by the increase and intensification of the consumption of football-related information and broadcasts, the growing personalization of this consumption experience, and the consideration of attending matches at the stadium as a festive recreational experience. In any case, this transformation of the relations between the fans and the football clubs has not weakened fans' feelings of identification with clubs; instead, it has strengthened them.

Fandom and the ownership and governance of Spanish football clubs

This section focuses on a specific aspect of Spanish football's transformation process: the evolution of clubs' ownership and governance from the point of view of the fans. Dealing with this aspect requires some initial considerations about what is known as the Sports Law (Law 10/1990 15 October), one of the main repercussions of which was the transformation of football clubs into Limited Liability Sports Companies (SAD).[18] The purpose of this law was to regulate the economic situation of professional football clubs, a situation that had reached alarming levels a few years previously. In January 1985, for example, the liabilities due from clubs in the First, Second, and Second B divisions totalled €124.5 million. Football clubs were in a complicated financial situation, due largely to the sizeable investment in stadiums required in order for the country to host the 1982 World Cup. Although the income from the event itself was initially expected to cover the cost of investment, this was not the case, and the financial clean-up plan later signed by the clubs and the Superior Sport Council did not have the expected effect.[19] The Sports Law was, in that context, an attempt to resolve the difficult financial situation in which the clubs found themselves. The question raised here, however is what the fans feel the football clubs' move to SAD status has meant.

The first thing that should be mentioned is that the majority of interviewees point out that fans are extremely confused about this question, and are not completely aware of the implications of the legal nature of the current SAD. Some interviewees think there is a combination of lack of awareness and a passion for the club that overrules all else. Others think fans do not really want to accept reality and prefer to deceive themselves, acting as if things have not changed.

> ... I think the fans are very confused about it; they're overcome by their feelings and by their identification with the club, the t-shirt and all that. It's like they don't want to know...

> ... We fans continue to act as if things were the same as before, and we don't want to know that there is a law of limited liability sports companies that allows someone to come and buy the club and make it his...

The situation of confusion or self-deception that characterizes the fans is confirmed by the survival in everyday language of a term that fits the situation which was prevalent before the Sports Law of 1990: the word 'member'. In the legal model prior to the Sports Law's coming into force, the clubs were composed of members who had the capacity to democratically choose a Board of Directors. The members could participate in the club's periodic assemblies and meetings, as long as they were up to date on payment of their quotas. In the current legal set-up of the clubs as SAD, such 'members' disappear, and the only forms of participation are the condition of shareholder – which means buying shares in the club – and season-ticket holder –which provides a pass that allows entrance to practically all the team's home games. However, both categories of participant, especially the season ticket holders, continue to use the word 'member' to describe their relationship with the club.

> ... I'm a member of the Valencia club; I go to all the home games and the away-games depending on where they play...

> ... I'm a member of the Levante club; every year I buy a season ticket...

And it is not strange that the word 'member' is still used, as in reality the fans continue to think of themselves as owners of the club. In some cases they do so in a strictly symbolic way, believing that no matter who the legal owner of the club is, the fans are the true *symbolic owners* and, therefore, can and must influence the life of the club. In other cases, a major part of the club's shares belong to a large number of fans, who become small shareholders and, therefore, continue to carry a certain weight in the club's ownership. This is the case for clubs whose capital is dispersed because no shareholders hold more than 10% of the capital:

> ... here in Valencia, but I think it's the same in other places, people still consider themselves the owners of the club; a football club isn't a company that only belongs to the one who buys it, but rather it belongs to its fans...

The feeling of symbolic ownership of the club is reinforced by a series of peculiarities of Spanish football that have a strong influence on the life and governance of clubs. The first has to do with the paternal and even populist tone taken by some of the people who have occupied the football clubs' presidencies, as has been the case for some of Valencia's and Levante's presidents:

> ... we didn't realize that the clubs belong to the one who buys them and we kept acting like they were ours, mostly because they made us think that by using big words and telling us we should contribute to save the club, but in reality what they wanted was to do their own business...

The local origin and regional roots of the majority of the football clubs' presidents have also contributed to this situation. Faced with the entrance of foreign investors, the fact that the presidencies of most of the clubs were held by local people with regional links meant fans did not fear their club would lose its identity, which they feel has happened to some English clubs; they have therefore continued to pledge their loyalty to their club.

> ... the people who control or have controlled the club are from here, so they're not going to change the club's identity or go against the club's traditions...

However, there is a second explanation for the many Spanish fans' feelings of symbolic ownership: the territorial link or regional representation the fans attribute to their clubs. The clubs are not perceived simply as SAD, but rather as a type of 'regional team' that represents a region, almost in the same way that the Spanish national team represents Spain. The clubs therefore have a socio-political function of which the fans are not necessarily aware, as, paraphrasing Michael Billig, it could be said that it acts as a sort of banal regionalism.[20] This role of regional representation therefore lies within the common sensibility and reveals itself as natural for the majority of the fans:

> ... the clubs aren't going to go broke because the politicians won't allow it. It if gets complicated, they'll have to give them money and fix the problems, because the clubs represent each region or city and they can't disappear...

In fact, the fans usually point out that on numerous occasions local and regional authorities have come to the economic rescue of certain football clubs, offering financial aid to avoid their bankruptcy and consequent disappearance:

> ... people don't seem to understand that the club is owned by investors because what they see is that the local and regional governments have come to the rescue of many clubs...

The connection between local or regional authorities and football clubs is reinforced even more in the imagination of the fans when they see that, at times, the public authorities have also acted directly or indirectly – that is, through financial entities that largely depend on or are controlled by regional or local authorities – to avoid foreign capital entering some football clubs.

This possibility has worried fans and the public authorities during the past few years, perhaps as a result of the public's negative view of Dmitry Piterman's time with Racing de Santander and Alavés.[21] In the opinion of some fans and sports journalists, the negative precedent set by Piterman's performance at Racing de Santander acted as a warning about what could happen in other clubs if they allowed the entrance of foreign investors who were not part of the tradition and sporting culture of the club:

> ... here the advantage is that there were some cases that ended up badly, like Piterman in Racing, I think this has made them pay more attention, that is, that the institutions and the people in the club have taken steps to make sure that there isn't a new case like the one with Piterman...

This situation, however, has changed since limits on the purchase of shares by foreigners, which the Sport Law had set at 25%, were modified.[22] Thus, during the current season, an investment of €36 million has seen Malaga acquired by the Qatari sheikh Abdullah Bin Nasser Al Thani, while Indian multi-millionaire Ahsan Ali Syed has acquired Racing de Santander through a €50 million investment. It now has the third highest expenditure in relation to hiring players, after Real Madrid and Barcelona FC. Recently, the possibility has been raised that Valencia FC, with a debt of more than €400 million, could be seeking to attract investment from a sheikh in the Persian Gulf who could help the club resolve its terrible economic problems.[23]

Some interviewees believe that these foreign investors' arrival in the game is inevitable and, moreover, desirable, given the complicated financial situation of Spanish football. However, they believe these investors should have to produce an economic offering that would make the club's viability possible, and would have to respect the club's culture and symbols:

> ... I think it's fine that some Arab sheikh buys the club as long as he brings a serious project to Valencia. Valencia, like many other Spanish clubs, is in bad shape. We can't get money anywhere. The only hope is foreign investment. Either that or the disappearance...

> ...the clubs are selling their shares to foreigners because they don't have any money. The shareholders sell because the clubs are unsustainable. The same thing happened in England and the results were good. If it's to avoid bankruptcy, I think it's fine...

Others, however, point out that the arrival of foreign investors would mean a loss of the clubs' identities, as these investors will not follow the same criteria as the Spanish owners. Such fans are resigned to what they believe will be a profound transformation in the culture and tradition of the clubs. It must be kept in mind that the possibilities for these investors are not as extensive as was the case in the English Premier League, as the two clubs with the greatest economic potential, Real Madrid and Barcelona FC (along with Athletic de Bilbao and Osasuna), are not

Limited Liability Sports Companies and, therefore, cannot be sold. The attraction of investing in Spanish clubs is limited, taking into consideration first that Real Madrid and Barcelona FC constitute most of the earning potential of Spanish football, and second that the enormous debts of teams like Valencia FC and Athletic de Madrid reduce the possibility of foreign investors viewing them as an investment opportunity. All of this determines and explains the fact that the Spanish League's level of internationalization is quite inferior to that of the English Premier League.

In sum, the fans are either not completely aware of the implications of clubs transforming into SAD, or they simply prefer to deceive themselves about it. A clear example of this is their continued use of the term 'member' to identify themselves or refer to those who, in reality, are shareholders or season ticket holders. The research has revealed the existence of a feeling of symbolic ownership of the club, the persistence of which is due to a number of things, such as the paternalistic tone or local origin of some leaders in Spanish football, the role of the majority of clubs as representatives of regional identity and, finally, local and regional governments' interest in keeping foreign capital or investors from taking control of a club.

Reactions to the process of commodification

The purpose of this last section is to analyse the reactions produced by the process of commodification of football among fans. More specifically, the aim is to examine fans' perceptions of the evolution of football in the past few years, the changes that have occurred in the way football is consumed and, finally, whether fans have developed responses or resistance initiatives in reaction to this process of commodification.

The majority of interviewees maintain that the transformations that have occurred in football in the past twenty years form part of the same evolutionary process that has taken place in Spanish society. Therefore, the transformation of football into a televised, plural and globalized phenomenon is inevitable, as this development has allowed not only football's survival, but also the maintenance of its hegemony as a social and sport phenomenon. Rather than proving fatal to the game, the current evolution of football is a sign of its superiority:

> ... I think the great success of football is that it has maintained its privileged place and overcome the competition, it has consolidated its hegemony at a time when there are a large variety of entertainment activities available...

These ideas, however, are not an obstacle to formulating a profound and unanimous negative rating of football clubs' management. The general feeling is that they are poorly managed, dedicated to an irresponsible dynamic of economic waste and personal interest, and removed from the control and supervision not only of the fans, but also of public administration:

> ... football could survive on its own, but the reality is that it is very badly managed...

This double impression is what we could call the *current paradox of football*: its growing role as entertainment produces great enthusiasm among the fans, but this enthusiasm coexists with the bitter sensation that the sport is on an irresponsible path which is extremely difficult to leave. The paradox, however, not only involves football as a social phenomenon. It also affects the fans, who on the one hand, complain about the economic situation of the clubs, but on the other demand that the owners pursue aggressive player-signing policies regardless of the cost.

Why does this logic end up prevailing? Some interviewees believe there is a combination of two factors behind it. On the one hand, the legal model of the SAD turns fans into mere spectators and relieves them of any responsibility for the club's progress. On the other, the pressure that fans can exert within the stadium can determine whether a club's president will stay or go. Thus, what finally triumphs is an irrational dynamic that involves an unsustainable expense:

> ... so then if you are used to the fact that football's money does not cause you problems, you don't mind if they spend all those millions hiring players...

What are the consequences of this dynamic in the relationship between fans and football? The clearest is the progressive separation between the sporting and social spheres.[24] Fans increasingly focus simply on the sporting sphere and distance themselves from any worry or interest, such as SAD status, related to the club as an organization. In other words, the fans are only interested in the sporting aspects of the club: the players' performance, the coach's decisions, the signing of new players, the playing style, the goals and the results of the matches.

> ... I think the evolution has been that the fans increasingly separate the economic-social management from the sport management, and they are becoming more interested in the sport and less in the other...

There are two reasons behind this progressive distancing from a club's social aspects and the consequent consolidation of the fan as a consumer of football information or shows. First, in recent years the fans have seen that the management of football clubs has become extraordinarily complex, involving technical–legal and economic peculiarities that are increasingly difficult to understand. Parallel to this, daily life has also become more complex for members of western societies as a result of the transformation of the world of work and the influence of individualization processes. It is not surprising, then, that fans are more interested in the fun and festive aspects of football, and avoid questions with a problematic or conflictive dimension:

> ...I think what is happening is that people think they already have too many problems in their own lives to get involved in the problems of an institution, no matter how much they care about it, in which they can't do anything...

Second, club management is increasingly based on considerations of a business nature – even though they might have to do with criteria *sui generis* – and less on the opinions, criteria and expectations of the fans. This leads fans to finally realize that the role designed for them in the new football scenario is that of a mere spectator:

> ... the management of the club is something that doesn't depend on us, in the sense that it is in the hands of the shareholders, and it is something we can't control, so even if the managers are pessimistic, in the end we realize that in those issues they don't count on us, so we can't do anything...

The reorientation toward strictly sport-related matters is also reflected in the type of information about football offered by news media. Newspaper articles and television reports increasingly avoid questions with economic and political implications in order to look more closely at purely sport-related aspects. This was verified by the journalists interviewed:

> ... the only thing people want to know is if the team works, that the coach is good, that the players are good and they sign up the best ones...

What are the effects of this progressive movement of the focus of fans and news media toward strictly sport-related questions? Based on the opinions expressed by the interviewees, this movement has signified their transformation into hyper-spectators. Thus, nowadays football fans are hyper-consumers of football entertainment and, compared to the 'members' of the previous era, are characterized by the display of a more hedonistic consumption of sport and an inability to be critical about the merchantilization process undertaken by the clubs.

Some interviewees point out that the role offered to the fan by the new football scenario should not always be evaluated negatively, as there are many fans who feel more comfortable with their role as mere spectators. Why? Because this role allows them to remain uninvolved in the club's problems and focus on the team's playing, enjoying their goals and triumphs in a completely relaxed way. Numerous interviewees testified in this regard:

> ... I want football to distract me from my problems, not create them. I go to football to be entertained and have fun, the same way I go to the movies to see a good film...

> ... I pay for my season ticket, I go on Sundays to watch my Valencia, and I don't want to know anything about problems or debts. I go there to be entertained and have fun, and I don't want to hear about problems...

All of this has given rise to the second differential characteristic of today's football fans: their lack of criticism. The interviewees point out that the consolidation of their role as spectators has caused them to distance themselves from decisions about the management and functioning of the club, things in which they do not feel involved. From this point of view, the current fandom involves going to the stadium to have a fun and entertaining experience, and the way it conceives this experience leaves no room for critical action or protest about the management and functioning of the club:

> ... we are less and less active, in reality we've been distancing ourselves and now we watch the matches and it ends there; we don't experience the club like before. The only thing we care about is winning games. Let the shareholders fix the club's economy; that's why they are the owners. ...

However, it would be erroneous to state that fans' lack of criticism of a club's management implies a lack of influence over its progress. In the recent history of Spanish football – including the cases of Valencia FC and Levante UD – there have been many situations in which fans have protested the path being taken by the club and called for the president's resignation, putting him under such pressure that he finally decides to leave. Interviewees recalled what occurred in 1997 when the Mestalla stadium called for the resignation of then-president Paco Roig:

> ... in the days of Paco Roig, which I lived through, the fans pushed the president to leave in a game against Salamanca when the whole stadium asked the President to leave and he did [...] I think at that moment, even though the SAD already existed, people still had the mentality of being members...

Nevertheless, two remarks must be made about Spanish fans' potential for protest. First, it is clear that this potential is only activated when there is an accumulation of negative sport results. It is not, therefore, a response of resistance to the economic functioning or management of a club. While the team plays well, makes goals and achieves victories, the fans do not express discontent:

> ... people protest when the team is not doing well and doesn't win games. They don't care about anything else, but the only thing that can make them get up and call for the president to resign is if the team loses games...

Second, it must be highlighted that quite probably, fans' critical capacity or potential for protest has become diluted in the past few years and is now only residual. This is basically because, as the years have gone by, the feeling of symbolic ownership of the club has also waned. Some interviewees mentioned that protest against a president when the team has a bad season or is playing far below the expected level are less and less frequent. Today, the fans' most common reaction when their team has a run of bad results or does not play football well consists of not going to the stadium. This is what a consumer does when he does not like a product any more: he stops buying it.

In sum, this section has described the *current paradox of football*, according to which fans' strong fascination with and attraction to the growing role of football as entertainment co-exists with the feeling that football is a poorly managed and unsustainable activity in today's terms. Fans resolve the tension between these two extremes by distancing themselves from the social and economic dimension of the club and consolidating their role as spectators. This process has meant the transformation of the supporter into a hyper-consumer of football entertainment, which restricts his participation in the club to the role of consumer. Thus, fans' potential for protest is now limited to those moments when the team has poor sporting results.

Conclusions

This article has focused on the social consequences of the commodification process in Spanish football culture. The analysis was based on interviews with 19 fans, six sport journalists and three professional sport managers. While the latter two groups were linked to television channels, newspapers and national organizations, the fans were supporters of Valencia FC and Levante UD, two clubs with very different characteristics whose fans can be considered to represent the most frequent experiences, opinions and attitudes seen in Spanish football.

The study has shown first that the process of commodification has not affected fans' feelings of identification with their clubs, although it has affected their repertoire of behaviours. A situation of *hyper-consumption* has been produced, which could be defined as an increase and intensification of the consumption of football information and televised broadcasts, parallel to the increase in football offerings in the media. This hyper-consumption explains the growing personalization of football consumption and an intensification of the entertainment-festive dimension of attending matches at the stadiums.

Second, the study has shown the existence of a sense of *symbolic ownership* of the club among Spanish fans that explains why the majority of them continue to consider themselves club 'members', even though the clubs' transformation into Limited Liability Sports Companies (SAD) has turned many of these fans into shareholders and/or season-ticket holders. Three elements contribute to the fact that fans are either unaware or fooling themselves about the implications of the clubs' move to an SAD model: the paternalism and local roots of the majority of the clubs' presidents, the clubs' strong regional symbolism, and local authorities' interest in keeping foreign investors from taking over the clubs.

Third, and finally, this study has proposed the existence of a *paradox of football*, where fans' fascination with football co-exists with the feeling that the clubs are poorly managed and economically unsustainable. The tension created by these two extremes is resolved by fans distancing themselves from any aspects of the club which are not strictly sport-related. Fans are transformed, then, into *hyperspectators:* consumers of the football show who voluntarily remove themselves from the social dimension of the club. They go to the stadium looking for a psychologically pleasurable experience and only react critically when their team goes through periods of bad sporting results, especially when, additionally, the playing style is not aesthetically pleasing to them.

Notes

1. Walsh and Giulianotti, 'This Sporting Mammon', 53.
2. Giulianotti, 'Supporters, Followers, Fans and Flaneurs'; Giulianotti, 'Sports Spectators and the Social Consequences of Commodification'.
3. Durán, *El fenómeno de las jóvenes hinchadas radicales en el fútbol;* Durán, *El vandalismo en el fútbol;* Adán, *Ultras y skinheads: La juventud visible*; Adán, 'Ultras, culturas del fútbol'; Viñas, *El mundo ultra. Los radicales del fútbol español*, Viñas, *Toleràncía zero*, Llopis-Goig, 'The Recent Evolution of Football Violence in Spain'.
4. Unzueta, 'Fútbol y nacionalismo vasco'; Colomé, 'Conflictos e identidades en Cataluña'; Díaz Noci, 'Los nacionalistas van al fútbol'; González, 'La cancha de las identidades, periodismo deportivo y fútbol gallego'; Llopis-Goig, 'Clubes y selecciones nacionales de fútbol: la dimensión etnoterritorial del fútbol español', Llopis-Goig, 'Identity, Nation-State and Football in Spain'.
5. Campo, 'Cuestión de Pelotas. Hacerse Hombre, Hacerse el Hombre en el Fútbol'; Llopis-Goig, 'Female football supporters' communities in Spain, Llopis-Goig, 'Learning and Representation'; Llopis-Goig, '¿Fuera de juego?; Llopis-Goig, 'Masculinidades inductoras'.
6. Llopis-Goig, 'Fútbol y televisión en España'.
7. Durán and Jiménez, 'Fútbol y Racismo: un problema científico y social'; Durán and Pardo, 'Racismo en el fútbol español (1ª y 2ª división)'; Viñas and Spaaij, *Medidas y políticas de intervención acerca del racismo y la xenofobia en el fútbol español*; Llopis-Goig, 'Racism and Xenophobia in Spanish Football'.
8. CIS, *Barómetro de Mayo de 2007*.

9. Llopis-Goig, 'El fútbol como ritual festivo'.
10. Conclusions of a report published by the Professional Football League, *The Impact of Professional Football on the Spanish Economy* (www.lfp.es). According to this report, professional football employs directly and indirectly nearly 66,000 people.
11. This is the report by Deloitte, *Football Money League 2008-2009*.
12. Gay de Liébana, *Fútbol y finanzas*.
13. Llopis-Goig, 'Identity, Nation-State and Football in Spain'; Llopis-Goig, *Fútbol postnacional*.
14. CIS, *Barómetro de Mayo de 2007*.
15. Lipovetsky, *La felicidad paradójica*.
16. Taking into account the extraordinary increase in information and audiovisual programming related to football, it is not surprising that 70.6% of the adult population consider that professional football receives excessive attention from the communication media (CIS, *Barómetro de Mayo de 2007*).
17. CIS, *Barómetro de Mayo de 2007*.
18. Although the Sports Law proposed the transformation, of a general nature, of all the clubs that participated in professional sport competitions, an additional disposition of this law contemplated the possibility that those who had a positive patrimonial balance in all the audits performed since the 1985/86 season by the National Football League (LNFP) would conserve their legal structure. This is what occurred with Real Madrid, Barcelona FC, Athletic de Bilbao and Osasuna (Barajas, *Valuation Model for Football Clubs*).
19. Barajas, *Valuation Model for Football Clubs*.
20. Billig, *Banal Nationalism*.
21. In January 2003, Dmitry Piterman acquired 24% of the shares of Racing de Santander, thus taking control of a league team with the permission of the other shareholders. He was a controversial figure, acting as coach in spite of not having the corresponding licence, which caused great debate at the heart of the League. At the beginning of the 2003/04 season, the business owner Santiago Díaz managed to regain control of Racing thanks to the support of the rest of the shareholders, meaning Piterman lost the control and later ended up without shareholder representation. In 2004 Piterman bought Deportivo Alavés, a Second Division team, and managed to raise it to the First Division. However, in the 2005/06 season the team descended again to the Second Division. After various arguments with followers of Alavés, relations between the players and the Alavés institutions worsened considerably. Already facing various economic problems and sentences for non-payment of salaries, in March 2007 Piterman left Alavés, after an investment group bought 51% of the shares. During his four years of management, the team's debt had multiplied by a factor of three, reaching €23 million.
22. This is a new version of article 22 of the Sports Law established by Law 50/1998 (article 109 four), in which mention of the nationality of the shareholder disappears. This aspect of the Sports Law of 1990 was already criticized at the time for being incompatible with the free circulation in the European Union treaties (Barajas, *Valuation Model for Football Clubs*).
23. Problems that in 2009 caused the entrance of a financial entity to assist in the club's difficult situation, which led to its having to mortgage the land of its current stadium, Mestalla, for €2.010 billion to refinance the debt. Among other measures, the club had to stop construction of the new Mestalla stadium and, later, sell two of its main football assets – David Villa, who was sold to Barcelona FC, and David Silva, who moved to Manchester City (*El Confidencial*, 17 March 2011).
24. With 'social sphere' understood as the legal and economic aspects of the club.

References

Adán, T. *Ultras y skinheads: La juventud visible*. Oviedo: Ediciones Nobel, 1996.
Adán, T. "Ultras, culturas del fútbol". *Revista de Estudios de Juventud* 64 (2004): 87–100.
Barajas, A. *Valuation Model for Football Clubs based on the Key Factors of their Business*. Pamplona: Universidad de Navarra, 2004.
Billig, M. *Banal Nationalism*. London: Sage Publications, 1995.

Campo, A. 'Cuestión de Pelotas. Hacerse Hombre, Hacerse el Hombre en el Fútbol'. In *Hombres. La Construcción Cultural de las Masculinidades*, ed. J.M. Valcuende and J. Blanco, 66–9. Madrid: Talasa, 2003.
CIS. *Barómetro de Mayo*. Madrid: Centro de Investigaciones Sociológicas, 2007.
Colomé, G. "Conflictos e identidades en Cataluña". In *Fútbol y pasiones políticas*, ed. S. Segurola, 169–74. Madrid: Editorial Debate, 1999.
Deloitte Consulting. *Football Money League: The Reign in Spain*, Sport Business Group at Deloitte, 2009.
Díaz Noci, J. 'Los nacionalistas van al fútbol. Deporte, ideología y periodismo en los años 20 y 30'. *ZER. Revista de Estudios de Comunicación* 9 (2000): 367–94.
Durán, J. *El fenómeno de las jóvenes hinchadas radicales en el fútbol. Su situación en España*. Madrid: Universidad Complutense de Madrid, 1995.
Durán, J. *El vandalismo en el fútbol*. Una reflexión sobre la violencia en la sociedad moderna. Madrid:: Editorial Gymnos, 1996.
Durán, J., and P.J. Jiménez. 'Fútbol y Racismo: un problema científico y social'. *Revista Internacional de Ciencias del Deporte* 2, no. 3 (2006): 68–94.
Durán, J., and R. Pardo. 'Racismo en el fútbol español (1ª y 2ª división); Temporadas 2004/05 y 2005/06'. *Revista Internacional de Ciencias del Deporte* 12, no. 4 (2008): 85–100.
Gay de Liébana, J.M. *Fútbol y finanzas: La economía de la Liga de las Estrellas*. Barcelona: Universidad de Barcelona, 2009.
Giulianotti, R. 'Sports Spectators and the Social Consequences of Commodification: Critical Perspectives from Scottish Football'. *Journal of Sport and Social Issues* 29, no. 4 (2005): 386–410.
Giulianotti, R. 'Supporters, Followers, Fans and Flaneurs. A Taxonomy of Spectator Identities in Football'. *Journal of Sport and Social Issues* 26, no. 1 (2002): 25–46.
González Ramallal, M. 'La cancha de las identidades, periodismo deportivo y fútbol gallego'. In *de las identidades. Medios de comunicación políticas y mercados de identidad*, ed. V. F. Sampedro and La pantalla, 259–84. Barcelona: Icaria, 2003.
Lipovetsky, G. *La felicidad paradójica. Ensayo sobre la sociedad de hiperconsumo*. Barcelona: Anagrama, 2007.
Llopis-Goig, R. 'Clubes y selecciones nacionales de fútbol: la dimensión etnoterritorial del fútbol español'. *Revista Internacional de Sociología* LXIV, no. (45) (2006a): 37–66.
Llopis-Goig, R. 'El fútbol como ritual festivo'. *Un análisis referido a la sociedad española'. Anduli, Revista Andaluza de Ciencias Sociales* 6 (2006b): 115–32.
Llopis-Goig, R. 'The Recent Evolution of Football Violence in Spain'. In *The Changing Role of Public, Civic and Private Sector in Sport Culture*, ed. H. Itkonen, A.K. Salmikangas, E. McEvoy. Jyväskylä: University of Jyväskylä, 155-62, 2007a.
Llopis-Goig, R. 'Female Football Supporters' Communities in Spain: A Focus on Women's Peñas'. In *Women Football and Europe: Histories Equity and Experiences* , ed. J. Magee, J. Candwell, and S. Scraton, 173–88. Oxford: Meyer & Meyer Sport, 2007b.
Llopis-Goig, R. 'Identity, Nation-State and Football in Spain: The Evolution of Nationalist Feelings in Spanish Football'. *Soccer and Society* 9, no. 1 (2008a): 56–63.
Llopis-Goig, R. 'Learning and Representation. The Construction of Masculinity in Football: An Analysis of the Situation in Spain". *Sport in Society* 11, no. 6 (2008b): 685–95.
Llopis-Goig, R. 'Fútbol y televisión en España. Análisis sociológico de unas relaciones de cooperación (y conflicto)'. In *Comunicación y deporte*, ed. V. Gambau, 77–82. Madrid: Librerias Deportivas Esteban Sanz, 2008c.
Llopis-Goig, R. '¿Fuera de juego? Las peñas de mujeres en el fútbol español'. *Sistema, Revista de Ciencias Sociales* 210 (2009a): 113–26.
Llopis-Goig, R. 'Racism and Xenophobia in Spanish Football: Facts, Reactions and Policies'. *Physical Culture and Sport: Studies and Research* XLVII (2009b): 35–43.
Llopis-Goig, R. *Fútbol postnacional. Transformaciones sociales y culturales del deporte global en Europa y en América Latina*. Barcelona: Editorial Anthropos, 2009c.
Llopis-Goig, R. 'Masculinidades inductoras. La construcción de la masculinidad en el fútbol español'. *Sistem* 217 (2010): 61–76.
Unzueta, P. 'Fútbol y nacionalismo vasco'. In *Fútbol y pasiones políticas*, ed. S. Segurola, 147–67. Madrid: Editorial Debate, 1999.

Viñas, C., and R. Spaaij. 'Medidas y políticas de intervención acerca del racismo y la xenofobia en el fútbol español'. *Sistema* 192 (2006): 51–76.
Viñas, C. *El Mundo ultra. Los radicales del fútbol español*. Madrid: Editorial Temas de Hoy, 2005.
Viñas, C. *'Tolerància zero. La violència en el futbol'*. Barcelona: Angle Editorial, 2006.
Walsh, A., and R. Giulianotti. 'This Sporting Mammon: A Normative Analysis of the Commodification of Sport'. *Journal of the Philosophy of Sport* 28 (2001): 53–77.

Supporters Direct and supporters' governance of football: a model for Europe?

Peter Kennedy

School of Business for Society, Glasgow Caledonian University, Scotland

> Supporters Direct, a sports policy initiative launched by the British Labour government in 2000, has consolidated its position in the intervening decade and experienced considerable success in setting up supporters' trusts. This success has encouraged the European football governing body, UEFA, to give its backing to the establishment of the Supporters Direct model across European leagues. This chapter develops a broadly Marxist political economy of football to explain how and why, despite the increasing pressure of commercialization, the football business remains founded on an unstable commodity structure in which the motive forces of exchange value and profit ultimately fail to dominate football as a community asset. The assumed progressive nature of Supporters Direct is premised on the view that football has been commodified. However, as the chapter will explain, the argument that football presents as an unstable commodity structure furnishes an alternative view of Supporters Direct: that it is an integral part of a social policy aimed at the preservation and extension of commodified social relations.

Introduction

In May 2006 the European Independent Review (EIR) published a report it had commissioned from Portugal's former Deputy Prime Minister, José Luis Arnaut. Arnuat's report, The Independent European Sports Review (IESR), presented a series of recommendations aimed at curbing and controlling the commercial 'excesses' which have been viewed as bringing professional football in Europe into disrepute.[1] Arnaut recommended a fit and proper persons test for all potential owners of football clubs – principally as a means of deterring clubs' use as money-laundering operations in Europe. He also suggested the need for a salary cap for players as an important measure toward securing a competitive balance between clubs. The report also called for the issue of player trafficking to be addressed, with Arnaut in favour of stricter controls on the licensing of football agents. A more even distribution of wealth generated by the game was also a key element of the report. To this end it is argued that 'central marketing' of the game (that is, national leagues collectively bargaining with TV companies over the sale of image rights to televise matches) is the most suitable vehicle to begin to bridge the gap in income between top clubs and others. The ultimate objective of these recommendations is to 'provide a comprehensive and robust legal framework'[1] for football's governance which allows

UEFA the authority to take a forceful lead on these issues, free from the threat of legal challenge to their efforts in the European Court.

However, one of the most eye-catching statements made by Arnaut with respect to football's governance is that supporters should have a greater say in the running of the clubs they support.[2] Arnaut believes that 'properly structured supporter involvement will help to contribute to improved governance' of football clubs.[3] The IESR highlighted the work carried out by Supporters Direct in Britain, an organization which aids in the foundation and development of football supporters' trusts.[4] Football supporters' trusts are committed to the principle of mutual ownership of shares in football clubs by their members, thereby gaining a greater voice in their football club's decision-making process. The report, noting the absence of a pan-European body representing the interests of supporters which UEFA could enter into structured dialogue with, advocates enquiring into the feasibility of 'rolling out' the British Supporters Direct model at a European level, while taking into consideration the different club ownership models that exist across Europe.[5]

What the IESR does not address is the particular political and economic context in which Supporters Direct was created. The organization was set up and funded by the British government of the time and, ideologically, sits within the framework of that government's attachment to the economic and productive virtues of the private sector and the role of the state in resurrecting communities and building social cohesion through market reforms. The 'economic and productive virtues' referred to by the British government in its economic policy deliberations derive from the commodity structure inherent to production in the private sector and, specifically, the well established practice that prioritizes the exchange value of goods and services and the profit motive as the primary aims and motivations of the business unit. Criteria of success and failure and appropriate and inappropriate forms of organization and goverenance find their premises here. However, when it comes to the business of football the premises are not so clear: in as much as the football industry expresses the dominance of the commodity structure found in the private sector, then one might understand Supporters Direct as part and parcel of the state's objective to resurrect communities and build social cohesion in the face of increasing commercial pressures acting on football. If, however, one disputes the idea that the football industry is an industry like any other (where exchange value and profit motives reign supreme), then Supporters Direct may be interpreted in a rather different light: as an institution that advances attention to economic imperatives of efficiency, responsible profits and, therefore, the view of football as an exchange value.

The argument of this chapter is that the commodity structure of football is fluid and unstable and that, as a result, the tendency towards commercialization has its limits as it comes up against the pursuit of football as a community asset. The speculatively rather than productively generated nature of profits, combined with the propensity to transform the money pouring into football into debt, bear some testimony to the *unstable commodity structure* of football. On this reading (to be detailed later), Supporters Direct has conflicting functions: on the one hand, it is a means of sustaining football as a community asset; on the other, it is a way of promoting football as an economic asset, where the result (if not necessarily the explicit aim) is more an attempt to consolidate the commodity structure of the football industry than to actually consolidate the community structure of football. Therefore, in what follows I argue that – contra the aspirations of IESR – Supporters Direct represents something more than the adoption of a different approach to football-club ownership. Before making this argument the chapter describes the background to the emergence of Supporters Direct and then explains the theoretical basis of the commodity structure of the economy and football in more detail, drawing on the works of two major figures to do so: Karl Marx and Karl Polanyi.

Background to Supporters Direct

The increasing level of commercialization of the British game during the 1990s is said to have run counter to the traditions of British football's historical development.[6] Professional football had been, indisputably, the national sport for over a century; watched weekly by hundreds of thousands of fans throughout Britain, and playing a vital part in sustaining the fabric of civil society. It has been pointed out that historically, the football authorities in Britain had 'recognised the twin dangers to football from unregulated market forces and private ownership of clubs' and took decisive action to avoid the very situation that has arisen latterly, whereby profit-seekers have entered into the ownership of clubs purely for financial reasons.[7] Principally, this was done by avoiding the payment of clubs' directors, preventing the sale of club assets, and setting in place 'a strong system of income-sharing to maintain competitive balance'.[8]

There is a debate over the primary motivation of professional football clubs taking the incorporation route. Steven Tischler, in particular, has made the case for seeing this transition in terms of the expansion of capitalist exploitative relations into what was for the most part a working-class cultural pursuit.[9] However, there seems to be a consensus within football historiography that the shift from club to club-company status had a more benign motive: incorporation as a means of raising capital to invest in a club as a competitive sporting organization, rather than to make profits for shareholders.[10] For the most part, football clubs retained their status as the members' organizations they had started out as. The not-for-profit, 'one game' principle held sway for a century prior to its dismantling and the opening up of football to market forces as another 'branch of the entertainment industry'.[11]

> The path that football had taken latterly, though, brought with it what were viewed as unacceptable socio-economic consequences, not only for football fandom, but also for the communities, which had traditionally supported professional clubs (Wragg, 1998). It was into this environment that the Football Task Force was launched. The Task Force's attempt to tackle the increasing trend toward commercialisation in football brought about a series of reports, and some of their recommendations were implemented.[12]

With little government appetite to impose a more radical, 'top-down' regulation of football club governance, a hoped-for grass-roots solution to the sport's ills was put into operation. Enter Supporters Direct. The 'bottom-up' regulation represented by the formation of Supporters Direct had the task of 'nothing less than the democratization of football clubs'.[13] The primary aim of Supporters Direct is to 'promote and support the concept of democratic supporter ownership and representation' in football clubs.[14]

To facilitate this objective, Supporters Direct – through legal advice and funding – help to form supporters' trusts at clubs, encourage the democratic representation of supporters' trusts on football club boards, and promote the idea of ownership by supporters' trusts of shares in clubs.[15] The advocated model of a 'football community mutual' for supporters' trusts is based on Industrial and Provident Societies.[16] Under the I&PS model, ownership of shares in a football club are held in common with other trust members, and these shares carry with them no rights for individuals involved in the trust to gain dividends. Dividend payments are ploughed back into the club through the purchase of more shares for the trust. In the event of a trust being wound up, any surplus left after paying debts goes to local charities or other not-for-profit organizations.[17] 'All of this means that a football mutual cannot be used as a vehicle for making profit and that its assets (which could include shares in a football club) cannot be cashed in by unscrupulous members in the future.'[18]

Supporters Direct established itself on the political landscape. The Labour government of the time viewed the Supporters Direct initiative as integral to its agenda to intervene in the social existence of community life in British towns and cities, where supporters' trusts are encouraged as a means to combat the social exclusion of marginalized groups within urban communities. As Kevin Rye, Supporters Direct's Development Officer, stated, 'the government values [Supporters Direct's] contribution to the game, and also acknowledges that football has a massive part to play in the health and social inclusivity agendas of, particularly, young people'.[19] Confirming this view, then-Labour Chancellor Gordon Brown, speaking at the Fourth Annual Supporters Direct Conference in October 2004, underlined the importance of Supporters Direct as 'a beacon of success for others to follow'.[20] Underlining the intimacy of Supporters Direct and the Labour Party was the fact that senior figures in Supporters Direct, such as Andy Burnham MP, the organization's former chairman, and Philip French, its former chief executive, had strong associations with the Labour government.

As noted, the confidence expressed in Brown's 2004 speech seems to be shared by the game's European authorities: Supporters Direct is seen by world governing body UEFA to be a suitable role model for clubs in other member countries to follow in terms of the ownership, control and management of football clubs.[21] But just how suitable is the model offered by Supporters Direct for forging greater fan democracy? Answering this question requires some understanding of the nature of the football industry itself. Much of the current political economy for the football industry accepts the logic of commercialization and commodification. The commercialization of football is not in dispute. However, commercialization and commodification are not one and the same and can run at different tempos: while one can extend markets and the langauge of markets into a domain and this will assist with commodifying the domain, commodification rests on more fundamental transformations in the basic relations of production and exchange in any given industry. With this in mind, in the next section I draw on the work of Karl Marx and Karl Polanyi to advance the argument that despite this increasing commercialization, the football industry has an unstable commodity structure, and Supporters Direct must be understood in the context of this instablity.

Marx, Polanyi and the political economy of the football industry

There has been quite a lot of focus on the effects of commercialization on supporters in recent years. Research to date has highlighted that, traditionally, supporters share strong bonds, a common identity and a sense of 'moral ownership' of their football clubs; but that increasingly, they are also 'market realists' when it comes to recognizing the financial exigencies of the clubs they support. Fans appear to be increasingly commercially savvy, with entrepreneurial sentiments toward the corporate affairs of their club developing in tension with longstanding traditional sentiments of 'moral ownership'. Overall, the ascendant view within the literature would appear to suggest that the relationship between football clubs and their supporters is becoming more narrowly defined in terms of producer and consumer[22] within an overarching trend towards commodification.

The research to date has expanded our understanding of the world of supporters. However, while there is a thriving research field focusing on the commodification of football and how this may be contested amongst fans, Marxist critical political economy rarely plays any central part in it – which is somewhat surprising, given the focus on commodification. Indeed, a Marxist critical political economy of football supporters is conspicuously absent from the literature. This absence means that any recognition of the fundamental dialectic between market processes and capitalist production relations is also absent from existing research into the dynamics of commodification. The theoretical origins of the existing literature are mostly drawn from a synthesis of Marx, Durkheim and Weber, under the rubric of 'classical sociological tradition'. Yet it is worth stressing that the defining feature of this synthesis is its *evasion* of Marx's central problematic –capitalist relations of production and the class struggle – in favour of placing priority on the forces of instrumental rationality as a means of understanding the dynamics of commodification.[23] Contrary to this synthesis, the market as the basis of understanding social relations is problematic – at the level of the market, the inner connections between things are difficult to grasp, because they are necessarily fragmented.[24] Present research into the commodification of football and football supporters accepts this fragmentation, whereby the football industry as a prism of class struggle is ignored in favour of descriptions and classifications of 'traditional' and 'gentrified' fans; where issues surrounding the extent to which the law of value actually operates in the football industry are at best marginalized by discussions about how exchange-value criteria (prices, costs, profits, merchandising, etc.) are influencing the game; and where commodification is ultimately understood in terms of the market.

Of course, there is recognition within the existing literature of the central tensions in football; for example, that football is increasingly defined in terms of producer–consumer relations, while also remaining very much 'more than a business'. However, the *exact nature* of what 'more than' means is never fully examined or explained. Explanations are pitched in terms of a conceptual shift back and forth between the binary oppositions of 'tradition'/'decommodification' versus 'commercialization'/'commodification', to the point where the blanket use of the concept of commodification 'blunts its usefulness as a descriptive and analytical tool, and may in fact serve as an obstacle to a more nuanced and contextual understanding of the ways in which markets and market logic are introduced into the game'.[25] Even when analysis is couched within a *cultural economy* approach, the articulation of *culture and economy* assumes a synthesis with the commodification of football as the end result. This is so despite the recognition by major theorists in this area[26] that there are 'two alternative causal claims' concerning trends in the relationship between culture and economy. The first of these is *culturalization* of the economy (where aesthetic orientations and symbolic meanings are increasingly integral to the 'economic' object). The second is that culture is becoming increasingly *commodified* (where instrumental–rational, calculative motivations are invading cultural practices). However, when it comes to applying this twin causal chain to football, the two alternative causes appear to be ignored in favour of one logic: commodification, with the sole caveat that the expansion of commercialization, and the attendant marketing and merchandising of all aspects of the game (which form the basis of commodification), depend less on economic calculus of costs to value than on the symbolic and iconic meanings attached to 'the consumption of football'. In other words, tradition and community serve as vehicles of commodification. The crucial point here is that the 'cultural' and the 'economic' are viewed essentially as being mutually constitutive of each other in developing commodification, within an overall theoretical framework in which market rationalization imperatives take the place of class struggle.

The challenge for Marxist critical political economy, which I will pursue below, is not so much the challenge of ignoring these conceptual dichotomies, as they add up to an understanding of football supporter attitudes, but of providing a dialectical, open-ended analysis of the fictitious and highly nuanced nature of both commodification and supporter references to community and tradition as vehicles of non-market sentiment, in opposition to commodification.

Marxist political economies of the sports industry had fallen out of fashion by the end of the 1980s, due in part to the influence of different academic paradigms such as post-structuralism, and in part to the ideological structure's perceived reductionism. When Marxism was influential in sports and football research, it tended to treat these industries simply as part of capital engaged in producing a commodity for profit (if not directly, then indirectly as an asset to be exploited for profit via media and advertising), and also as a means of ideological control over the working class (by inculcating capitalist values of consumerism, competition and the celebration of iconic footballer brands), in much the same way that any other commodity reproduces this domination.[27] This treatment certainly has resonance with the work of Marx. In *Capital*, Marx and Engels wrote of laws as tendencies acting with iron necessity,[28] and in *The Communist Manifesto*[29] they stated their confidence that the laws of capital accumulation would penetrate all industry.

Nevertheless, their emphasis on the struggle over the working day would also suggest that law-like tendencies remain just that: *tendencies open to struggle* and transformation, in which case the outcome is never certain. Moreover, when Marx wrote on commodity fetishism (the category underpinning commodification – rarely mentioned in current literature), he was very much aware of how situations in which 'the social relations between men appear to them as an object'[30] were never fixed states or categorical imperatives, but rather points of intense *collective and individual struggles*[31] appears to endorse this more open-ended view when it comes to the football industry, arguing against any 'capital logic reading of football' by pointing out that it is not an area of capital accumulation, but more a utility-maximizing capital absorber that is best seen as the institutionalization of working-class and bourgeois social relations around a form of weekend entertainment. Yet having noted this economic peculiarity, Taylor never once questions the commodity structure of the football industry.

For Marx, the inability of capital to penetrate an industry must influence the commodity structure. Commodities are capital manifest, and capital is class struggle manifest. Commodities are also manifest use values and social needs, which are also products of class struggle. Capital accumulation provides the motive force to ensure that exchange value dominates over use value: generally, the greater the scope for accumulation the more powerful are processes of commodification; and where accumulation is weak or non-existent, commodification motives lose power relative to use value and social need, which may or may not then become dominant motive forces within the particular industry in which this occurs. Following Marx, one can say that in capitalist society, objects, practices and relations (such as in the field of football) are always in motion; always *becoming* commodities, but never fully commodified, because they are also *becoming* use values. Likewise, while they are *becoming* use values, they rarely develop their full capacity as use values, because they are also *becoming* commodities designed for exchange and with profit in mind. The governing motive force from the side of capitalists is the capacity for capital accumulation in any given industry; if this is weak, the commodity structure will tend to be unstable relative to industries in which it is strong.

Following the above lines of thought, a Marxist political economy of the football business has the potential to provide a dialectic account of football more aware that its relations of production and consumption have *never fully developed to the point at which they are commodified*. The football industry is one in which the dominance of capital is still relatively weak and where, as a consequence, the commodity structure is highly unstable and so open to interpretation, manipulation and, on occasion, outright challenge (an argument extended below). I tend not to read too much about this sort of Marxist view of the commodity structure of industries because it continues to be marginalized by approaches that treat capitalist relations and categories as fully formed entities. Yet what Marx stated about the commodity structure, picked up by Polanyi's[32] observations concerning the 'fictitious' nature of some commodities, can add to a Marxist political economy of the dialectics, dynamics and tensions of the football business. Polanyi understood the limits to economic rationality underpinning the commodity structure of the economy, arguing 'that the most basic human characteristic—the need to relate to other humans, to feel part of a larger community'[33] offers natural limits to commodification. He was the first to use the concept of 'fictitious commodity' with reference to labour, money and education. The concept refers to a struggle between economy and society in capitalism, and specifically to the stripping away of a community asset, or community need, from its wider social relations and its reinsertion within a market-mediated activity where business motives dominate, corrupt and distort the community asset.[34] For example, people's labour power is the classic example of a 'fictitious commodity', because labour activity has a wider social meaning that becomes narrowed into an economic category – wage labour – which inscribes labour's commodity form of existence in capitalist society and negates its direct social usefulness.

The idea of 'fiction' arises as a way of explaining that labour power is never commodified but always in the process of *becoming* commodified, while at the same time also *becoming* something entirely different: an activity for its own intrinsic usefulness to the individual and society. This implies a capitalism-embracing economy–society dialectic close to Marx's original meaning: the commodity structure is permanently in existential doubt, but the circuit of capital accumulation is sustained by powerful social forces that assist in maintaining its dominance, both materially and ideologically, through money capital. Moreover, reflecting on Polanyi's account of the fictitious commodity and reinterpreting this through his reference to a 'double movement' in capitalism enables us to forge a Marxist political economy applicable to illuminating the dialectics of football supporter attitudes.

Polanyi argues that historical transformations in market capitalism take the form of a *double movement*, in which market relations become disembedded from society, producing anomie and dislocation, and then re-embedded, with market imperatives subordinated or harmonized with wider social values and traditions related to production, consumption and distribution. The embedding and disembedding is viewed broadly by Polanyi, and in dialectical rather than linear terms. However, the dialectics of disembedding and re-embedding can also be understood as a daily occurrence in describing *micro processes* of containment and resistance to commodity fetishism. Doing so allows us to relate the latter to the construction of 'fictitious commodities' and related non-market 'fictions' based on tradition and community.

First, 'fiction' is equated with the social construction or reconfiguration of natural resources, manufactured/useful objects and social needs into commodities or exchange values. Second, implicit to the double movement is another fiction usually treated as 'fact' by Polanyi and followers: the fiction of re-embedding or subordinating market relations to 'social needs' and 'traditions'. The latter are fictions because, as Marxists point out, social needs and traditions remain framed by the overarching power of capital, no matter how we 'embed' them in market relations. Polanyi and his latter-day followers tend to play down or else ignore this 'double fiction' emerging from market and non-market relations, largely due to their commitment, whether explicitly or implicitly formulated, to restoring capitalism through either regulation or reform of liberal and neoliberal forms of capitalism, respectively.

This idea of a 'double fiction' highlights the fragility of commodity fetishism and the 'fictional' or constructed nature of non-market alternatives of 'community' and 'traditions' (which are nevertheless hidebound by the market) and is, therefore, particularly apt in understanding the football industry and football supporter attitudes. One can argue, as we will below, that the tensions and contradictions emerging from this 'double fiction' are particularly acute in industries such as football, where the profit motive is weak or non-existent, and so the power of capital over the commodity structure of the industry is correspondingly weaker and open to contestation. With respect to this latter point, football clubs (even English Premier League [EPL] clubs, where most of the capital is concentrated) appear to be guided much more by the dictates of moral ownership than by economic ownership and capital accumulation as, urged on by fans, they pursue top players and success on the pitch. EPL clubs rarely make a profit and even more rarely go out of business; for the most part, they exist in a situation of debt. Hence it is an industry in which capital accumulation as the principal motive force – and with it the rule of capital over the commodity structure – is weak: in the period between the 1998/1999 and 2005/2006 seasons, only Liverpool FC, Manchester United FC and Arsenal FC achieved pre-tax profits in more than four of those years, while the majority of Premiership clubs on average earned pre-tax profits in only two years.[35,36]

Since 2004/2005, profits at the big four clubs have doubled to £166m. The rest of the division has seen its financial situation shift from profits of £53m to an operating loss of £117m (excluding the newly promoted clubs). In practice, these figures imply that the only business model for EPL clubs outside the Champions League is to keep selling to richer owners (a kind of art-collector model).

What the above indicates is that football is 'more than a business', and this implies that the usual rules of producer–consumer relations do not apply quite so strictly. Football supporters continue to be part-producers, while they have much more than a consuming role to play in the overall functioning of the club. Supporters help 'produce' football, not only by adding to the match-day atmosphere and so exerting an influence on the game itself, but also by extending the role and importance of football in the local community through after-match dialogue and debate, taken up and disseminated through the internet and the local media. Moreover, supporters continue to 'consume' football even when the 'commodity' proves to be an 'unsatisfactory' or unsuccessful one. The nature of production is both less and more than the roles narrowly depicted for it in economic literature. The boundaries between production and consumption of economic and community assets when it comes to football are broad and porous, as are the identities and attitudes shaping supporters' beliefs (a claim which is elaborated on in the sections that follow).

For all the above reasons, the perspective of viewing football as an enterprise in the production and consumption of 'fictitious commodities' presents one with a more realistic, open and dialectic appraisal of the situation. Under the conceptual rubric of fictitious commodity, the 'present tense' of the football business as it becomes the subject of increasing commercialization is one characterized as *possibility* rather than fact: it is a possible economic asset and a possible community asset, without fully realizing either. More to the point, it is not simply that one 'asset' corrupts the other, but that one provides the necessary ground for the other to flourish, *while also simultaneously providing the ground from which the corruption of both possibilities occur*. In this sense, football offers supporters a double fiction – unrealizable commodification and mythical tradition.

Using Marx and Polanyi to contextualize Supporters Direct

The above analysis brings us back to Supporters Direct. The 'present tense' double fiction, or dialectic, of corruption, outlined above is recognized, if perhaps not fully understood, by the creation of the Football Taskforce,[37] out of which came Supporters Direct, a government-sponsored supporters' agency that attempts to harness both possibilities. Brown points out that the Taskforce 'steadfastly refused to intervene against the interests of business by supporting the much bolder vision of new regulatory bodies with statutory power'.[38] The fact that the Taskforce, out of which Supporters Direct emerged, was a compromise favouring football as an economic asset bears testimony to the argument that the possibilities of realizing football as a community asset are inextricably linked with the continuing commercialization of football as an economic asset; a 'present tense' making for difficult compromises from Supporters Direct and the supporter trust movement. It is this 'present-tense' dialectic that makes possible a fuller appreciation of not only 'mutualism' as a 'solution'[39] underpinning the political economy of Supporters Direct[40] but, more pertinently, also of the struggles of and compromises made by football supporters as they wrestle with the possibilities of football as both economic and community asset; where the basis of accumulation is weak in favour of speculative profits, and where, therefore, the grounds for realizing both are weak, and for corrupting both are stronger.

In one very real respect, the benefits argued to flow from supporters' trusts seem undeniable. They hold out the prospect of football supporters taking an active part in the running of their clubs and, eventually, taking over their full ownership and control. Moving to a mutual structure may be more reflective of the emotional.[41]

Mutualization does, of course, hold the potential to promote supporters into positions where they can exercise participatory democracy and to extend supporters' involvement in their clubs to include some level of legal ownership of it. As a result of the activity of individual supporters' trusts, a small number of lower-league English and Scottish clubs are now owned outright by their supporters. This type of development marks significant progress for supporters from their traditional status as, at best, 'consulted customer' and, at worst, that of passive and manipulated 'consumer'. In this sense supporters' trusts may aspire towards a more embracing citizenship that allows the dreams and aspirations of fans to prosper.

However, is it this same premise that makes supporters' trusts such powerful 'techniques' for colonizing supporter relations along a more commodified pathway? In particular, a supporter's sense of moral ownership of their club can become blurred by the diktats of economic ownership, converting the traditional feelings of emotional solidarity between supporters in their attachment to the club into more instrumental and quantifiable forms of attachment. It ought to be stressed that mutualization, even in the most favourable conditions – for example, where there is a statutory commitment to governance by mutuality – creates only the *potential* for participatory democracy; it does not simply arise out of the establishment of mutuality.[42] Mutuality could just as well revert to the more passive and, on many occasions, manipulative relations of producer–consumer that are inherent to profit shareholder forms of governance. After all, mutuals must still derive profits so they can invest in the organization in order to keep up with the competition, to develop and to survive. Democratically elected boards must deliver and execute business plans based on an economic rationality which may well come into tension with parallel social objectives.[43] Such is the capitalist context within which mutual forms of governance must be located. The point here is that such pressures provide fertile ground for the democratic potential inherent in mutualization to become compromised and even negated, as it becomes a technique for use in the move towards commodification. As supporters are drawn deeper into football as a business within an industrial complex, there is clearly the potential that they will be inclined to view performance with an eye to the consequences for the latest club audit.

Indeed, it can be argued in this respect that Supporters Direct – in its role as mentor to football trusts – provides the impulse to deepen and extend relations of commodification between supporter and club. Research indicates that the majority of supporters' trusts make cash donations to their football clubs, with almost half of the trust movement viewing such activities as an 'important' or 'very important' part of a trust's activities. (Perhaps tellingly, almost 80% of football clubs surveyed believed supporters' trusts should fundraise for their clubs.)[44] This contradicts the view propounded by Supporters Direct that there is a major difference in this respect between the roles of the traditional supporters' clubs and supporters' trusts – the latter being more typically associated with the concept of donating to the club cause.[45] These donations take the form of supporters' trust membership fees, individual cash donations, fundraising at local community events, and applications for community grants and awards.[46] The football industry's auditors, Deloitte and Touche, underline the importance of these revenue sources as an opportunity for value creation opening up to football clubs: 'There is an increasing amount of supporter involvement in the ownership and operation of clubs... Primarily, this has been driven by the supporters' trust movement... A strong relationship between club and community is also good for business.'[47] The case being made in this statement is that while there are community benefits to this engagement strategy – such as greater youth involvement in football and the elimination of racism from football grounds – as important is supporters' trusts ability to access 'revenue streams' that are inaccessible to PLCs by pioneering such campaigns.[48] This thought is echoed by former Supporters Direct Chief Executive, Philip French: 'Clubs are beginning to understand that supporters' representation and strong trusts are not a threat but a much valued necessity improving the operation and running of clubs.'[49] [50]

There is, then, an apparent contradiction concerning the supporters' trust movement: its 'levelling' ideology is counterbalanced by a willingness to be utilized for commercial purposes by the club hierarchies trusts seek to replace. This contradiction, we believe, has implications for the development of the movement. Evidence suggests that there is an ambiguous attitude among grassroots supporters with regard to how progressive the trust movement is and how much it can achieve.

Football supporters and supporters' trusts

Certain indicators suggest that ordinary supporters remain favourable toward the principle of supporters' trusts becoming involved in the running of football clubs. Many talk of their presence as being a long-overdue intervention which can bring about 'a measure of democracy to football clubs',[51] suggesting that they are 'a much better way of running [clubs]'[52] and an obvious starting point for supporters looking to constructively improve their lot, rather than simply complaining about being exploited.[53]

There are, however, emergent signs that at least some sections of football supporters are questioning the legitimacy of the trust movement. This relates to trusts' ability to put into action their objective to effectively redress the balance of power at football clubs, and thereby remain outside the orbit of influence of club hierarchies and their financial agendas.

It would be difficult to challenge the assertion that supporters' trusts are only given the option to become central stakeholders in a club when it is in a situation of financial crisis and forced to turn to hitherto unconsidered sources of investment. As David Conn[54] asserts in relation to fan control of the bigger clubs in particular, such 'heady thoughts of "rolling back the PLC"... have melted into the realization that mutualising the big clubs is currently impossible'. The trust movement's failure of to make significant inroads into the governance of football clubs has been recognized by football supporters, and it is clear that some now doubt the possibility of reforming football from the situation where 'fat cats in boardrooms count notes'[55] to a position in which clubs are run successfully along democratic lines. Indeed, trust ownership of shares demonstrates that relatively few hold significant amounts of shares in their clubs.[56] There is a perceptible growth in the feeling that trusts continue to be 'locked out' and 'wield limited influence' in club decision-making processes,[57] and this appears to be generating a degree of apathy regarding the value of trust membership.[58] Only in the lower divisions of football (and here in only a fraction of clubs) is there anything like a substantial overlap between trust membership and club support.[59]

This lack of influence in club affairs seems, in some instances at least, to have persuaded trusts to pursue the controversial tactic of allying with individuals holding large amounts of club shares (or seeking to gain large amounts). This has led to suspicion developing between trusts and other supporters. For example, The

Owls Trust (the Sheffield Wednesday supporters' trust) became entangled in Leeds United chairman Ken Bates' takeover bid for Sheffield Wednesday in 2004. The Owls Trust were accused of coming to an arrangement with Bates in his bid for ownership in return for increasing their own influence in the club, and were strongly condemned by many Sheffield Wednesday supporters for their actions.[60] The Celtic Trust was criticized for using shares owned by Simple Minds singer and Celtic supporter Jim Kerr in order to force motions at a Celtic AGM. Kerr had previously been part of a proposed consortium seeking to take control of Celtic FC in 1998, and there was speculation amongst Celtic supporters that the Celtic Trust was being used as 'a vehicle for increasing the power and influence of a number of prominent individuals who currently sit outside the boardroom'.[61] At Peterborough United, The Posh Trust were allotted a place on the board and worked very closely with Barry Fry's regime when his consortium took over ownership of the club in 2003,[62] despite Fry's obvious unpopularity among the club's supporters.[63]

Such examples could be argued to be atypical of the response of supporters' trusts to the problems they face in wielding influence within football clubs. They could, however, also be argued to be the logical actions of organizations working within the parameters of a government agency, Supporters Direct, whose fundamental role is to manage – if not extend – the commodification of football. Indeed, the actions of these named trusts may be considered a harbinger for the future direction of the trust movement. For instance, in the recent past supporters' trusts have been encouraged to cast off their I&PS status and embrace the structure and rules of Community Interest Companies (CICs). CICs can be described as a halfway house between a traditional mutual (such as an I&PS) and a private limited company. CICs (organizations are given this status by proving that they add 'social value' to communities) encourage private investment in return for dividend payments on shares bought and/or interest payments on loans made.[64] CICs can be used as an asset base for attracting loans (debt), making them an attractive proposition for business investors. In the words of Supporters Direct, the philosophy of the CIC 'attempts to reconcile the aims underpinning a social enterprise – community benefits, community need, environmental concerns – with the needs of the investors who have the capital needed to enable these social enterprises to grow and flourish'.[65] This model of organization is increasingly being advocated for supporters' trusts due to examples of trusts taking control (or having the opportunity to take control) of failing clubs, but finding themselves unable to financially support their ambitions.[66] Despite Supporters Direct's assurances that the CIC model offers a democratic alternative to the use of private capital, a move toward such a model – a joint venture between supporters and commercial entities – would undoubtedly provide the potential for problems in company decision-making regarding community and investment objectives, and compromise the original ideals which won the trust movement favour in many quarters.

Conclusion

The aim of this paper has been to offer a Marxist critical political economy of football that gives priority to the unstable commodity structure of the football business, and to offer suggestions about how this critical political economy can help explain the nature of Supporters Direct and the suitability of their model of supporter involvement in football club governance. In this respect, the paper has argued that a more fruitful way of understanding Supporters Direct emerges from a perspective which views the football business as both producer and consumer of a 'fictitious commodity'[67] – creative, enduringly communal and a basis for collective identity, which must be continually bent out of shape until it looks more like (but never quite like) something one invests in, exploits, sells or purchases as a consumer in the marketplace. However, as I have also argued, the fiction is double-edged – part of a dialectic of disembedding and re-embedding market ideology and traditional rhetoric that can also be understood as a daily occurrence in describing the micro-processes of containment and resistance to commodity fetishism. It is to be noted that the 'apparent contradiction' alluded to earlier concerning the supporters' trust movement – its 'levelling' ideology being counterbalanced by a willingness to be utilized for commercial purposes by the club hierarchies that trusts seek to replace – is tangible and very real, and ought to be considered with care before the Supporters Direct model is rolled out beyond the United Kingdom and into mainland European leagues.

Notes

1. Conn, D. 'The Beautiful Game', 2005; Bower, T. 'Broken Dreams'.
2. Arnaut, 'European Union Report', 71–2.
3. IESR, 72.
4. Supporters Direct, 2001.
5. IESR, 72.
6. Hamil et al, *The Changing Face of the Football Business*; Burnham, 'Regulation, Redistribution and Mutualisation', 14–5.
7. Burnham, 'Regulation, Redistribution and Mutualisation', 14.
8. Burnham, 'Regulation, Redistribution and Mutualisation', 14–5.
9. Tischler, in 'Footballers and Businessmen',, more especially makes the case that football club directors were in a prime position to exploit their own clubs by providing certain business services, such as food, refreshments or building services in the guise of vendors to the club.
10. Mason, 1980. 'Association football and English society 1863–1915'; Holt, R. 1989, Sport and the British: a modern history.
11. A phrase taken from the 1991 Football League document *One Game, One Team, One Voice*, which called for, as a means of counteracting the commercial instincts of the elite clubs, the unification of the Football League and Football Association to preserve the unity of the English game's 92-club structure and a commitment to the historic sharing principle regarding the game's revenues.
12. In particular, the Task Force report and recommendations on tackling the problem of racism at football grounds saw the passing of a law in 1999 criminalizing racist chanting inside football stadia. See S. Hamil et al., *The Changing Face of the Football Business*, 38.
13. Hamil et al, *The Changing Face of the Football* Business, xi.
14. Supporters Direct, Newsletter, 2001.
15. Supporters Direct, Newsletter, 2001.
16. IPS, 'Registrar of Friendly Societies'.
17. Jaquiss, 'Mutualism rules: The Community in Football', 51–6.
18. Supporters Direct, 2004a, 4.
19. Supporters Direct, 2006, 10.
20. Arnaut, *European Union Report*, 71–2.

21. Tapp and Clowes, 'From "carefree casuals"'; Tapp, 'The Loyalty of Football Fans'; Adamson, Jones and Tapp, 'From CRM to FRM'; Giulianotti, 'Sport Spectators and the Social Consequences of Commodification'.
22. Giulianotti, 'Sport Spectators and the Social Consequences of Commodification'.
23. Marx, *Capital, Volume 1*.
24. Moor, 'Sport and Commodification: A Reflection on Key Concepts', 132.
25. du Gay and Pryke, 'Culture and Economy: Cultural Analysis and Commercial Life'; Warde, 'Production, Consumption and 'Cultural Economy'.
26. Brohm, *Sport: A Prison of Measured Time*; Wheeler, 'Organized Sport and Organized Labour'; Beamish, 'Sport and the Logic of Capitalism'.
27. Marx, *Capital, Volume 1*.
28. Marx and Engels, *The Communist Manifesto*.
29. Marx and Engels, *Capital, Volume 1*.
30. Polanyi, *The Great Transformation*.
31. Taylor, I. 'Professional Sport and the Recession: The Case of British Soccer', 1984.
32. McQuaig, *More than Just Consumers*, 2.
33. Polanyi, *The Great Trasformation*.
34. Football Economy, 'Football Club Financial Profiles and Article Archives'.
35. Fry, 'The Real Business of Football'.
36. Football Taskforce, 'Football: Commercial Issues'.
37. Brown, 'A Task of Two Halves'; Brown, 'Football and Communities', 2006.
38. Michie, *New Mutualism*.
39. Kennedy and Kennedy, 'Preserving and Extending the Commodification of Football Supporter Relations'.
40. Michie, *New Mutualism*, 15.
41. This is a point made by Dominic Malcolm in 'Football Business and Football Communities in the Twenty-first century', 109. Malcolm points to the danger of supporters' groups becoming 'dominated by an active minority' that is unrepresentative, demographically speaking, of the wider club support. See FGRC (2003a) where the social complexion of the vast majority of seven West Midlands supporters' trust boards were found to be overwhelmingly white, middle-aged males. See also M. Jackson and P. Maltby, 'Trust in Football', 6.
42. Reid, 'Charitable Trusts'.
43. FGRC, 'The State of the Game', 62–3
44. In particular, this donor aspect to supporter's trusts is rebuffed by Supporters Direct's Deputy Chief Executive, Dave Boyle: 'Gone were the days when would simply hand over money. That is not their role'. He was speaking at Peterborough Supporters' Trust AGM, 11 September 2006. See Posh Supporters' Trust.
45. FGRC, 'The State of the Game', 58–9.
46. Supporters Direct, 2001, 9.
47. Hamil, 'The Third Annual State of the Game Survey of Governance at Professional Football Clubs', 38.
48. Supporters Direct, 2005b, 5.
49. Closer analysis reveals that Supporters Direct is highly instrumental in its approach to supporters outside the trust movement too, positioning them in market relations: supporters display 'a degree of customer loyalty that is unprecedented in other lines of business'; 'football fans contribute to the "output" or "value"' generated by clubs over and above the money they spend on tickets; 'packed and atmospheric stadiums… make the matches more attractive to broadcasters and increases their value' (Hamil, 'The Third Annual State of the Game Survey of Governance at Professional Football Clubs', 25). Indeed, the relationship between supporters, clubs and the community is highly commodified in the language deployed by Supporters Direct. The following statement highlights this point to good effect:'Most supporters' trusts include among their objectives strengthening links between the club, supporters and the community, fundraising for the club, attaining a shareholding and promoting youth involvement, equal opportunities and anti-racism initiatives. All of these activities can help widen the revenue base of clubs and/or increase clubs share capital' (Hamil, 'The Third Annual State of the Game Survey of Governance at Professional Football Clubs', 36).

50. One Touch Football, 'The Self Disgust of the Modern Football Fan'.
51. Urban 75 Forums, 'Has There Ever Been a Co-Op Run League Club?'
52. One Touch Football, 'Black Balloons'; Big Football Forum, 'General Football Forum, Supporters Clubs/Trusts'.
53. Conn, 'The New Commercialism', 31.
54. Urban 75 Forums, 'Has There Ever Been a Co-Op Run League Club?'.
55. As noted in the FGRC report 'The State of the Game', 'significant' share ownership refers to anything over 1% of share capital in a listed PLC; anything over 5% of share capital in private limited companies or PLCs not listed. The figures published in the report for share ownership of trusts also includes shares not owned by the trust but are proxied to them for voting purposes. The number of clubs where trusts 'own' significant amounts of shares, then, could be inflated.
56. One Touch Football, 'Black Balloons'.
57. Big Football Forum, 'General Football Forum, Supporters Clubs/Trusts'.
58. FGRC, 'The State of the Game', 52–5.
59. One Touch Football, 'The Self Disgust of the Modern Football Fan'.
60. E-Tims, 'It's a Matter of Trust'.
61. Supporters Direct, 2004a, 16.
62. Peterborough Today, 'Your Comments'.
63. CIC, 'Community Interest Companies'.
64. Supporters Direct, 2005b, 6.
65. Supporters Direct, 2006, 2.
66. Polanyi, *The Great Transformation*.
67. A Supporters' Trust could, however, adopt a constitution where the voting rights that go with share ownership could be transferred by proxy to be used by the Trust board but whereby dividends accruing from shares owned would pass to the share owner.

References

Adamson, G., W. Jones, and A. Tapp. 'From CRM to FRM: Applying CRM in the football industry'. *Database Marketing & Customer Strategy Management* 13, no. 2 (2005): 156–72.

Arnaut, J.L. 'European Union Report: UK Presidency of the EC', *Independent European Sports Review*, 2006.

Beamish, R. 'Sport and the logic of capitalism'. In *Sport, Culture and the Modern State*, ed. RS Gruneau and H. Cantelon. Toronto: University of Toronto Press, 1982.

Big Football Forum. 'General Football Forum, Supporters Clubs/Trusts', 13 January. http://www.big-football-forum.co.uk/forum/

Bower, T. *Broken Dreams: Vanity, Greed and the Souring of British Football*. London: Pocket Books, 2003.

Brohm, J.M. *Sport: A Prison of Measured Time*. London: Inklinks, 1978.

Brown, A. 'A Task of Two Halves'. Democratic Socialist, 2002. www.democraticsocialist.org.uk

Brown, A. et al. 'Football and Communities: Final Report', Manchester, Football Foundation, 2006. http://www.footballfoundation.org.uk/news-and-media/publications/football-and-its-communities-final-report

Burnham, A. 'Regulation, Redistribution and Mutualisation: A Red-In-Tooth-and-Claw Cure For Football's Ills'. In *Trust in Football,* ed. Matt Jackson and Paul Maltby. London: The Institute for Public Policy Research, 13–9, 2003.

CIC. 'Community Interest Company Regulator'. http://www.cicregulator.gov.uk

Conn, D. 'The New Commercialism'. In A Game of Two Halves? The Business of Football', ed. Shaun Hamil, et al. London: Mainstream, 1999.

Conn, D. 'The New Commercialism', cited in 'The Changing Face of the Football Business', *Soccer and Society* 1, 3 (2000).

Conn, D. 'The Beautiful Game?: Searching the Soul of Football'. London: Yellow Jersey, 2005.

du Gay, P., and M. Pryke. *Culture and Economy: Cultural Analysis and Commercial Life*. London: Sage, 2002.

E-TIMS. 'It's a Matter of Trust'. E-TIMS. http://www.etims.net
FGRC (Football Governance Research Centre). 'The State of the Game: The Corporate Governance of Football Clubs'. Research Paper 3, Birkbeck University of London, 2005.
Football Economy. 'Football Club Financial Profiles and Article Archives'. www.footballeconomy.com
Football Task Force. 'Football: Commercial Issues. A Submission by the football task force to the minister of sport'. London: Football Task Force, 1999.
Fry. R. 'The Real Business of Football'. *Business Life*. http://www.babusinesslife.com/Tools/Features/Football-finance.html
Giulianotti, R. 'Sport Spectators, the Social Consequences of Commodification Critical Perspectives from Scottish Football'. *Journal of Sports and Social Issues* 29, no. 4 (2005): 386–410.
Gruneau, R.S., and H. Cantelon, eds. *Sport, Culture and the Modern State*. Toronto: University of Toronto Press, 1982.
Gruneau, R.S. *Class, Sport and Social Development*. Amherst: Massachusetts University Press, 1983.
Hamil, S. et al. ed. 'Recent Developments in Football Ownership', *Soccer and Society* 1, 3 (2000): 1–10.
Hamil, S. The Third Annual State of the Game Survey of Governance at Professional Football Clubs. London: Football Governance Research Centre, Birkbeck, University of London, 2003.
Holt, R. *Sport and the British: a Modern History*. Oxford: Clarendon Press, 1989.
IPS (Industrial Provident Societies). 'Registrar of Friendly Societies'. IPS. http://www.vikingsc.f9.co.uk/About_IPS.htm.
Jackson, M., and P. Maltby. *Trust in Football*. London: The Institute for Public Policy Research, 2003.
Jaquiss, K. 'Mutualism Rules: The Community in Football'. *Soccer and Society* 1, no. 3 (2000): 51–6.
Kennedy, D., and P. Kennedy P.. 'Preserving and Extending the Commodification of Football Supporter Relations: A Cultural Economy of Supporters Direct'. *Sociological Research Online* 12, 1. http://www.socresonline.org.uk/12/1/kennedy.html
Malcolm, D. 'Football Business and Football Communities in the Twenty-first century'. *Soccer and Society* 1, no. 3 (2000): 102–13.
Marx, K. *Capital, Volume 1: A Critique of Political Economy*. London: Lawrence and Wishart, 1954.
Marx, K., and F. Engels. *The Communist Manifesto*. London: Penguin Books, 1998.
Mason, T. *Association Football and English Society 1863–1915*. Brighton: Harvester Press, 1981.
Michie, J. *New Mutualism: A Golden Goal? Uniting Supporters and their Clubs*. London: Cooperative Party and Trafford Press, 1999.
Moor, L. 'Sport and Commodification: A Reflection on Key Concepts'. *Journal of Sport and Social Issues* 31, no. 2 (2007): 128–42.
McQuaig, L. *More than just Consumers*. Karl Polanyi Institute of Political Economy. http://artsandscience1.concordia.ca
One Touch Football Forum. 'Franchise: A Matter of Trust'. One Touch Football Forum. http://www.onetouchfootball.com
One Touch Football Forum. 'Black Balloons' http://www.onetouchfootball.com
One Touch Football Forum. 'The Self Disgust of the Modern Football Fan' http://www.onetouchfootball.com
Peterborough Today. 'Your Comments'. write in here - Peterborough Today. http://www.peterboroughtoday.co.uk
Posh Supporters Trust. http://www.theposhtrust.com/minutes/agm2006.htm
Polanyi, K. *The Great Transformation: The Political and Economic Origins of our Time*. Boston: Beacon, 1957.
Reid, G. 'Charitable Trusts: Municipal Leisure's "Third Way"?'. *Managing Leisure* 8 (2003): 171–83.
Supporters Direct. 'Newsletter', 2001. Supporters Direct. http://www.supporters-direct.org/englandwales/library.htm

Supporters Direct. 'Newsletter', 2004a. Supporters Direct. http://www.supporters-direct.org/englandwales/library.htm

Supporters Direct. 'Newsletter', 2004b. Supporters Direct. http://www.supporters-direct.org/englandwales/library.htm

Supporters Direct. 'Newsletter', 2005a. Supporters Direct. http://www.supporters-direct.org/englandwales/library.htm

Supporters Direct. 'Newsletter', 2005b. Supporters Direct. http://www.supporters-direct.org/englandwales/library.htm.

Supporters Direct. 'Newsletter', 2006. Supporters Direct. http://www.supporters-direct.org/englandwales/library.htm

Tapp, A., and J. Clowes. 'From "Carefree Casuals" to "Professional Wanderers": Segmentation Possibilities for Football Supporters'. *European Journal of Marketing* 36, no. 11–12 (2000): 1248–69.

Tapp, A. 'The Loyalty of Football Fans: We'll Support you Evermore?'. *Database Marketing & Customer Strategy Management* 11, no. 3 (2004): 203–15.

Taylor, I. 'Professional Sport and the Recession: The Case of British Soccer'. *International Review For the Sociology of Sport* 19, no. 19 (1984): 7–30.

Taylor, R. *Inquiry by Right Honourable Lord Justice, The Hillsborough Stadium Disaster: Final Report.* London: HMSO, 1990.

Tischler, S. *Footballers and Businessmen: The Origins of Professional Soccer in England.* New York: Holmes and Meier Publishers, 1981.

Urban 75 Forums. 'Has There Ever Been a Co-Op Run League Club?'. Urban 75 Forums. http://www.urban75.net

Wagg, S. 'Sack the Board, Sack the Board, Sack the Board'. In *Production and Consumption of Sport Cultures: Leisure, Culture and Commerce*, ed. U. Merkel, G. Lines, and I. McDonald. London: LSA Publication No 62, 1998.

Warde, A. 'Production, Consumption and 'Cultural Economy''. In *Culture, Economy: Cultural Analysis, Commercial Life*, ed. P. du Gay and M. Pryke. London: Sage, 2002.

Wheeler, R.F. 'Organized Sport, Organized Labour: The Workers' Sports Movements'. *Journal of Contemporary History* 13 (1978): 191–210.

Walking alone together the Liverpool Way: fan culture and 'clueless' Yanks

John Williams

University of Leicester, Leicester, UK

> Historically, supporters at Liverpool football club have shown relatively few signs of collective supporter radicalism. Indeed the belief among the club's followers that there is a highly specific and culturally embedded approach to managing the club's affairs, one which positively emphasises consensus and privacy – the Liverpool Way – actually has its roots in the ruthless, autocratic control practised by its directors in the 1950s. This relative supporter passivity slowly began to change, initially and culturally, after the appointment of Bill Shankly as Liverpool manager in 1959, and then more formally and more 'politically' following the Heysel Stadium disaster in 1985. More recently, under the auspices of two distinctive and very different locally based supporter campaigns *Share Liverpool* and *Spirit of Shankly*, Liverpool fans have displayed an unusual level of collective organisation and militancy to oppose and help unseat the dilatory and profiteering Anfield regime of two American venture capitalists, Tom Hicks and George Gillett. This article explores the tensions between the necessarily global nature today of this sort of popular opposition, the recent hyper-commodification of the Premier League and its clubs, and the emphasis among supporter groups in Liverpool on maintaining 'authentic' forms of local cultural practice and identity formation around football in the face of the sometimes grim realities of globalisation and foreign ownership.

The strange absence of supporter 'activism' in Liverpool football – a brief history

Liverpool is probably popularly known – perhaps especially among those from *outside* the city – for its various urban disturbances, often flavoured by sectarianism; for its non-conformist popular revolts; for vivid stories of army gunboats and anti-government riots; for striking workers and, in the 1980s, for confrontational, radical Militant local government; for periodic 'race' uprisings; and for its generally carnivalesque expressions of collective opposition to impositions of authority from outside the city. An orderly and pacified attitude in community and political affairs is probably not regarded as the typical Liverpool Way. So one might expect organized football *activism* among Liverpool football spectators also to be deeply etched into the consciousness and history of its people when, actually, the opposite is more true: conservatism and collective *inaction* among fans has been much more typical. This relative passivity of football fans in the city was perhaps especially true historically of supporters of Liverpool FC: followers of near neighbours Everton benefited from more democratic club structures and a rather more inclusive boardroom philosophy.[1]

Indeed, it was probably the very early mythologizing of the Spion Kop which, in some important senses, 'filled' this local identity void at Anfield by establishing a creatively collective and satisfyingly liminal supporter profile for Liverpool fans. Supporter songs and chants, for example, were a very early feature of Anfield fan cultures.[2] Liverpool supporters soon shaped this football terrace in the Red half of the city, in Ray Oldenburg's words, as an authentic and native 'third place':[3] one constructed out of 'the many little episodes of personal interaction between guests, mediated by dialogue as well as visual contact, by bar-room slogans as well as sophisticated conversation – they are symbolic and signifying forms and worlds of socialization.'[4] But it was especially the Kop's near-unique relationship with the Liverpool players, established first in the 1920s through its 'communing' with the Reds' long-serving Ulster-born goalkeeper Elisha Scott, which marked off the great terrace as a very special public site – as an authentic collective cultural space for public expression and exchange among working-class people and their symbolic representatives. It led in 1932 to the *Liverpool Echo* actually sending its football correspondent Bee to stand on the great terrace – an early glimpse 'inside' the world of British working class football supporter culture. A typical Kopite was described by Bee as 'loyal to the core [...] he goes on talking his matches, debating his matches'. 'This spectator', said Bee, 'is matchless'.[5]

This sort of unquestioning Liverpool fan loyalty would be severely tested many times. Indeed, in the 41 years between 1923 (the last Elisha Scott title) and 1964 (the first Bill Shankly championship) Liverpool FC won just one major trophy (a scrambled League title in 1947), to balance a humiliating relegation to the Second Division in 1954. The club's conservative (and Conservative) board repeatedly hired malleable young 'puppet' managers in the post-war era and refused to meet transfer fees, while the directors selected the team, often with catastrophic consequences. Moreover, the Liverpool board quite ruthlessly manipulated the club's Annual General Meetings in the 1950s in order to ensure minimal fan opposition to their own ineffective stewardship.[6] Liverpool supporters could rarely challenge their own directors – Everton's more widely spread shareholders would be more confrontational with theirs[7] – reverting instead to comforting Kopite tropes about loyalty and stoic support; which would be lavishly embellished, of course, under Bill Shankly in the new television age of sport in the 1960s.[8] Thus the celebrated modern notion of the 'Liverpool Way' – conducting club business efficiently, consensually and in a dignified manner, carefully and privately out of the glare of publicity (a trait so carelessly traduced later under Hicks and Gillett) – ironically comes directly out of a period when Liverpool supporters were relatively powerless, and certainly both passive and ineffective in opposing the club's autocratic custodians.

Some early stirrings

Just as the 1960s swept away some of England's aged conservatism and the deference and austerity of previous decades, Bill Shankly's arrival at Liverpool in 1959 challenged the club's own alarmed directors, charmed the game's emerging TV partners, finally loosened the Anfield purse strings, and mobilized the club's young followers both at home and, increasingly, in Europe in ways that would eventually transform the modern profile of Liverpool Football Club.[9] Shankly identified especially strongly with the growing, irreverent, youthful exuberance of the city and the native wit, passion and 'exceptionalism' of the club's supporters. He spoke especially about the unbreakable bond that existed between the Liverpool team and its followers on the Kop. In this sense Shankly endorsed the wider, idealist views of the Marxist sociologist Ian Taylor about English football at this time: that supporters and professional players shared a distinctive class membership and a common experience of democratic *participation*, in this case in the regeneration of the modern Liverpool FC.[10]

But in the 1970s the local focus for signs of *oppositional* football cultures at Liverpool moved elsewhere, as younger male fans began to relocate from the Kop to be closer to rival fans at the Anfield Road end of the stadium. At the same time, the city of Liverpool began to incrementally lose even its residual role as a 'complete seaport economy', becoming instead a 'decentred' city with no obvious unifying trading or manufacturing focus.[11] Neoliberal policies and the collapse of the Fordist regime of accumulation in the 1970s and 1980s exacerbated Liverpool's increasing disconnection from the networks which had previously maintained its position of global trading significance.[12] Simultaneously – and indeed partly for precisely these sorts of reasons – football hooligan rivalries in England intensified.

New synergies between music, football and street style offered young male supporters from Liverpool a form of distinction in an emerging working-class cultural elite, one reinforced by the symbolic economies growing up around the interconnected casual clothing contestations and the English terrace rivalries of the late 1970s and early 1980s.[13] Liverpool's European success in the 1970s and 1980 meant that its young fans dominated these domestic 'style wars': foreign sports gear and new hairstyles – liberated from Italy, German, France and Spain – circulated freely in the city from the late 1970s.[14] But what was also important here was the overtly *political* gesturing involved in some of these developments in the city. The fanzine *The End*, for example – an acute early music/football hybrid, edited by Peter Hooton (later of the band The Farm) – ruled ruthlessly in Liverpool, dictating the essence of Scouse terrace style while trashing hooligans from elsewhere, Kop 'out-of-towners' and Liverpool FC 'anoraks'.[15]

In the 1970s and 1980s Hooton was a key young member of a small, but influential, group of inventive street cultural intermediaries in the city – writers, musicians and others – who brilliantly articulated the strong links that had been established in Liverpool between local resistance to external constraints, working-class masculinist cultures, football and other creative forms, including art, music and literature.[16] Significantly, a number of these characters, including Hooton and Anny Road regular Nicky Allt, would resurface as important figures in the Spirit of Shankly protests against Hicks and Gillett almost 30 years later. Author and playwright Allt testified to the perceived 'rebelliousness' of foreign football tours following Liverpool FC in the seventies and eighties with the 'Anny Road boys', which, in his words, were about 'not wanting to be held down or held back by your social background; being absolutely determined not to let a lack of cash tie you to a job centre lifestyle that successive Tory governments were trying to impose on you'.[17]

The tragedy at the European Cup final in the Heysel Stadium in Brussels in 1985 – a result of UEFA bungling, inadequacy on the part of Belgian authorities and, especially, the atypical behaviour of some Liverpool followers, causing the deaths of 39, mainly Italian, supporters – was followed by a ban on English fans in Europe. Inevitably it stemmed these near-chaotic and highly pleasurable foreign excursions; Liverpool has never dominated European football in the same way since. But the accusations aimed at the city after Heysel also produced, by way of local response, not simply protests and *cultural* patterns of resistance, but instead – and for the first time – residual, formal organization of fans in the city to challenge the international governance of the sport. It came in the shape of the national Football Supporters Association (FSA) and was echoed in important respects later by fan mobilizations around the local 'justice' campaigns following the Hillsborough Stadium disaster in 1989. The key instigator of the FSA in the 1980s, its Liverpudlian chair Rogan Taylor, would also appear more than two decades later as the driving force behind the Share Liverpool supporter scheme aimed at an unlikely buyout of the club by Liverpool fans.

Interviewed recently, Taylor recalled the FSA in 1985 as emerging directly out of a deeply felt angst which informed a piece of writing he completed about Heysel for a broadsheet newspaper, not so much from a cogent and organic collective response in the city to the inadequacies of the game's governance. Heysel, in this sense, was experienced by Taylor as trauma: 'This feeling of unhappiness in the body [which] was like periods of adolescence that felt so sort of meaninglessly awful that you just wondered what you were doing – and what you could do.'[18] Here was a highly personal – and in some ways quite visceral – response to the extant frustrations which existed in the 1980s about the lack of an effective supporter voice in the sport. The burgeoning football fanzine movement carried forward the FSA message, but the FSA spawned no subsequent collective supporter structures or fan uprisings on Merseyside in the 1990s.

The transformation of English football

So what transformed Liverpool supporters' initial conservative acquiescence and their historically largely cultural articulations of collective fandom into the sort of organized collective protest and the complex and cogent forms of grassroots fan opposition to Hicks and Gillett which emerged in the city from late 2007? Clearly, a number of things are involved – not least the economic and governance transformations of the game in the 1990s, as English club football rapidly became a cultural product of considerable seductiveness, global significance and enormous commercial value.[19] This is by now a well known story, but it is worth rehearsing a number of points briefly here.

Historically, English football clubs had provided their owners and directors with forms of 'psychic income' in the shape of influence and local power. The early Football League was characterized by a philosophy of 'mutual protection' in which a fixed national maximum wage coupled with a penal retain-and-transfer system effectively shackled players to their clubs.[20] Even post the maximum players' wage, top English football clubs remained essentially small local businesses run on a largely hand-to-mouth basis. At the very height of its football powers in season 1978/79, for example, Liverpool FC, recently double European champions and also Football League champions, could boast only a £71,000 annual seasonal profit on a turnover of £2.4 million. Chairman John Smith described Liverpool's finances as 'absurd.' 'While we are very successful in football terms', Smith told anyone who would listen (though few cared), 'in economic terms we are broke'.[21] Liverpool also had little time for modernizing its administrative procedures under Smith and those who followed: the club was 'a collection of tattered rags hanging from a diamond tip' – holding data on season ticket holders, for example, in shabby cardboard boxes long after electronic storage was in vogue.[22] While Liverpool was a prime case, these archaic administrative and ownership arrangements for football clubs – and the failure to establish any obvious causal connection between commercial acumen off the field and success on it – actually characterized much of the first 100 years of professional football in England.[23]

However, as neoliberal economic and social policies began to dominate wider political agendas in the UK in the 1980s, so English football became immersed in a series of crises relating to fan behaviour and spectator provision[24], and the more traditional 'custodian' English football club director began to attract growing public and political criticism for lacking sufficient commercial dynamism and the sort of leadership the sport was now deemed to require.[25] A new breed of football entrepreneur began to push for a market-driven breakaway of the elite (more profitable) league clubs and the evasion of long-established FA limitations on income generation and potential profit-taking by directors. In 1983, after listing on the Stock Exchange, Tottenham Hotspur set up a parent company to evade the FA's rules on dividends for shareholders and payment for directors, thus critically weakening the game's historic governing body.[26]

Partly in order to try to regain some of this lost ground, ironically it was the FA itself which, in 1992, enthusiastically sanctioned the formation of the new, TV-driven FA Premier League. In doing so it catastrophically overstated its own regulatory powers and misguidedly detected potential synergies between the new corporate interests of club owners, the FA's own commercial ambitions, and the future of the England national team.[27] In fact, the new League would – predictably – be controlled and regulated by a networked governance structure made up of its 20 members, not by the FA.[28] Burgeoning income streams provided by new satellite television conglomerates, the judicious use of new technologies, much more efficient forms of consumer marketing, and the allied growth in the cult of celebrity in a new globalized marketplace[29] all helped to fuel the expansion of the Premier League and its elite clubs. Its star players became part of the increasingly valuable 'economy of the aesthetic', plundering growing transnational markets in the process. In short, the stage was set for the Premier League and a small number of its clubs and star players to become powerful global brands in seemingly 'borderless' markets. According to international sports marketing agency *Sportspro*, in 2009 Liverpool football club was the ninth most valuable single sports club brand in the world, worth an estimated £801 million.[30] Cue the arrival at Liverpool FC, at the beginning of 2007, of two hyper-ambitious American corporate investors, George Gillett and Tom Hicks.

Yanks in...

I have written elsewhere about the arrival of Hicks and Gillett at Liverpool and some of the reasons why, initially at least, these Americans were offered a relatively warm welcome by most Reds fans on Merseyside.[31] I do not want to rehearse that again here beyond saying that in some respects, the American heritage of the new buyers and their powerful rhetorics about 'heritage', 'community' and the 'family' were all seen locally as important signs of *continuity*, given the city's traditions and the local sense of its own trans-Atlantic exceptionalism.[32] Hicks and Gillett had also publicly 'guaranteed' that their purchase of Liverpool FC was no leveraged buyout, thus avoiding the conflictful, debt-laden fate suffered by hated rivals and north-west neighbours Manchester United following the club's sale to the Glazers.

But two other factors are more important here: firstly, the almost complete trust placed by Liverpool supporters in the club's administrators – chairman David Moores and chief executive Rick Parry – to manage the sale of the club to reliable and responsible new owners, men who understood the cultural significance of the 'Liverpool Way'. This trust derived, at least in part, from the uneasy synthesis between traditional Liverpool supporter conservatism and the later Shankly credo about the exceptional relationship that existed between Liverpool supporters and the club. Crucially here, both Parry and Moores were seen locally as old-style club custodians who were also well-known Liverpool *fans*. The latter represented a local family dynasty of long-term investors in the club and was widely regarded on Merseyside as someone whose strength lay more in his care for the team, the fans and its players than in sophisticated financial acumen or effective leadership of Liverpool FC. Moores sold Liverpool because the club now needed new owners with the kind of wealth required to invest in a possible £400 million stadium development, planning permission for which had already been agreed on nearby Stanley Park.[33]

Rick Parry had been the first chief executive of the Premier League, but he also had impeccable Merseyside area and LFC credentials and was reassuringly uneasy about the dangers of the new commercial forces in the game, often citing Manchester United as an example of the risks of over-commercialization.[34] Together, Moores and Parry had publicly agonized over the sale of the club for many months, apparently waiting for the ideal bidders – new owners who understood the core principles of the club – to come along. They had rejected local suitors and more substantial bids from both Thailand and the Middle East in the process. Later, of course, this delay – and, especially, Parry's domination of the process and his clumsy attempts to protect 'Liverpool values' – would be read locally more as bungling indecision than good judgment. Worse, it was seen as compounding Liverpool's existing long-term competitive disadvantage, as the club had stagnated commercially while recovering from the human aftermath of the two terrible stadium disasters – at Heysel and Hillsborough – that had engulfed it. Thus, what had previously been regarded as the core Liverpool strengths – its tight-knit administration and relative eschewing of commercialism – had come to be regarded as a glaring weakness, as Spirit of Shankly's Graham Smith confirms:

> There was a sense in which the Liverpool Way was a 'corner shop' mentality. What happened [on the commercial side in the Premier League] was like a tsunami, it took them clubs away and we couldn't keep up. The received wisdom – and he would admit it himself – was that [Rick] Parry was a control freak who had to be in charge of everything. Because of that he was spread too thin.[35]

The second factor in the sale of Liverpool, and the one that *really* mattered to most supporters at the time, was simply the recognition that in an age of open borders and global sporting capital flows, non-local financing – and probably the additional commodification that went with it – was now necessary for the club to be competitive again. With major foreign capital apparently finally on offer, financial realism rapidly overcame any residual local idealism. As Jay McKenna, secretary of Spirit of Shankly, recalled later, by this stage most supporters in the city were simply desperate for new investment, thus ruling out any more than a cursory examination of the credentials of these American gift horses – men who had, after all, been vetted and endorsed by trusted club custodians, Parry and Moores:

> When the Americans came in we thought it was alright, if we were honest. Let's not rewrite history here[,] we can't be revisionist about it. We welcomed them with open arms, because Man United and Chelsea had their slice of the pie and we wanted ours. They came in with all the promises and we'd fallen so far behind Man United and Chelsea, and even Arsenal to an extent, that we wanted our share. [...] It was a combination of supporters wanting the best and Parry, and Moores the chairman, telling us that they couldn't do it no more. We, as loyal Liverpool fans, didn't want to be left behind.[36]

Hicks and Gillett had worked together in business (but not in sport) in the USA and each had separate experience of owning NHL and baseball franchises in the United States, so they certainly had a relevant track record of sorts. But the two men knew nothing about English soccer and had rejoined forces to buy Liverpool only when Gillett called on Hicks to invest in 50% of the shares on 2 February 2007, some five days before completing the purchase.[37] It seemed, at best, like a shotgun wedding. The figures bandied around at the time in the press estimated the American investment at £400 million, including money allocated towards a new stadium, but more realistically the new owners probably paid around £185 million for the Liverpool shares. They borrowed some £350 million from the Royal Bank of Scotland and Wachovia to cover the purchase, the current Liverpool debt (then estimated at around £80 million) and further investments in the club, securing £105 million against the club and some £245 million against the parent company Kop Holdings – whose only asset was Liverpool Football Club. These details remained carefully under wraps as the new owners made a different case in public, though Hicks in particular was well versed in the use of leveraged buyouts to buy new businesses – borrowing capital, laying the debts on the acquisition and using profits from the company purchased to service interest payments. He had previously purchased soft drinks and cereal companies using this investment technique.[38] Liverpool Football Club at last had their long-awaited new saviours, but they were not what they seemed.

Supporters out...

Crucially for Parry and Moores, and for Liverpool supporters, Hicks and Gillett had also promised 'a spade in the ground within 60 days' to get the much anticipated and much delayed new Liverpool stadium underway. But then the new owners decided they wanted a completely revamped and improved design to the one painstakingly prepared for the club, thus delaying the start of construction – eventually indefinitely. On the field, under the 'stewardship' of the Americans and Spanish club manager Rafa Benitez, Liverpool – perhaps surprisingly – reached the final of the Champions League in May 2007, losing narrowly to AC Milan. But even here there was supporter unrest; Liverpool fans angrily protested in the city over their limited ticket allocation for the final, suggesting a combination of UEFA, Liverpool shareholder and corporate malpractice.[39]

A more general sense of Liverpool supporter unease began to take concrete form in the summer of 2007, when stories began to emerge about disagreements between their distant US owners – were these two men partners or rivals? – and complaints from Benitez that funds were not forthcoming for transfers (although Fernando Torres was purchased for £20 million in July). Later that year it became clear that the Americans and Rick Parry had held secret meetings in the USA about replacing the Liverpool manager, thus revealing an alarming insouciance about and lack of understanding of local sensibilities on the part of the largely absent American owners. Benitez enjoyed considerable popular acclaim in Liverpool, where the cult of the club manager, post-Bill Shankly, is arguably more profoundly rooted than anywhere else in Britain.

When it finally became clear in January 2008 that, despite all previous promises, the purchase of Liverpool had indeed been a Glazer-style leveraged buyout, one which would require paying interest on loans from club profits, a local storm broke. A supporters' meeting was called for 31 January 2008 at The Sandon pub in Anfield – the site of the club's founding back in 1892. Present were some of those key Liverpool supporters drawn from the terrace tear-ups and cultural expressions and 'resistances' of the 1970s and 1980s. These were supplemented by younger recruits, including the key figure of 21-year-old Jay McKenna, a local civil servant and union rep, and the whole project drew impetus from the loose organizational structures established for Hillsborough 'Justice' campaigning in Liverpool over the previous decade.

The language and terms used at this initial, 300-strong meeting are significant. The group initially decided on *Sons of Shankly* for a title – soon changed to *Spirit of Shankly* (SoS), presumably to deal with accusations of masculinist exclusion – but the emphasis from the start was that this would be an organic, proudly local Supporters' *Union*, not a corporatized and bureaucratic Supporters' Trust. It was aimed at being assiduously non-hierarchical and democratic and was, in some ways, a highly politically attuned and certainly a profoundly local 'Scouse' and 'classed' social movement. It was agreed that SoS would have popular protest and supporter rights at its heart, as SoS community/youth officer Paul Gardner later remembered:

> It was important it was a grassroots initiative – not having a go at people who are Trusts and so on - but things like Supporter Trusts make it sound too official. It sounds a bit more higher level. It's not that there is anything wrong with that, but it's not something from the supporters on the ground.[40]

Early meetings of SoS were certainly heavily masculinist; they were dominated by men and hosted in Olympia, an austere and gloomy boxing venue on West Derby Road about a mile from the stadium. In part this approach was almost certainly a conscious response to the planned launch by Rogan Taylor of the Share Liverpool website on the same day, 31 January 2008. The latter – an internet-driven cooperative, initially aimed at raising an unlikely £5,000 from each of 100,000 Liverpool supporters worldwide to buy-out the American owners for £500 million - was perceived by SoS, rather unfairly, to be detached and elitist, too dependent on 'big money' and on input from outside the city, and also personality-driven: 'If you ask anyone about Share Liverpool they will say Rogan – they don't know anybody else.'[41] Instead, Spirit of Shankly aimed at recruiting a mass Liverpool membership (eventually agreeing on a joining fee of £10) and carefully meshed traditional forms of 'hot' street mobilizations – supporter demonstrations, protests and marches, 'the physical things' – with new, 'cooler' and more measured 'repertoires of action' for the digital age.[42]

SoS also drew on some of the supposed radical working-class traditions, general cultural practices and dominant local 'structures of feeling' in the city[43] – 'What Liverpool people are like' – characteristics which, as we have seen, had actually been largely absent from much of the early supporter history of the club. This opting for the use of new media techniques, combined with forms of mass supporter action which drew directly on highly oppositional *local* traditions, was regarded by those involved as an inescapable outcome of the first Sandon gathering:

> It was how people were feeling at the time. When we had that first meeting Nicky Allt stood up and said that it was strange that for a politically motivated city, for a city that's often been very radical, the football supporters have never had a union. We have never had a collective body of supporters... In terms of the protests against Hicks and Gillett we had to do physical things that were very 'old', but there were also modern functions to it: Internet forums; the use of social media; Facebook and Twitter. We recognised we had to do a lot more modern things. People were sending emails to RBS, we bombarded the Premier League. It's just based on what Liverpool people are like.[44]

Bill Shankly's famous dictum about football and politics – 'The socialism I believe in is everyone working together, everyone having a share of the rewards' – accordingly adorned the SoS homepage, thus simultaneously raising and defusing concerns about the Merseyside-specific *political* underpinnings of the new body. It was Shankly who had pronounced Liverpool supporters the club's greatest asset, and in March 2008 his granddaughter Karen Gill publicly commended SoS's campaign and its attack on the 'corporate gluttony' allegedly dogging the sport.[45] Nevertheless, using a discourse of socialism – even one cloaked in a reverential local football frame – was both daring and risky. Even in the grim aftermath of the failures of Blairite politics it was deeply unfashionable in Britain to proselytize about 'socialist' action and principles – at least outside the city of Liverpool. SoS committee members were well aware of the term's historic echoes and its potential divisiveness, perhaps especially on Merseyside:

> But not everyone agreed with the language we were using; socialism and the union, for example. It is socialism with a small 's'. A lot of people get frightened by the word 'socialism' and all its connotations. They look back to Liverpool in the 1980s and there is almost a feeling of 'Oh, here we go again.' Recently we [SoS] put on a bus to the TUC and there were a few comments from the membership, one in particular who said that 'You are all about socialism.' But if you actually look at what our aims and objectives are, about community and regeneration, it's a completely linked issue.[46]

Added to this, the initial forceful emphasis on the importance of the Scouse roots of SoS clearly recalled earlier supporter debates and informal campaigns around Anfield – on the Kop, in fanzines and on websites – on keeping alive more 'traditional' forms of fandom by addressing concerns about integrity, localism and supporter 'authenticity'. These included the Keep Flags Scouse (KFS) initiative from 2001 and the more recent Reclaim the Kop (RTK) campaign from January 2007.

The latter was aimed at tutoring the club's followers on rooting out 'plastic' Reds fans (often out-of-towners or day trippers who consumed excessively from the club shop and wore it products); accentuating the specifics of locally acceptable Liverpool styles of support (original songs, no crass goading of opponents); and stressing that supporters properly honour the *city* of Liverpool and its people, and especially those fans who had died at Hillsborough.[47]

In this important sense, then, *coming from* Liverpool was deemed by those involved in setting up SoS – predominantly upwardly mobile male Scousers; men with authentic Liverpool accents and origins mainly in working class or lower-middle class backgrounds – to be the surest way of ensuring the new organization was organically rooted in the body politic of the city, its working people and the club. But it was also perceived as a way of responding to the unique selling proposition Liverpool FC offered its many non-local followers – cultural assimilation into the club's prized and acutely Scouse textures, cultures and traditions. As Graham Smith of SoS put it:

> Having a Scouse core to it [SoS] was crucial because those thousands of Liverpool supporters from outside Merseyside who bought into it did so because they bought into the culture of the club – which of course is basically a Liverpool culture... They may not always buy into the 'Keep Flags Scouse' thing, but they are buying into the Istanbul spirit or the Hillsborough situation, into that pool of Liverpool references. If you buy into that or one element of another than fine, you're in.[48]

This rather reductionist view also helped produce a basic structural philosophy for the founding of SoS – led and driven in policy terms by local, 'authentic' Scousers, but supplemented and legitimized by a global Reds backing. This frame also later underpinned the eventual federalized spread of SoS branches outside Liverpool, coupled with the use of video technology and the internet to offer its global members access to proceedings and votes on SoS agendas for action.

Finally, all this also meant that for all the socialist rhetoric and the early SoS militant chutzpah – its first posting on 6 February 2008 issued 'A Call to Arms' – SoS recognized from the outset that political idealism must, in the end, necessarily be tempered by hard-headed realism in the new corporate age of transnational sport. This view also informed SoS's scepticism about the global reach of Share Liverpool and its 'dream' of fan ownership. 'Supporters wanting it all perfect' were now engaged in simple nostalgia, no longer fit (if it ever was) as a viable option for large, successful late-modern football businesses. Fully embracing this position meant, first, confounding the expectations of the American owners concerning the credibility of the men leading SoS – people who had allegedly been labelled by one Liverpool official after a fractious meeting as 'sons of strikers'[49] – and second, responding effectively to the existing crisis, not to one imagined by SoS or its members. 'I don't think they expected us to organize or know what they were facing when SoS met Gillett in September 2008', recalled Paul Gardner of the first fans meeting with the Americans. 'Basically, they wanted us to introduce ourselves, and it was: 'Chief executive', 'playwright', 'chief executive.' I think Gillett was expecting to meet a plumber, an electrician...'[50]

These well-educated, reflexive 'post fans'[51] were charged locally with devising effective strategies to 'wear down' the new owners, but also with making appropriate connections between previously opaque financial matters such as leveraged investments and developments on the pitch. The primary longer term focus was ensuring owner accountability, but also prioritizing economic sustainability for the club: that is, protecting its long-term financing over chaotic, short-term expediency and profiteering. But, as Jay McKenna explained, SoS were focused on having an active say in shaping the new 'glocalized'[52] economics of network football and in managing their consequences for local people, rather than harbouring vague ambitions – as Share Liverpool seemed to – about fashioning an alternative to its corporate structures, ownership elites and global reach. In this sense, even for SoS's more confrontational actors, football had 'moved on' even from Bill Shankly's day:

> [When] we looked at what our principles should be[,] our objectives and aims… that's where Shankly came in, with his quote about socialism. It's about everybody working together. It's not *about* socialism; it's not that they [the club's owners] can't be rich and they can't make money. It's about whatever decisions *they* make, we have all got to be pulling in the same direction. It can't be the club at all costs, making as much money as possible, leaving the supporters behind. And it can't be supporters wanting it all perfect – we are *never* going to get it perfect. Football doesn't work like that now; it has changed and moved on. But supporters shouldn't be left behind. The chase for consumerism, new markets and bigger stadiums sometimes leaves the core supporters behind.[53]

The rocky road to the Fenway Sports Group

The forms of opposition mobilized by SoS against the new Liverpool owners in the months which followed its formation reveal not only the strength of its collective supporter mobilization, but also its impressive cultural creativity and considerable media-awareness. They included mass meetings of Liverpool supporters in a variety of local venues, mainly sports clubs and bars; meetings between SoS representatives and club officials, including initially with Hicks and Gillett; the setting up of SoS branches outside the city; calls for a boycott of club merchandise; a symbolic SoS 'dig' at the proposed new stadium site; a staged supporter 'repossession' of the Anfield stadium aimed at local media sources; anti-Hicks and Gillett posters, leafleting and beer mat campaigns around the Anfield area; extensive use of new media, including blogs, podcasts and social network sites; organized mass letter-writing, telephone and email messaging to disrupt the business of RBS, Hicks and Gillett's main financers, and, via *Kop Faithful*, to urge other financiers to shun the Americans;[54] public rallies and supporter celebrations and regular protests and marches, often before Liverpool home fixtures – up to 4000 were involved before the match against Manchester United on 13 September 2008. But the ownership crisis was also used by SoS as a rationale for addressing a range of basic 'consumer' issues facing local Liverpool supporters – among them ticketing matters, local community sports provision, and the costs of official travel to away matches. SoS coaches were laid on for fixtures, club officials were interviewed for the SoS website, and in the summer of 2009 free SoS summer coaching camps were launched in Crosby, to the north of the city – implicitly offering a critique of the club's inadequate investment in regeneration and local community projects, especially in the more disadvantaged white working-class neighbourhoods of north Merseyside.

In June 2009, figures released by Liverpool showed that due to the club's debt-laden status it had made an unprecedented loss of £42.4 million on a turnover of £164.2 million in season 2007/08, even though Hicks and Gillett had also invested money in the club.[55] As Rogan Taylor memorably put it later, it was now clear that '[a] stranger had come into the Liverpool house and was rifling through its drawers.'[56] As the ownership crisis deepened, in July 2009 SoS signalled the resolution of some of its core philosophical and practical differences with Share Liverpool by agreeing to support a revised supporter ownership proposal, part of which was aimed at attracting up to 25,000 fan shareholders each paying a lower price of £500 for a single vote-bearing share (delivering £11 million in equity). Share Liverpool had not raised any income from its backers at this point but it claimed to have nearly 10,000 registered members globally, over 6000 of whom had said they were willing to subscribe £5000 under the original share scheme. Share Liverpool also had ambitious plans, in a hostile economic climate, to raise a further £200 million from banks and commercial investors. SoS was reported to have 2500 members at this time, with 'very little overlapping between the two groups.'[57] Discussions continued about a possible merger of the two bodies, and in December 2009 SoS was nominated for the European Football Supporters Award for its work with supporters and in Merseyside communities.[58] But on 4 June 2010 SoS announced that no agreement could be reached on a merger; instead it set up a Credit Union so that 'ordinary' people could save toward their share, and/or as a means – for local people at least – of purchasing a Liverpool season ticket on credit.[59]

The two supporters' bodies continued to exist separately, but now they exchanged committee members and had a shared long-term goal of developing supporter equity and representation inside the club. However, when representatives of SoS met in the summer of 2010 with Barclays Capital, who had been engaged by RSB to help find a new buyer for the club, the familiar stumbling block of providing evidence of adequate finance raised from supporters remained: 'They were saying we are not letting you into the process unless you can show you've got the money and we were saying, well, unless you announce you are letting us into the process we can't raise the money.'[60] This seemed like a potentially insurmountable barrier to new forms of supporter investment at Liverpool.

By March 2010 Hicks and Gillett, still hounded by fan protests and in financial meltdown in a gloomy global economic climate, were desperately trying to raise £100 million to reduce the £237 million debt they still owed RBS, now a majority publicly owned bank. A firm of US fund managers, the Rhone Group, offered a reported £110 million for a 40% share of equity in the club, but this valued Liverpool some way below Hicks and Gillett's reported figure of some £500 million.[61] In April 2010 RBS insisted that in order to extend the loan by a further six months from the June repayment deadline, an independent chair – Martin Broughton, chairman of British Airways – should be appointed under the auspices of Barclays Capital to manage the sale of the club for any 'reasonable' offer.[62] Crucially, Broughton and two other independent Liverpool directors, Christian Purslow and Ian Ayre, were allocated powers under this new arrangement to outvote the other two existing directors on the Liverpool club board – the American owners Hicks and Gillett.

With the threat of Liverpool slipping into administration, and the humiliation of the subsequent docking of league points that this would entail, this unusual settlement paved the way in October 2010 for Broughton and his directors to agree to sell Liverpool, against the wishes of Hicks and Gillett, to the Boston-based group New England Sports Ventures (NESV, later Fenway Sports Group, or FSG) for £300 million. The sale survived a dramatic High Court hearing and claims from the owners that it constituted an 'epic swindle': Broughton himself judged that Hicks and Gillett had lost around £144 million on their investment in the club.[63] However, estimates drawn from guidelines provided by analysts Deloitte suggested that by applying the same formula that Hicks and Gillett had initially used in valuing the club when conducting their own takeover, Liverpool Football Club was actually worth some £295 million in 2010.[64] Epic swindle it was not.

SoS and Share Liverpool together celebrated the sale of the club, stressing it had never been the *nationality* of the past owners which had been problematic, simply their financial mismanagement, devious lies and broken promises. John W Henry of NESV spoke immediately with Liverpool fan representatives to show that he had clear plans for the future of the club and to confirm that theirs was no leveraged buyout. NESV had recently revived the Boston Red Sox baseball franchise, a sports body which seemed in the USA to have some of the locally venerated characteristics of Liverpool FC.[65] Liverpool's debts were finally lifted, though the *Guardian*'s headline of 7 October 2011, 'Exit Americans. Enter Americans', summed up how much – and how little – had changed.

Some conclusions

So what role did the Liverpool fan protests play in the fall of Hicks and Gillett in October 2010, and what sort of future did Liverpool and its supporters now face? It must be said that despite concerted supporter opposition, the Americans had seemed determined to hold onto their Liverpool investment, but by early 2010 their financial problems had simply become intolerable. They were offloading businesses in the USA and could no longer afford to manage their debts in the UK. In this sense it was the global economic crisis which began in 2008 that eventually did for the Anfield ambitions of Hicks and Gillett, rather than local supporter opposition.

However, it was also clear that the Americans *were* deeply unsettled by the relentless popular hostility expressed toward their presence at Liverpool, and perhaps particularly the capacity and determination of SoS to respond through new media to virtually every public utterance made by Hicks and Gillett about the club and their role in its governance between 2008 and 2010. Crucially, these interventions were organized by media-savvy Liverpool supporters, some of whom were performers, musicians, film-makers or writers – cultural actors who were well experienced in the use of viral campaigns operating mainly from the backrooms of pubs and houses in the city. These SoS sympathizers and members had the necessary contacts, technological capital, developing knowledge about global football finance and, perhaps above all, the sheer passion and determination required to manage the manipulation of the key media narratives concerning the Liverpool crisis. They did this palpably more effectively than their multi-millionaire American nemeses and their PR advisors. None of Hicks and Gillett's US business or sporting ventures had ever attracted quite this sort of media vortex. When a clearly shaken Gillett was tracked down by SoS members to the Crowne Plaza Hotel in Liverpool on 1 February 2009 and was asked why he had gone into partnership with Hicks to buy Liverpool, he muttered that the pair 'had worked together well for six years on other businesses' but that 'this [the Liverpool investment] is different because the media are involved.'[66] He was right.

The Americans had little strategic direction or support for their own media outpourings, which often lacked guile and coherence and which were instantly paraded on websites and deconstructed by SoS. 'They'd rush into saying something in responding [to us] and caused themselves more problems', recalled a scathing Jay

McKenna. 'For us [at SoS] it was good, but if you look at it objectively you'd say: Do you know what you're doing? How are *you* a billionaire? How can Tom Hicks be friends with one of the most powerful men in the world, George W. Bush? Because you really just don't get it, do you: you are clueless.' Ironically, given their initial successes, the closer Liverpool supporters got to their opponents the more these global capitalists seemed like men with feet of clay, at least in terms of media management.

The future for Share Liverpool, SoS and fan investment in Liverpool FC seems far from clear-cut today. Operating on a war footing when the very future of the club is at stake is rather different to remaining active and relevant for the new football peace under more benign owners. How to keep supporters focused on the dangers which may yet still lie ahead? The abiding image of SoS raises spectres of discontent which most Liverpool fans now want to put behind them: 'It's hard for [Liverpool] people to think about SoS now because every time our name is mentioned it's: "Here we go again, are we gonna have another march?"'[67] For all their promising early talk, the new US owners FSG have chosen a limited route for increasing supporter involvement at Liverpool, inviting a range of fans to join a new Anfield supporters committee. The initiative has merit, but it is also risks being seen locally as a mechanism for managing consumer dissent more than one for advancing real supporter representation.

The 'Liverpool Way' – the unblinking and unreflexive supporter loyalty shown historically towards the club's administrators and managers – has arguably been one of the more prominent casualties of recent events. A poorly performing Liverpool manager, Roy Hodgson, was a victim of the new assertiveness (and impatience) of Liverpool supporters, being unprecedentedly booed by the Kop and eventually sacked by the FSG board in January 2011.[68] As a Parliamentary Commission examines the economics and inert governance of the English game, so SoS and Share Liverpool enviously eye the licensing system, restraints on foreign owners, sustainable economics, cheap ticket prices and fan representation which characterize the structures of German football today.[69] Unsurprisingly, perhaps, there seems little appetite among elite Premier League club owners for this sporting model of commercial restraint. The relative lack of European success for club sides in Germany – with no Champions League winners since 2001 – may also make it difficult to sell the concept to some English club supporters. Meanwhile, the Liverpool fan bodies are cautiously supporting the new Anfield fans' initiative. Share Liverpool hopes its model might still find favour with FSG – perhaps for a 10% fan stake – but SoS fears the owners are already gearing up to marginalize the very local people who played a part in paving the way for their successful takeover of the club.

> Slowly but surely the club are chipping away at what is their product. It is what makes people come from all over the world to here; the unique nature of the Liverpool experience [...] These new fellahs [FSG], when they came in, all the talk was about 'engagement'. At the moment the jury is out because they have certainly sidelined us. And the 'engagement' they are offering is very much at arm's length.[70]

Thus, this strange Merseyside case of 'Yanks out' and 'New Yanks in' has no guaranteed happy ending for Liverpool football supporters, and many of the tensions which emerged in the city between grassroots (local) supporter action and (global) fan ownership between 2008 and 2010 remain unresolved. The 44 months under

Hicks and Gillett provided dire warnings but no obvious solutions to the ownership and governance questions which continue to plague marketized English football in the age of globalization.

Notes
1. Williams, *Red Men*.
2. Williams, *Red Men*, 105–6.
3. Oldenburg, 'The Great Good Place'.
4. Jacke, 'Locating Intermediality', 332.
5. Williams, *Red Men*, 202.
6. Williams, *Red Men*.
7. Kennedy, Class, Ethnicity and Civic Governance
8. See Williams, *Red Men*.
9. Ward, 'Bill Shankly and Liverpool'.
10. Taylor, 'Soccer Consciousness and Soccer Hooliganism', 142.
11. Munck, 'Introduction: The City, Globalisation and Social Transformation', 5.
12. Cohen, *Decline, Renewal and the City in Popular Music Culture*, 43.
13. Williams, 'Having an Away Day'.
14. Hewitson *The Liverpool Boys are in Town*.
15. See Williams, 'Kopites, Scallies and Liverpool Fan Cultures', 108.
16. Allt, *The Boys From the Mersey*.
17. Allt, *The Boys from the Mersey*, 83.
18. Interview with the author, 11 April 2011.
19. Williams, 'Protect Me from what I Want'.
20. Taylor, *The Leaguers*.
21. Kennedy and Williams, *Kennedy's Way*, 120.
22. Interview with Rogan Taylor of Share Liverpool, 11 April 2011.
23. Tomlinson, 'North and South'.
24. Taylor, 'English Football in the 1990s'.
25. King, *The End of the Terraces*.
26. Williams and Hopkins, 'Over Here'.
27. Ward and Williams, *Football Nation* 289–97.
28. Millward, *The Global Football League*, 20.
29. Rojek, *Celebrity*.
30. Millward, *The Global Football League*, 28.
31. Williams and Hopkins, 'Over Here'.
32. Lane, *Liverpool City of the Sea*.
33. Williams and Hopkins, 'Over Here', 169.
34. Williams, *Into the Red*, 153.
35. Interview with the author, 23 April 2011.
36. Interview with the author 23 April 2011.
37. Millward, *The Global Football League*, 92.
38. Donegan, 'Loan Ranger Hicks Kops the blame', 5.
39. Williams and Llopis, *Rafa*.
40. Interview with author, 23 April 2011.
41. Interview with Graham Smith, 23 April 2011.
42. Millward, *The Global Football League*.
43. Williams, *The Long Revolution*, 132.
44. Interview with Jay McKenna, 23 April 2011.
45. Spirit of Shankly, 'Statement from Bill Shankly's daughter Karen Gill'.
46. Interview with Graham Smith, SoS, 23 April 2011.
47. Millward, *The Global Football League*, 56–8.
48. Interview with the author, 23 April 2011.
49. Interview with Jay McKenna, 23 April 2011.
50. Interview with Paul Gardner 23 April 2011.
51. Giulianotti, *Football*, 148.

52. Giulianotti and Robertson, 'The Globalisation of Football'.
53. Interview with author, 23 April 2011.
54. Millward, *The Global Football League*, 105.
55. Conn, 'Liverpool's American Dream looks a Dead End', S6.
56. Interview with author, 11 April 2011.
57. Spirit of Shankly, 'Share Liverpool Proposal Supported by SoS'.
58. Spirit of Shankly, 'Spirit of Shankly up for European Football Supporters Award'.
59. Spirit of Shankly, 'Supporter Ownership Announcement'.
60. Interview with Graham Smith, 23 April 2011.
61. Barrett, 'Rhone Group makes Official Anfield Offer', S2.
62. Kelso, 'Americans Prepare to Cut their Losses' S9.
63. Conn, 'Broughton saves Bombast for Last as Quiet Man Wins Out'.
64. Smith and White, 'Hicks and Gillett Ready to Sell Liverpool', S7.
65. Shaugnessy, 'Sold Towne Team', 32.
66. Spirit of Shankly, 'SoS Meeting and Action'.
67. Interview with Graham Smith, 23 April 2011.
68. *The Telegraph*, 'Liverpool Fans Instrumental in Roy Hodgson's Sacking'.
69. BBC Sport, 'German Model Highlights Man United Dilemma'.
70. Interview with Graham Smith of SoS, April 2011.

References

Allt, N. *The Boys From the Mersey: the Story of the Annie Road Crew Football's First Clobbered-up Mob*. Chatham: Milo Books, 2004.

Barrett, T. 'Rhone Group makes Official Anfield Offer'. *The Times*, March 15, 2010, S2.

BBC Sport. 'German Model highlights Man United Dilemma'. BBC Sport. http://news.bbc.co.uk/sport1/hi/football/europe/8589872.stm

Cohen, S. *Decline, Renewal and the City in Popular Music*. Aldershot: Ashgate, 2007.

Conn, D. 'Broughton Saves Bombast for Last as Quiet Man Wins Out' *The Guardian*, October 14, 2010, S2.

Conn, D. 'Liverpool's American Dream Looks a Dead End'. *The Guardian Sport*, June 2, 2009, S6.

Donegan, L. 'Loan Ranger Hicks Kops the Blame'. *Observer Sport*, June 7, 2009, S5.

Giulianotti, R. *Football: A Sociology of the Global Game*. Cambridge: Polity, 1999.

Giulianotti, R., and R. Robertson. 'The Globalization of Football: A study in the 'Glocalization' of Serious Life'. *The British Journal of Sociology* 55, no. 3 (2004): 545–68.

Hewitson, D. *The Liverpool Boys Are in Town: the Birth of Terrace Culture*. Liverpool: The Bluecoat Press, 2008.

Jacke, C. 'Locating Intermediality: Socialization by Communication and Consumption in the Popular-cultural Third Places of the Music Club and Football Stadium'. *Culture Unbound* 1 (2009): 331–48.

Kelso, P. 'Americans Prepare to Cut their Losses'. *The Daily Telegraph*, April 14, 2010, S9.

Kennedy, A., and J. Williams. *Kennedy's Way: Inside Bob Paisley's Liverpool*. Edinburgh: Mainstream Press, 2004.

Kennedy, D. 'Class, Ethnicity and Civic Governance. A Social Profile of Football Club Directors on Merseyside in the Late-nineteenth Century'. *The International Journal of the History of Sport* 22, no. 5 (2006): 840–66.

King, A. *The End of the Terraces: The Transformation of English Football in the 1990s*. London: Leicester University Press, 1998.

Lane, T. *Liverpool City of the Sea*. Liverpool: Liverpool University Press, 1997.

Millward, P. *The Global Football League: Transnational Networks, Social Movements and Sport in the New Media Age*. Basingstoke: Palgrave, 2011.

Munck, R. 'Introduction: The City, Globalisation and Social Transformation'. In *Reinventing the City: Liverpool in Comparative Perspective*, ed. R. Munck, 1–22. Liverpool: Liverpool University Press, 2003.

Oldenburg, R. *The Great Good Place*. New York: De Capo Press, 1999.

Rojek, C. *Celebrity*. London: Reaktion, 2001.

Shaughnessy, D. 'Sold Towne Team: Harrington had Great Chance to Hit Home Run for Sox Fans, but he Whiffs he Blew a Great Chance'. *Boston Globe*, December 21, 2001.

Smith, R., and D. White. 'Hicks and Gillett Ready to Sell Liverpool'. *The Sunday Telegraph*, April 11, 2010, S7.

Spirit of Shankly. 'Supporter ownership announcement'. Spirit of Shankly. http://www.spiritofshankly.com/news/Supporter-Ownership-Announcement.html.

Spirit of Shankly. 'Spirit of Shankly up for European Football Supporters Award'. Spirit of Shankly. http://www.spiritofshankly.com/news/SOS-up-for-European-Football-Supporters-Award.html

Spirit of Shankly. 'Share Liverpool proposal supported by SoS'. Spirit of Shankly. http://www.spiritofshankly.com/news/ShareLiverpool-Proposal-_-Supported-by-SOS.html.

Spirit of Shankly. 'SOS meeting and action – Sunday 1st February 2009'. Spirit of Shankly. http://www.spiritofshankly.com/news/SOS-Meeting-and-Action-_-Sunday-1st-February-2009.html

Spirit of Shankly. 'Statement from Karen Gill, Bill Shankly's grand-daughter'. Spirit of Shankly. http://www.spiritofshankly.com/karen-gill.html

Taylor, I. 'English Football in the 1990s: Taking Hillsborough Seriously?' In *British Football Social Change: Getting into Europe*, ed. J. Williams and S. Wagg, 3–24. Leicester, London and New York: Leicester University Press, 1991.

Taylor, I. 'Soccer Consciousness and Soccer Hooliganism'. In *Images of Deviance*, ed. S. Cohen, 134–63. Harmondsworth: Penguin, 1971.

Taylor, M. *The Leaguers: The Making of Professional Football in England*. Liverpool: Liverpool University Press, 2005.

The Telegraph. 'Liverpool Fans Instrumental in Roy Hodgson's Sacking, says Phil Thompson'. *The Telegraph*. http://www.telegraph.co.uk/sport/football/teams/liverpool/8247821/Liverpool-fans-instrumental-in-Roy-Hodgsons-sacking-says-Phil-Thompson.html

Tomlinson, A. 'North and South: the Rivalry of the Football League and the Football Association'. In *British Football Social Change: Getting into Europe*, ed. J. Williams and S. Wagg, 25–47. Leicester, London and New York: Leicester University Press, 1991.

Ward, A. 'Bill Shankly and Liverpool'. In *Passing Rhythms: Liverpool FC, the Transformation of Football*, ed. J. Williams, S. Hopkins, and C. Long, 53–76. Oxford and New York: Berg, 2001.

Ward, A., and J. Williams. *Football Nation: Sixty Years of the Beautiful Game*. London: Bloomsbury, 2009.

Williams, J. *Red Men: Liverpool Football Club, the Biography*. Edinburgh: Mainstream Press, 2011.

Williams, J. 'Protect Me from What I Want: Football Fandom, Celebrity Cultures and 'New' Football in England'. *Soccer and Society*, 1(2006): 96–114.

Williams, J. 'Kopites, Scallies and Liverpool Fan Cultures: Tales of Triumph and Disasters'. In *Passing Rhythms: Liverpool FC, the Transformation of Football*, ed. J. Williams, S. Hopkins, and C. Long, 99–127. Oxford and New York: Berg, 2001.

Williams, J. 'Having an Away Day: English Football Spectators and the Hooliganism Debate'. In *British Football Social Change: Getting into Europe*, ed. J. William and S. Wagg, 160–84. Leicester: Leicester University Press, 1999.

Williams, J., and R. Llopis. *Rafa: Rafa Benitez, Anfield and the New Spanish Fury*. Edinburgh: Mainstream Press, 2007.

Williams, J., and S. Hopkins. 'Over Here: "Americanisation" and the New Politics of Football Club Ownership'. *Sport in Society: Cultures, Commerce, Media, Politics* 14, no. 2 (2011): 160–74.

Williams, R. *The Long Revolution*. Harmondsworth: Penguin, 1965.

From community to commodity: the commodification of football in Israel

Amir Ben Porat

Department of Behavioral Sciences, Ben-Gurion University of the Negev, Beer Sheva, Israel

> This paper chronicles the process of football's commodification in Israel. The contours of the football story in Israel were sketched by the dominant society. In 1948, the year the State of Israel was established, football was a political–community project. The local club was controlled by the club's members and by the specific sports federation (there were three state-wide political federations), which was affiliated with a particular political party in Israel. Many of the fans, who were also members of the club, were involved in electing the club's management. This correlation between politics and football was natural at that time because during the first decades of the State, politics was the dominant force in Israeli society. In the late 1980s, when Israel became a capitalist society and the dominant force in society shifted from politics to the economy, football's status changed; clubs of the first and the second leagues were privatized, players were purchased and sold by their exchange value, and many fans turned into customers. Israeli football eventually became commodified.

Commodification as history

In the first volume of *Capital*, Marx says:

> The mysterious character of the commodity-form consists therefore simply in the fact that the commodity reflects the social characteristics of men's labour as objective characteristics of the product of labour themselves[...] through this substitution, the product of labour become commodities...[1]

Commodity, according to Marx, is the elementary form of wealth in capitalist societies.[2] In particular, commodity and its 'historical embodiment', commodification, are paramount concepts in Marx's conception of capitalism as a historical mode of production. Apparently, Marx's sociological perspective of the process of becoming capitalist can be epitomized in the concept of commodification, even if it does carry a hint of determinism: capitalism's ultimate ongoing goal is to turn virtually everything into a commodity – labour power included – because when something is commodified, it is assigned an exchange value and then succumbs to the logic of the market. The road from here to the historical aim of capitalism, that of making profit – the prime motive of the social order – is inevitable.

Essentially, the concept of commodification in the relevant literature refers to the process by which something that does not have an economic value becomes, as noted above, subject to the rules of the market.[3] However, it should be noted that for Marx, commodification is a historical phenomenon. It is embedded in a definite historical context: the process of becoming a capitalist society. Also, according to Marx, commodification is assigned a double function: it is a critical mechanism of transformation from pre-capitalist to capitalist mode, and it is a definitive element of capitalism. Marx insists that it is impossible to comprehend commodification outside a definite historical context.

Therefore, the story of football's commodification occurs in the particular historical 'realm of opportunities' that is subject to the major economic, political and cultural parameters that shape the structure of the relevant society.[4] The foundation of the professional English football league in 1885 was made possible because the major process that shaped English society at that time was the accelerated process of becoming capitalist. The English FA's objections were met by threats from some club owners that they would withdraw from the association. In fact, the realm of opportunity in England at that time offered and encouraged the option of professionalism (commodification), and the FA was compelled to yield.

In order to recount the story of football's commodification at any place and time, one should begin with the relevant society, assuming that football's development is relatively autonomous. Football is constrained by the social system it exists within, but it is also granted a certain degree of freedom to create and consolidate itself. Ultimately, because of the domination of capitalism, commodification of football is virtually inevitable. However, although football's process of commodification is basically the same everywhere, certain local characteristics (for example, those of the nation in which it exists) such as cultural or political elements mark the specificity of this process and shape its context. The bottom line is that the specific relationships between the capitalist context and the political and cultural context(s) influence and even determine the present and future of football.

The context – that is, the historical realm of opportunity and its basic parameters – is described and explained in brief following Althusser's concepts of 'instances', 'relative autonomy' and 'determination/domination'.[5] Althusser argues that every social formation consists of three prime instances: political, economical and ideological (Althusser adds a fourth; the scientific instance). The factors that integrate these instances into a social formation in a specific society (a state) are domination and relative autonomy.

Therefore, it is assumed that with regard to the specific historical realm, any instance of the above could exercise 'domination in the structure' over the society in question's other instances. This domination is associated with the relative autonomy of both the dominant instance and the dominated ones. Furthermore, even in a society that is in the process of becoming capitalist, there may be certain reasons for the relative autonomy of politics to become highly effective; thus, politics projects constraints on the economy. It should be noted that Althusser rejects Marx's mono-causal model in which the economy determines the content and form of the superstructure. However, Althusser maintains the priority of the economy by adding the concept of 'in the last instance'; that is, although other instances may be dominant in the social formation, the economic instance remains determinant. Nevertheless, this determination is in effect only rare, and is distanced.[6]

These clusters of concepts suggest that although commodification of football is inevitable, its formation may take different avenues. Indeed, the relevant literature that deals with the development of football supports this assumption. The process of football's commodification in various countries is similar to the process of becoming a capitalist society, yet it is also formulated by the specific characteristics of the particular society.[7]

The story of football's commodification in Israel is therefore a derivation of the history of Israeli society. In essence, the story of Israeli football is integrated in the major underlying processes of Israel's becoming a state and a capitalist society, in this order. The following offers a brief description of Israel at the time when it was dominated by the political instance and continues by describing the transformation of Israeli society into a neoliberalist market economy. Football in Israel began as a community project, and was then privatized and turned into a commodity: the name of the game was, and is, capitalism.

Football: a community project

When Israel was established as a state in May 1948, politics became the dominant instance. This was not a new phenomenon. Politics (and ideology embedded in Zionism) was a dominant instance before the establishment of the state. Almost every political institution and organization that existed prior to May 1948 'migrated' to the new state, in which it resumed its previous position. It is worth mentioning that the domination of politics characterizes the period of 'nation building'. Politics' domination of the social formation appears to have been inevitable in almost every society undertaking a process of state/nation building.[8]

The domination of politics in Israel in the 1950s and later (until about the mid-1980s) was carried out by the political regime under the tutelage of the Labour Camp, led by *Mapai* (the Workers of Israel Party) and a few other left-wing (and Zionist) political parties. Most importantly, the Labour Camp established (in 1920) and controlled the Federation of Trade Unions, the Histadrut, which was a multi-functional organization: aside from being the host of almost all the trade unions in Israel (membership in 1948 numbered up to 70% of employees), the Histadrut owned approximately one-fifth of the country's economy, including the largest health organization at that time, as well as primary and high school education systems. It maintained various cultural institutions and was involved in several other areas, including sports.

The priority of politics in Israel at that time was in effect regarding other instances of this society, particularly that of the economy, that is, the political institutions decided the allocation of economic resources. Therefore, the mobilization (import of capital) and distribution of economic resources was determined by political priorities, while, it should be noted, the Labour Camp enjoyed a relative majority in the Knesset (parliament) and the government. As a consequence, the political instance was dominant in the context and determined the degree of freedom of any other instance in Israel at that time. Correlatively, the Labour Camp had a highly effective influence on the evolution of different domains and a direct or indirect (by means of intermediary organisations) decisive influence on sports in the country, football included.

Like most other institutions that were formed prior to the birth of the state, sport also 'migrated' to the new state. From its very beginnings, even before the establishment of the State of Israel, sport was affiliated with politics, and this association continued and developed after statehood. Sports in Israel in the 1950s and onward was organised by three state-wide sports federations, each affiliated with a particular political camp: Hapoel sports federation was affiliated with the Labour Camp by means of the above-mentioned Histadrut;[9] the Maccabi sports federation was affiliated with the political party of the bourgeoisie; and the Beitar sports federation was affiliated with a right-wing political party. At that time, Hapoel was the largest federation according to number of clubs and membership. Its affiliation with the Labour Camp, which was dominant in the state's political institutions (the Knesset and the government), consolidated its power in the country's sports institutions, including the Israel Football Association (IFA). Two other small federations were also present at that time: Alizur, a sports federation affiliated with the Zionist-religious sector in Israel, and ASA (established in 1953), a sports federation composed of university students. Every sports institution in Israel (such as IFA) was based on the above federations: the elected (or nominated) representatives constituted the general assembly and the managements of these institutions. Sport, as noted above, was subject to politics, and football, because of its popularity, was closely supervised by political functionaries.

Every sports federation had affiliated clubs all over the country. Hapoel, Maccabi and Beitar made great efforts to establish their sports clubs in almost every community in Israel, including in Arab towns.[10] The 'hidden' motive was political: relative representation in the management of the country's sports institutions, most importantly the IFA, was based on the number each federation's sports clubs. Moreover, sports clubs were instrumental for the purposes of political propaganda and support.[11] But the point that is most relevant to the subject of this article is that the sports club was enmeshed in the local community. The membership was composed of local people who, besides taking part in its various activities, by the power vested in them as members of the club and more often with the involvement of certain political parties, elected the management of the local club. Although the local club embodied various different sports, football was the most prominent spectator sport at that time, and the majority of the club's resources were channelled to its football team.

A brief portrayal of the local Hapoel club may offer some insight regarding football as a community project. Primarily, Hapoel was an independent organization. Its central management institutions were elected by the representatives (also elected) of the various clubs. Individuals (mainly hired employees) were encouraged to join the local club, pay membership dues, and participate in the various popular sports offered (gymnastics, volleyball, swimming, and so on), and also to cast their vote every few years in the election of the local club's management. According to Hapoel regulations, the elected managements of the clubs became the electorate body of Hapoel governing institutions. These institutions were accountable to the local clubs, who were in turn accountable to their local membership. Hence, even though politics was involved in Hapoel at the local and state levels by means of the political parties mentioned above, and even though Hapoel was affiliated with (but did not belong to) the Histadrut and was supported financially by it, in formal and in practical terms the local club belonged to the Hapoel local community and was endowed with relative autonomy regarding its policy. This was projected on the club's football team.

Football in the 1950s was an amateur sport. The players received no material remuneration. Clubs' management was also based on voluntary participation – the elected directors did not receive any material compensation for their efforts. The IFA regulated the league's games and the policy regarding the players' status. In fact, amateurism was functional to the federations and their local clubs because at that time they had no resources to reward players. Running a football club was not an expensive enterprise; a small proportion of the club's staff (the coach, the maintenance staff) were paid employees. The stadium plot was allotted to the club by the local municipality, which usually also took care of its maintenance. Aside for a limited number of stadiums in the big cities, most of the stadiums were extremely modest. The football pitch was made of sand and surrounded by a few stands. The dressing rooms, if any, were makeshift: more often a kind of storeroom that barely served the needs of the football team.

As said, the players had amateur status. They worked in various jobs as hired employees or they were self-employed. The list of players' occupations at that time indicates that football players came from Israel's working and lower-middle classes.[12] They lived in the same neighbourhood as the teams' fans, in small, mainly rented flats in the cities, towns and villages. Their income was reasonable but not high. They travelled to the football stadium by public transport. Financial payments and other material compensation were forbidden by the IFA; the adoration of their fans had to be sufficent payment.

The clubs' fandom was composed of three groups: those who were club members and watched almost every home game and some of the away games, those who were not members but identified with the football team and watched almost every home game, and those who lived in the neighbourhood and occasionally walked to the ground to watch a game. Watching the games in the stadium was the only way to have any involvement, as the radio did not broadcast football games, and television was not available at that time. The first group of fans were motivated by a specific ideology: in Giulianotti's categories of football supporters, they were very close to the 'traditional hot supporters',[13] and they also had political reasons for backing a football team. Almost every game between Beitar and Hapoel football clubs was considered a political struggle by the supporters. The traditional hot supporters were possessive of their football team – after all, they paid their membership dues to the club and elected its management.

The second group was motivated by the love of the game. These people were loyal, but not members of a particular club. They supported the club because it was compatible with their ideological-political inclination, or because members of their family supported the club, or because it was the only club in their neighbourhood. The third group of fans resembled Giulianotti's category of *flaneurs* – supporters who occasionally watched (consumed) a team play but had no special attachment. Although surveys of fans and their motivations were not available at that time, so there is no systematic evidence to rely on, it is possible to suggest that, bearing in mind the domination of politics in Israel in its first decade, politics played a crucial role in football fandom behaviour in the 1950s and later. Fans were at least aware of the connection between 'their' club and Israeli politics: the colour of the club's uniform was carefully selected to suit the club federation's political orientation, such as the colour red being used for Hapoel football teams.

Stages of commodification

Football's process of commodification in Israel occurred in two related domains: that of the players, and that of the clubs and the leagues. The process began in the former domain before it was seen in the latter one and comprised three consecutive stages signalling the formation of 'the power of production'; that is, the player as producer of the game: amateurism, professionalism, and commodification. The period of amateurism covered above is the point of departure. The story of the commodification of football players in Israel begins with the disintegration of amateurism because of certain conditions that offered alternative options for the football players and forced the local clubs' management to change their practices while overlooking IFA and their particular federation's policy.

In October 1953, *Sport La'am* – a sports magazine issued by Hapoel Federation – informed its readers that Joshua Glazer, a highly valued Maccabi Tel Aviv and Israeli national team player, had been offered a contract by the Turkish club Panerbachze for a fair but undisclosed sum.[14] Formally, neither Maccabi nor the IFA had any legal means by which to stop Glazer from signing the contract and playing (for money) for the Turkish club. After pressure was exerted by Maccabi and the weight of public opinion (using Zionist and Maccabist motives), Glazer decided to remain with Maccabi Tel Aviv. The above magazine insinuated that 'Glazer was tempted by his wallet'. In February 1955, a football player from Nicosia (Cyprus) was invited to play for Maccabi Haifa. Although no mention of payment was made, it was obvious that some money had changed hands. Several other non-Israeli players joined first-division football clubs in the late 1950s; all were paid for their participation. In 1961, the IFA issued a decree that prohibited the participation of non-Israelis in the football league, but the deed was done: the Israeli player had realized that amateur status constrained his career. Some sought alternatives outside Israel's borders.

In 1960, Rafi Levi, a prominent player with Maccabi Tel Aviv, travelled to South Africa to become a professional player. Levi defended his move by citing the poor wages that he earned as a garage employee. Several other players travelled to play in South Africa, whose football federation was not a member of FIFA. Some players moved to Australia.

The Israeli economy was improving in the early 1960s, and footballers were frustrated; their non-footballer friends and neighbours were earning more money than them. The rules of amateurism affected their income. Some football stars of the era 'sold' their image to commercial advertisers, for which they were scolded by the IFA. Players opposed and began to confront their clubs, demanding compensation. A Maccabi Netanya player (Netanya was a first-division club) refused to step on the pitch, demanding that the club organize employment for him. Two Maccabi Haifa players followed suit and demanded that their club organize employment for them. The newspapers stated that senior players were treated well by their clubs, whether through financial or other compensation, yet the clubs' managements and the Federation's leadership continued to behave as if the rules of amateurism remained intact.

The rumours of football players receiving material rewards from their clubs eventually became fact. In 1965, the IFA conducted an audit of the first-division clubs' books, which revealed that clubs offered financial loans, goods and payments –disguised as compensation for training time and sick leave – to their players. Some clubs also encouraged their fans to establish 'supporter circles' that collected money which was then channelled to the players' pockets. The football authorities and the state political institutions could not remain indifferent, but they encountered a dilemma: how to reconcile the welfare of the players, the position of the clubs, and the practical necessity of amateurism that allowed Israel's participation in international sports?

A radical idea was raised by several football officials in the early 1960s – to turn the first-division leagues (12 clubs) into a semi-professional league, thereby changing the player's status from amateur to club employee. As early as 1961, a representative of Hapoel in the IFA directorate calculated that each first-division club needed 15,000 to 18,000 Lirots (the Israeli currency at that time) just to compensate the first-division club players for the working hours they lost to training in the 10 months of the league's season. Abraham Epstein, a director of Hapoel Tel Aviv FC, concluded that a first-division club needed 42,000 to 60,000 Lirots per year to pay its players a reasonable monthly salary. Overall, concluded Epstein, the first-division league needed two million Lirots per year. This was a fair sum; however, neither the clubs nor the sports federations could find such an amount of money. Only the state would be able to provide these funds, but the state had other priorities. Essentially, the problematic issue of amateurism remained political rather than economic – amateur football run by voluntary organizations (the sports federations and the clubs) was preferable to football run by the state, which struggled to balance the economic situation. This was short-lived, however. Eventually, the political parties affiliated with particular sports federations and state institutions such as the Knesset (parliament) were compelled to demonstrate their interest. Football was not just a domestic issue. Israeli clubs travelled to play in Europe, European and non-European football teams came to play in Israel, and the Israeli national team had become a national symbol and an effective instrument for integration in Israeli society and for the state's international relations.[15]

Football was the most popular cultural-social event in Israel in the 1950s. This game was almost the only event that connected and even integrated the various different groups in Israel: veterans, new immigrants from different countries who did not speak much Hebrew and were estranged to the local-native culture, and Arabs. The league's games offered the peripheries certain opportunities to meet the cosmopolitan centres. The national team became the most important secular icon[16]. Football fans did not care much about the formal status of the players: fans came to the games for the fun. However, the politics that ruled the football institutions could not ignore the signs that amateurism was disintegrating. The name of the game, as noted above, was politics, and politics set the degrees of freedom for football in Israel. Thus, in order to remove certain constraints from football's management – that is, to modify amateurism – the interested party, the players, had to target the political institutions and/or the leadership. But players had very little influence on the latter. Their best and only option was the club, and indeed the players' status began to change at that level, as elaborated below.

As said, football in the 1950s belonged to the local community. It is worth noting that the community's control over a particular club was by no means absolute. The relevant and affiliated political parties were involved in nominating and electing their clubs' management. However, political intervention in the clubs' management was based on the *local* people and the *local* branches of certain political parties. Almost every football club in Israel (Hapoel, Maccabi and Beitar) carried a surname (that of the federation) and a name (that of the locality); for example, Maccabi Haifa, Beitar Jerusalem. The surname was dominant in the 1950s and the 1960s, which meant that although the local club was an independent body (belonged to its members), it was subject to the particular sports federation. This relationship would change in the coming decades.

The second stage: semi-professionalism

In September 1972 Deputy Minister of Education Aharon Yedlin, who also served as the IFA chairman at the time, published an article in *Yedioth Hapoel* (Hapoel's sports magazine) on sports and amateurism, stating: 'Amateurism is not ideology... for me the issue is economic... we could not maintain a league with many teams based on high payments... football should finance itself from its own resources, and not by the state...'.[17] The writer's political and public position (Yedlin was a member of Mapai, the dominant party in the government) endowed the article with added significance: amateurism as the leading sports model was devalued by the author. If football could finance itself, it should be allowed to become professional, as in other countries. The deputy minister/IFA chairman was aware of the increasing gap between amateurism and reality, but he refused to eliminate this gap with the state's money. Thus it was not amateurism but the real option of professionalizing the players' status which turned public discussion toward the economy of football.

Indeed, the option of professionalizing the players (while the club remained a public organization) depended on the economic situation. Who would foot the bill?

The chairman of Hapoel, Joseph Inbar, estimated in 1970 that 7,500,000 Israeli Lirot were required for professional players in a league of 16 teams – a substantial amount of money that no sports organization would or could afford at that time. A survey initiated by the Histadrut and Hapoel concerning the latter club's finances concluded that in the early 1970s the first division league clubs covered only 75% of their current expenses through their economic resources (mainly the support of the particular federation), while formally adhering to the amateur model – that is, not remunerating their players.

Inbar also ruled out the option of semi-professionalism – that is, the player working part time and the club supplementing his income – arguing that this model would not eliminate under-the-table payments and the migration of football players abroad. Nevertheless, as noted above, the main deterrent against professionalism in football was no longer solely political-ideological, but was now also economic. In the end, the academic debate indicated the first step in the professionalism and commodification process.

As in other countries where football was the most popular game, in Israel a grass-roots change was initiated by the players. The players in the various clubs complained that they were not receiving the compensation they deserved. They wanted more than occasional material rewards: they demanded that football players be recognized and registered as an occupation *de jure*. In 1968, the footballers established the Players Union, challenging the status that was forced upon them and arguing that the relationships between player and club constituted employee–employer relations. The IFA rejected this definition. The players therefore refused to continue with their amateur status – that is, to participate in league games without payment.

In November 1968, a Beitar Jerusalem FC player refused to participate in his club's games. He demanded a monthly salary of 300 Lirot (a substantial sum at that time), bonuses for the team's victories, and a private car (private cars in Israel at that time were not prevalent). Several months prior to that event, a Shimshon Tel

Aviv FC player demanded 35,000 Lirot from his club to purchase a membership share in a public bus corporation. The club's management offered him only 22,000 Lirot.[18]

The football players increased their pressure on the clubs. The editor-in-chief of *Hadashot Sport* (sports news) magazine informed his readers that the ongoing negotiations between the clubs and the players regarding payment were being openly conducted. In October 1968, Hapoel representatives in the IFA directorate met to discuss the state of amateurism. They informed each other of the growing sums of money involved in an unofficial players' market, where some players had already become contracted players receiving monthly salaries during the league season. The officials of Hapoel, Maccabi, and Beitar realized that the money they channelled to their clubs was being used to remunerate players and came to the conclusion that the amateur code was obsolete and should therefore be abolished, enabling the clubs to pay their players a monthly salary (between 600 and 2000 Lirot). In fact, semi-professionalism was recommended as the leading model. However, one question remained open – that of money. The sports federations and the state supplied some, and the clubs raised some capital. Money for players' wages was indeed scant, but the clubs continued to remunerate at least their favoured players. This was a point of no return. In practice, amateurism was demoted forever.

Although the political institutions set the degrees of freedom for football, the critical arena of the game was the local club. This was because the local club was the core of the three major participants in football: the management, the players, and the fans. It can be suggested that precisely because of the strong association between football and politics, the club was located at the frontier; where politics met the people. Often, players' disgruntlement and the anger of the fans were aimed at the club's management. The management, which – as noted above – consisted of elected-volunteer individuals, was considered responsible by both the players and the fans for the team's successes and failures. In the last instance, the fate of the football team was contingent upon the individual club, regardless of its surname.

Frustrated players voted with their feet. More of them left their clubs and travelled to play as professionals in South Africa and the USA. The clubs' management invented various ways to remunerate their footballers: compensation for training hours, 'gifts' in the form of apartments for players' families, loans to open small businesses, and payments made under the table. They realized that the football economy was becoming the critical issue, and that the policy concerning amateurism was just pretence.

The IFA, apparently supported by the sports federations, was involved in trench warfare, yet was gradually retreating from amateurism. Reluctantly, semi-professionalism was adopted at the club level – players received material rewards for their participation, but football players were not recognized as having an occupation *de jure*. The individual clubs decided on the amount they paid their players. Football institutions such as the IFA and the club directorate were still managed by volunteers: the elected leadership of the above did not receive payment for their efforts. Therefore, it appeared that at the institutional level, the policy as well as the practice reflected that amateurism in football was still intact.

The next decade, the 1970s, was a turning point in the history of the commodification of football in Israel. Subsequent to changes that occurred throughout Israeli society, politics' hold on football began to weaken. The IFA was informed (mainly by the newspapers) that players were being paid for their participation. Many received monthly salaries that exceeded the average market salary in Israel at that time. Some senior players received handsome sums of money in the form of wages or bonuses. It was estimated that in 1975, the first division league clubs paid their players a sum of 4,800,000 lirots. The sources of this money were not disclosed.[19] Facing pressure from below, the IFA determined a new policy: Israeli players who played as professionals outside of Israel could now play in the Israeli league. National-team players received bonuses for their performance in international matches. Most importantly, 'football player' became a registered occupation. Essentially, club–player relations became, albeit not yet legally, employer–employee relations.

The semi-professional type of football that was consolidating in the late 1970s and the early 1980s was a hybrid: politics and economics were interwoven in its management. In fact, players were professionals because football was their main and often only source of income. Players were bought and sold according to their exchange value. At the club level, IFA politics still reigned, but the die was cast. Israeli football never looked back. The future was commodification at the organizational and institutional levels of the game.

The inevitable transformation

The underlying assumption of the story of Israeli football's commodification process is the relative autonomy of the above vis-à-vis the entire social structure – in other words, that the development and changes in Israeli football were subject to the major parameters shaping the whole of Israeli society. Therefore, semi-professionalism was encouraged and enabled by exogenous factors such as changes in the state's economy in the 1960s; most importantly, those that were in effect after the Six Day War (1967). This section, which deals with the most recent stage of commodification, begins with a very brief description of the critical changes in Israeli society that occurred in the late 1980s – the accelerated process of becoming a capitalist society. These changes are responsible for the transformation of Israeli football from community to commodity.

During the second half of the 1980s, Israel faced an economic crisis. The government coalition, which included the two major parties at that time, Likud and Labour, made a major – and, retrospectively, a critical – move toward a policy that enhanced the domination of the market. Within a very short period of time, the public sectors that controlled approximately 40% of Israel's economy collapsed. The most significant matter regarding football was the radical decrease of the Histadrut's finances. The name of the new game in the Israeli economy was privatization of public organizations – those of the Histadrut and those of the State. During the last decade of the previous millennium, a major proportion of the Israeli economy – industry, finance, media, certain natural resources, and more – was owned by private individuals and/or corporations. Considering the known characteristics such as the class system, the concentration of capital, the division of labour and so forth, Israel by definition became a capitalist society.

The change of the dominant instance, hence the accelerating domination of 'market economy', affected football's status. Basically, the sports federations lost their economic power vis-à-vis their clubs; their economic sources were dwindling. The political parties could no longer support them. The government refused to channel any more money to sports by means of the above federations. The Histadrut, which was Hapoel's major financial supporter, was barely able to maintain the level of its finances. Maccabi and Beitar could no longer lean on their political patrons.

Consequently, the individual clubs had to seek economic support in order to survive. Even the big clubs – those with relatively strong fan bases – were struggling to maintain their position in the first division. If the former name of the game was political-economical, the current name was strictly economical.

The football realm of opportunity was shrouded by ambiguity. Although the clubs remained public organizations run by volunteers, albeit politically affiliated and mostly non-professional managers, they had to continue paying their players and signing new contracts. The directors tried a soft move: the position of club chairperson was offered to individuals with business experience, regardless of their political orientation. However, facing a poor economic situation, this was just a temporary solution. Commodification – that is, privatization – was already knocking at the door.

In May 1992, the directors of Maccabi Haifa FC voted in favour of transferring the club to Ya'akov Shahar, a wealthy businessman. In fact, Shahar acquired only the 'managing rights' of the club. Its legal status was that of a non-profit organization and by Israeli law, this type of organization could not be sold. Nevertheless, the transformation of Maccabi Haifa FC was a breakthrough in the history of Israeli football. Commodification had reached the organizational level of the game, signalling that everything had become a commodity: the players, the staff, and the club.[20]

In 1993 Maccabi Haifa's staunch rival, Hapoel Haifa FC, was acquired by businessman Robbie Shapira. In 1994, the management responsibilities of Maccabi Tel Aviv FC were handed to 'Mofeth', a group of businessmen. Not long after, Maccabi's 'management rights' were transferred to Lonny Herzikowitz, who became the club's owner and chairman. In 1995, businessman Eli Lahav acquired Hapoel Be'er Sheva FC. By January 2000, all but two of the premier league (first division) football clubs had been privatized. Although formally the clubs were not the legal property of the assumed owner, he/she had *de facto* absolute authority over the football club's management.

The transference of ownership from public to private hands was not pre-planned. It was imposed on the clubs because of changes in the parameters of Israeli society. Encountering a radical change in the status quo, the IFA, which was still a public organization, feared losing control over the clubs. Its reaction to the changing situation was reasserting regulation. In 1995, the IFA reaffirmed the status of the individual club, stating that a football club is a non-profit organization and therefore cannot be sold. It is worth noting that clubs had virtually no physical assets; the land or the stadium remained the property of the municipality or that of the particular sports federation. Thus, the commodification of football was restricted to club level; that is, the football team alone. Nevertheless, the new directors of the first and second-division football clubs (the professional leagues) had plenty of room for manoeuvre. Aside from selling the club to a third party, the management rights allowed them to behave like owners in every other respect, such as buying and selling players, nominating the coach and the maintenance staff, determining the club's financial policy, and so forth.

The new directors changed the prime orientation of the privatized club: football economics became the leading factor in the club's management. Achievements on the pitch became instrumental to the club's economy: league championships, cups and most importantly, participation in UEFA projects enriched the club's box office. Private money in various forms (such as sponsorships), including that of the owner, became a major factor in clubs' economies. Public money in the form of television payments or the football lottery is still important, but less than before. Since the establishment of the Premier League, the clubs that won the championships and the state cup, and that made it to the UEFA games, have been the four or five clubs with the biggest budgets. Indeed, private money made the difference between winning and losing both symbolic and material rewards on the football pitch.

When business people (or corporations) took over the reins of a football club, their motives were divided. Some believed that football was a business and eventually the game would make a profit. Others were less economically optimistic and defended their move by stating their love of the game.[21] Since the inauguration of the Premier League in 1992, the total financial investment in it has exceeded its total income. Very few clubs generate enough income in a given season (mainly because of participation in UEFA projects) to balance their budget.[22]

During the 2008/2009 football season, private investment in the Premier League reached an all-time high. This is explained by the upgrading of ownership. Three tycoons acquired football clubs: Arkadi Gaydamak bought Beitar Jerusalem FC, Alexander Schneider acquired Maccabi Tel Aviv FC, and Daniel Yammer bought Maccabi Netanya. It is worth noting that this was the first time that non-Israeli (albeit still Jewish) money had been invested in Israeli football.

In spite of the constraints limiting the options of Israeli football club owners, the process of commodification, or the transformation of football from community to commodity, matured during the first decade of the current millennium. Players, staff and clubs are now basically evaluated by their exchange value. Football in Israel is now playing by two sets of rules: those formulated at the inception of modern football, which have been supervised by FIFA since around 1904, and those imposed on the game by the capitalist system.

The ordeal of the football fans

The commodification of Israeli football has had a critical impact on the fans. More precisely, commodification has had a differential impact on the different groups of fans: those who were/are highly committed (the 'hot traditional') and those who were/are less committed (the 'cold traditional'). But in fact, the process of this game's commodification changed the orientation and behaviour of generations of Israelis who had embraced football as a beloved game. To reiterate, the change was not initiated by the fans. The dependency of Israeli football on the major parameters of the entire society also placed certain boundaries on the autonomy of the fans. Primarily, they had to adjust to the changes in the organization and operation of their football club.

The economic orientation that underlay the policies of the new football club owners and the nominated new directors that in effect run clubs was also directed toward the fans. As elsewhere in the world of commercialized football, the 'ideal' image of the fan was that of a customer. However, the Israeli football club owners were aware that football fandom is a unique asset: whatever happens to the owners or to the club, the hot traditional fan's commitment never wavers. Although this type of fan represents just one part of the actual and potential football crowd, it is the most important part, because in the owner's perception, this fan is the 'ultimate customer', who buys the season ticket and the club's merchandise and follows the team to away games. This fan is responsible for the atmosphere in the stadium, which is crucial to the game and to television broadcasts. This fan is also a recruiter: he brings family members or friends to watch the club's games, and they in turn often become loyal fans. Hence, club owners in Israel vacillate between attracting fans and maintaining their loyalty on the one hand, and being reluctant to involve the fans in the club's management on the other hand. The Israeli owner realizes that managing a football club is quite different from managing a supermarket. While the customers of the latter go to the competition if they are dissatisfied with a product, the former stick by their club through thick and thin. Nevertheless, the loyal/committed fan is opinionated about how the club should be managed. Fandom as consumerism is a unique phenomenon and even the less committed fan bears little resemblance to the regular market customer.[23]

During six decades of football in Israel, the fans have experienced changes in the organization of the game and, most importantly, the management of the club, which have had an effect on fans' relationships with their clusb. In historical terms, Israeli football fandom began as a form of membership of a certain community in Hapoel, Maccabi or Beitar, when the sports club was woven into this community. As a member of this local community, he also participated in the operation of the club's management. Events that occurred throughout the years and that were not under his control changed his relationship and attitudes toward his club. These included the increasing power of politics – that is, of the specific political parties to which the certain federation was affiliated with – to the point where the party (or parties) determined the management of the club, the management of the federation, and the composition and policy of the IFA. Membership in a particular club then was beneficial solely for participating in the various sports that were operated by the club, and for reduced-price tickets to home games.

When players began demanding material compensation in the 1960s and onward, the fan was faced with a dilemma. On the one hand, he tended to support the players' demands, probably because he wanted them to remain at the club. On the other hand, he was afraid that the players' demands might be detrimental to the operation of the club and to the team on the pitch. Fortunately, he did not have to dwell on this dilemma. As outlined above, the players and the club reached a certain *modus vivendi* in the form of *de facto* semi-professionalism, which later matured to commodification. No one consulted the fans about it and, aside from a few small groups, the fans did not complain about it.

However, the fan was involved, sometimes integrally, in his club's ventures. For example, he was involved when the club was under threat of relegation, or when a beloved player decided to move to another club. The history of football in Israel also tells the stories of fan revolts and militant demonstrations concerning their clubs, of aggressive encounters between fans of rival clubs, of fan demonstrations against certain IFA policies, and so forth. Ever since the resumption of the football league after the 1948 War, the *local club* was and still is, the fan's major interest: many Israelis keep a 'overseas sweetheart', an admired football club in Europe or South America (Barcelona or Manchester United, for example), but the local club is the real fan's home.

The commodification of Israeli football seems to have incited fans' interest in their club. The club became the focal point of reference and commitment: players are highly mobile between clubs, sometimes even within the same season. Jobs,such as coaching positions, are temporary. Ownership changes hands, but the club is as stable as ever. Israeli fans are cognitively and emotionally invested in the one thing that, while commercialized, has remained loyal to them. The football stadium is still a home for the fans. Relegation affects the players, the staff and the owners, but the clubs do not fold. For the (fortunate) fans whose club participates in UEFA projects (Israeli clubs joined UEFA in the 1990s), the emotional value increases tenfold. The bottom line is that irrespective of anything else, including the national team, the commodification of football turned the local club into the central life interest of Israeli fans.[24]

Conclusion

The process of football's commodification is almost universal – mainly because of the results of the process, which turn the building elements of the game into commodities, thereby dictating its management, its new aims and its relationships with the fans. This was and still is the story of football's commodification in Israel.

The story of football in Israel has three chapters: it began as a community project under the tutelage of national political sports federations. Carried along on the winds of change in the entire society, commodification was forced upon Israeli football, as it had been forced on football elsewhere. When the market economy became the dominant instance in Israel and when privatization became the major mechanism, the individual club could no longer lean on the support of the sports federations or the state and had to initiate its own transformation, which manifested in new owners, new directors, new relationships with the players and staff, and new attitudes toward the fans. Although the position of the individual club has some unique cultural characteristics, in terms of the basic elements of commodification, the picture of Israeli football is a carbon copy of football elsewhere: an Israeli football club could be introduced to one of the European leagues and be completely assimilated after only a few adjustments.

Notes

1. Marx, *Capital*, 164–5.
2. Osborn, *How to Read Marx*, 13
3. Giulianotti, 'Supporters, Followers, Fans and Flaneurs'.
4. Gruneau, *Class, Sport and Social Development*; Hargreaves, *Sport, Power and Culture*.
5. Althusser, *For Marx*.
6. Ricoeur, 'Althusser's Theory of Ideology'.
7. Eg Goldblatt, *The Ball Is Round*.
8. Eg Alvi, 'The State in Post-Colonial Societies; Pakistan and Bangladesh'.
9. In formal terms, Hapoel was not part of the Histadrut, but a separate independent organisation. However, the Histadrut financed Hapoel. See later on in this paper.
10. The Arab community in Israel in the 1950s (those who stayed in the country after the 1948 War) amounted to 150,000 people. This community was subject to a military government (abolished in 1966) that constrained almost every aspect of its life. Nonetheless, this community established football clubs that have played in the Israeli leagues since 1950.
11. Ben Porat, *How did Israel Become Capitalist?*.
12. Ben Porat, *From a Game to Commodity*.
13. Giulianotti, 'Supporters, Followers, Fans and Flaneurs'.
14. Ben Porat, *From a Game to Commodity*, 138.
15. Ben Porat, *How Did Israel Become Capitalist?*.

16. Ben Porat, *Oh, What a Delightful War!* Haifa, 2007.
17. Ben Porat, *From a Game to Commodity,* 155.
18. Ben Porat, *From a Game to Commodity,*157.
19. Ben Porat, *From a Game to Commodity,* 208.
20. The IFA remained a public organization. Politics in the form of the sports federations and even political parties still has a significant influence on the IFA institutions but private club owners currently have a substantial influence on IFA policy.
21. Ben Porat, *The Passion, The Game and Exchange Value.*
22. Ben Porat, *The Passion, The Game and Exchange Value.*
23. However, Giulianotti points to the 'flaneur', which is a non-committed football consumer.
24. Ben Porat, *Oh, What a Delightful War!.*

References

Althusser, L. *For Marx*. London: Verso, 1969.
Alvi, H. 'The State in Post-Colonial Societies; Pakistan and Bangladesh'. *New Left Review* 74 (1974): 59–81.
Ben Porat, A. *From a Game to Commodity: Israeli Football 1948-1999*. Sde-Boker: Ben Gurion University Press, 2002 (in Hebrew).
Ben Porat, A. *Oh, What a Delightful War!* Haifa: Pardes, 2007 (in Hebrew).
Ben Porat, A. *How did Israel Become Capitalist?* Haifa: Pardes, 2010 (in Hebrew).
Ben Porat, A. *The Passion, The Game and Exchange Value* (forthcoming).
Giulianotti, R. 'Supporters, Followers, Fans and Flaneurs'. *Journal of Sport and Social Issues* 26, no. 1 (2002): 23–46.
Goldblatt, D. *The Ball Is Round*. New York: Riverhead Books, 2006.
Gruneau, R. *Class, Sport and Social Development*. Amherst: University of Massachusetts Press, 1983.
Hargreaves, J. *Sport, Power and Culture*. Cambridge: Polity Press, 1985.
Marx, K. *Capital Volume 1*. London: New Left Review, 1976.
Osborne, P. *How to Read Marx*. New York: W.W. Norton & Company, 2005.
Ricoeur, P. 'Althusser's Theory of Ideology'. In *Althusser*, ed. G. Elliot, 44–72. Oxford: Blackwell, 1994.

Index

AC Fiorentina 3
AC Milan 106
AC Parma 3
Academic Sport Association (ASA), Israel 120
administration 3–4, 111
AFC Wimbledon 53
Airdrie 56
Al Thani, Sheikh A. 74
Alavés 74
Alizur 120
Alkmaar Zaanstreek (AZ) 3, 12n
Allianz Arena 42–4
Allt, N. 102, 108
Althusser, L. 118
amateurism 35, 121–5
Andrews, D., and Ritzer, G. 53
Anfield 20, 100–2, 107–13
Annan, K. 33
Arab-Israeli War (1948) 129
Arnaut, J. 5, 83–4
Arsenal FC 57–61, 90, 106; TV channel 61
AS (Associazione Sportiva) Roma 62–3
Asia 55
Associazione Calcio (AC) clubs 3, 106
Athletic de Madrid 3, 67–8, 75
Auge, M. 58 ; and non-place 58
Australia 122
Ayre, I. 111

Bairner, A., and Sugden, J. 34
bankruptcy 3–8, 13n, 36, 39, 73–4
Barcelona FC 3, 12n, 44, 54–6, 61–2, 67–8, 74–5
Barclays Capital 111
Basque country 69
Bates, K. 94
Baudelaire, C. 55
Baudrillard, J. 54
Bavaria 37
Bayer 45
Bayern Munich 37–9, 44
Beckenbauer, F. 47

Beitar Jerusalem FC 124
Beitar sports federation 120–1, 125–9
Belgium 102
Ben Porat, A. 8–9, 117–31
Benitez, R. 106–7
Berlin 33, 36, 42
Bertelsmann 37
Best, G. 55
Bielefeld 36
big five leagues 1, 13n; revenue growth **2**
Billig, M. 73
Blair, Prime Minister A. 33, 108
Blatter, S. 5
Bohemen 60–1
Borussia Dortmund 37–8
Boston Red Sox 112
bourgeoisification 39, 43
branding 4, 23, 26, 37, 104
Brann 61
Braunschwieg 36
break even requirement 6
Britain 5, 10–11, 34–6, 39, 42, 45, 51–9, 66, 74, 83–99, 118; Liverpool FC 100–16, *see also* English clubs
British government 10, 24–6, 83–6, 91, 94; Conservative 102
broadcasting deals 1–5, 12n, 37–9, 46, 51–3, 56, 83, 129
Broughton, M. 111
Brown, A. 91
Brown, G. 86
Brown, R., and Goodman, G. 25
Brussels 102
BSkyB 53
Bundesliga 1, 4, 7, 12n, 60; commodification 33–50; statutes 45
bureaucracy 25
Burnham, A. 86
business ethic 22–6, 76
BV Veendam 3

Camp Nou 56
Canada 34

INDEX

capital accumulation 88–90
Capital (Marx and Engels) 88, 117
capitalism 9–10, 25, 51–3, 62, 85, 89–92, 117–19, 128; production relations 87
Cataluña 69
Catholicism 62
Celtic AGM 94
Celtic FC 54, 56, 58, 62, 94
Celtic Trust 94
Centre for Sociological Research (CIS) 67, 69, 71
CF Barcelona 56
Chelsea 23, 106
civil society 35, 85
Clarke, G. 29
class 34–5, 40–1, 47, 51–2, 55–6, 85–7, 101–2, 108–10, 121
club presidents 73, 77–9, 104
commerce adoption 15–32
commercial rationality 19, 23–5
commercialization language 7, 11, 15–32; findings analysis 23–5; previous findings 17–19; recent findings 19–23; theoretical reflections 25–8
commodification 6–10; Everton supporters 15–32; Germany 33–50; Israel 117–31; Marxism 87–9; Spain's social consequences 66–82
commodity structure 28, 83–5, 88–90, 94; fetishism 88–90, 95
commonsense concept 24–6, 30n
communicative discourse 26
communities 6–8, 14, 19–21, 27–8, 35, 84–95, 111; Germany 33–50; inter-community interaction 51–6; Israel 117–31; sociality 52, 57–61; Spain 67
community asset 83–4, 89–91
community business 51–65; fan action 52–3; hypercommodification 56–9; spectatorship 54–6; virtual sociality 59–61
Community Interest Companies (CICs) 94
Conn, D. 93
Conservative Party (UK) 56
Critcher, C., and Taylor, I. 52
Crosby 110
culture 19, 24–7, 34–6, 40–3, 47, 51–65, 74, 78, 87–8; defiance 39–44, 103; fan subcultures 39–44, 51–4, 59–60; Germany 35, 39–47; Liverpool 100–16
Culture Media and Sport Select Committee 29

Dead Ball 57
debt 1–6, 12–13n, 28–9, 68, 74–5, 80n, 84, 86, 90, 106, 110–12
decision-making process 84, 93–4
Deloitte 15, 27, 92, 112

democratic participation 34, 46, 85–6, 92–4, 102
Dortmund 44–6
double fiction concept 90–1
DSB Bank 3, 12–13n
Dutch Football Association (KNVB) 3

economy 18–28, 37–8, 55, 71, 77, 85–9, 118–19; Germany 38; Israel 8–9, 117–19, 122–7; Spain 68
Edinburgh teams 56–7
Edinburgh United 56
Electoral Reform Society 16
Elstone, R. 22
Emirates 58; Cup 58
The End (Hooton) 102
Engels, F. 88
English football clubs 35, 39, 42, 45, 54, 60–3, 73, 92, 103–4, 113–14; *see also* Everton FC
English national team 46, 104
English Premier League (EPL) 3–7, 12n, 15, 22, 28–9, 53–6, 74–5, 90, 100, 104–5, 118
Epstein, A. 123
Eredivisie league 3
European Court 5, 84
European Football Supporters Award 111
European Independent Review (EIR) 83
European Parliament 6
European Union (EU) 1, 4–5, 80n
Everton FC 7, 15–32, 61, 101; board of directors 16–17; commercial language adoption 15–32; stadium relocation background 16–17

Fan Projects 43
fanzines 56–7, 102–3
FC St. Pauli of Hamburg 8, 41–2
FC United of Manchester 53
Fever Pitch (Hornby) 51
fictitious commodity 89–91, 95
FIFA (Fédération Internationale de Football Association) 5, 122, 128
financial context 1–14, 30, 68–77, 81, 111; revenue growth (big five European leagues) 2
flaneur 55–6, 59, 63, 121
Football Association (FA) 53, 95n, 104, 118
Football and Finances: The Economy of the League of Stars 68
Football Supporters Association (FSA) 103
Football Task Force 85, 91, 95n
Football World Cup 33, 55, 63; 1974 World Cup 38; 1982 World Cup 72; 2006 World Cup 33–4, 46; 2010 World Cup 45, 58
foreign investors 73–5, 79, 100–16
France 12n

Franco, Francisco 69
free market 55
French national team 46
French, P. 86, 93
Fry, B. 94

Gardner, P. 107, 109
Gaudi, A. 56
generational transmission 69
German football 33–50; commercial football axis emergence 35–8; fan resistance 38–9; league model 44–6; national team 33–4, 38, 45–6; symbolic rebellions 39–44
German Football Association (DFB) 35–7, 43, 45
German Football League (DFL) 39, 45–6
Germany 1, 4, 7–8, 60, 113; Empire 36; fans and clubs 33–50; match fixing scandal (1971) 37–8; patriotism 34; Telecom 37
Gill, K. 108
Gillett, G. 100–14
Giulianotti, R. 30n, 51–5, 60–3, 121; and Robertson, R. 63
Glasgow 56, 58, 62
Glazer, J. 122
Glazer, M. 53, 105, 107
global recession 1–4, 21, 53, 111–12
globalization 9, 18, 53, 59–63, 100, 114
glocalization 53, 110
Goodison Park (Liverpool) 7, 15–32
Goodman, G., and Brown, R. 25
Gorgie (Edinburgh) 56
governance 7–8, 11–13, 21–3, 29, 53, 103–4, 112–14, 125; Spanish clubs 71–8; supporters 83–99
Gramsci, A. 7, 30n, 34
grobalization 53
Gruenau, R. 34
Guardian 112

Habermas, J. 7, 15–16, 25–8
Hadashot Sport 125
Hamburg 38, 41, 54, 61
Hapoel Be'er Sheva FC 127
Hapoel Haifa FC 127
Hapoel sports federation 120–9, 130n
Hapoel Tel Aviv FC 123
Hargreaves, J. 34, 52
Heart of Midlothian 56–9
hegemony theory 7, 34–50
Henry, J. 112
Herzikowitz, L. 127
Heysel stadium disaster 100, 102–3, 105
HFC Haarlem 3
Hibs 56
Hicks, T. 100–14
High Court 111

Highbury 58
Hillsborough Stadium disaster 52, 56, 103, 105, 107, 109
Hisadrut (Federation of Trade Unions) 119–20, 124–7, 130n
Hodgson, R. 113
Hognestad, H. 9–10, 51–65
Holland 3
hooliganism 52, 102
Hooton, P. 102
Hornby, N. 51
hybridity concept 47
hyper-commodification 30n, 43, 51–65
hyper-consumers 10, 66–82; personalization 70–1, 79
hyper-spectators 77, 79

identity 9–11, 30n, 40, 51–6, 59, 63, 66–75, 79, 91, 95; Everton FC 17–20, 24–7; Liverpool 100–1
ideology 9, 11, 22, 28, 30n, 34–5, 54, 84, 88–9, 93–5, 121, 124
Inbar, J. 124
Independent European Sports Review (IESR) 5, 83–4
Industrial and Provident Societies (I&PS) 86, 94
information presence 70, 77
internationalization 75
internet 43, 109
ISPR agency (German sports marketing company) 37
Israel 8–9, 117–31; sports organisation 119–20
Israeli Football Association (IFA) 120–9, 131n
Israeli football commodification 117–31; commodification stages 121–4; community project 119–21; football fans ordeal 128–30; history 117–19; semi-professionalism 124–6; transformation 126–8
Israeli government 119, 126
Israeli League 9, 128–9
Israeli national team 122–3, 130
Italy 4, 12n, 35, 42, 54, 60–1; national team 63

Jägermeister 36
Johansson, L. 5
Jones, D. 1

Keegan, K. 38
Keep Everton In Our City protest group 17, 29–30
Keep Flags Scouse (KFS) 108–9
Kennedy, D. 7, 15–32; and Kennedy, P. 1–14, 53, 63

INDEX

Kenwright, B. 16
Kerr, J. 94
Kick-Off (*Anpfiff*) 37
Kirch media 8, 37, 39
Kirkby (Knowsley) 7, 15–32
Klanen (supporter's club, Norway) 60
Klinsmann, J. 33
Knesset (Israeli parliament) 119, 123
Knowsley (Merseyside) 7, 15–32; Borough Council 16
Kop Faithful 110
Kop Holdings 106

La Liga 3, 12n, 29, 68, 75
Labour Camp (Israel) 9, 119–20, 126
Labour Party (UK) 83–6, 91, 94
labour power 89, 117
Lahav, E. 127
Lazio 63
Leeds United FC 4
Leith, A. 57
Leith (Edinburgh) 56
Levante UD 3, 10, 67–73, 77–8
Leverkusen 42, 45
Levi, R. 122
life world concept 7, 15–16, 25–30
Likud (political party, Israel) 126
Limited Liability Sports Companies (SAD) 71–9
Lipovetsky, G. 70
Liverpool 7, 15–32, 59–60; City Council 21
Liverpool Echo 101
Liverpool fan culture 100–16; beginnings 101–3; club's sale 104–6; English football's transformation 103–4; Fenway Sports Group 110–12; history 100–1; post-sale reactions 106–10
Liverpool FC 11, 20, 90; Annual General Meetings 101; collective supporter radicalism 100–16
the Liverpool Way 100–16
Livorno 54
Llopis-Goig, R. 10, 66–82
London 53, 57–8

Maccabi Haifa 122, 127
Maccabi Netanya 122
Maccabi sports federation 120, 122, 125–9
Maccabi Tel Aviv 122, 127
McKenna, J. 106–7, 110, 112–13
McLuhan, M. 54
Malaga 74
Manchester City 23, 62
Manchester United FC 20, 29, 53, 59–63, 90, 105–6, 110
Mapai (Workers of Israel Party) 119

market 86–7, 90, 95, 104, 117–19, 126; economy 18, 22, 126, 130; forces 84–5; realism 27–8, 37, 86
Marx, K. 85–93, 117–18
Marxism 34, 52, 83, 91–3, 102; critical political economy 86–91, 94
Mast, G. 36
media 37, 40–2, 59–63, 70–1, 79, 108–13, 122; news 77
Mercer, W. 56
merchandising 4, 36, 41, 68, 88
Merkel, U. 7, 33–50
Merseyside 103–4, 108–13
Mestalla stadium 68, 78, 80n
middle-class 35, 52, 55, 109, 121
Millerntor Stadium 41
Millwall FC 58
Milton Keynes 53
modernization 56
Mofeth 127
Moores, D. 105–6
moral ownership 86–7, 90–2
Morgan, W. 28
Munich 42, 46
mutual ownership 5, 10, 21–2, 84–6, 85, 91–3

Nazi history 34
New Den 58
New England Sports Ventures (NESV) 111–12
Nice Declaration 5
Nicosia (Cyprus) 122
Northern Ireland 34
Norway 9, 51–2, 59–63
Norwegian FA 59
Norwegian Premier League 61–2
Nuremberg 44

Offenbach 36
Oldenburg, R. 101
Olympia 107
Orth, S. 41
Oslo 60
The Owls Trust 94

Panerbachze 122
Parry, R. 105–7
peñas (fan communities) 67
Persian Gulf 74
Peterborough United 94
Piterman, D. 74, 80n
Platini, M. 4, 6
players' reputations 38–9
Players Union 124
Polanyi, K. 85–93
political economy 1, 8–10, 28–9, 34, 38, 83, 91, 94; Marxism 86–91

INDEX

politics 41, 51, 104, 109, 118; activism 41–3, 52–3, 102; Blairite 108; Israel 117–31; left-wing 42, 54, 119–20
Portsmouth FC 4
The Posh Trust 94
Premiere 39
professionalism 9, 23, 34, 85, 104, 118, 124–6
protests 43, 51–65, 77–8, 102–3, 106–12, 129
pubs 59–61
Purslow, C. 111

Racing de Santander 74, 80n
Rangers 56, 62
Rauball, R. 45
RC Celta Vigo 3
RC Deportivo La Coruña 3
RCD Mallorca 3
Real Madrid 3, 12n, 67–8, 74–5
Real Sociedad 3
Reclaim the Kop (RTK) 108–9
Red Army Faction 40
Reeperbahn 41
Rhone Group 111
Ritzer, G., and Andrews, D. 53
Robertson, R. 53; and Giulianotti, R. 63
Robson, G. 58
Rochdale 53
Roig, P. 78
Rome 62–3
Ronaldo, C. 55
Rosenborg 61
Royal Bank of Scotland (RBS) 106, 110–11
RTL plus 37
Ruhr area 45
Rummenigge, K. 38
Russell, D. 52
Rye, K. 86

Sage, G. 34
St. Pauli of Hamburg 54, 60–1
Salamanca 78
Sat.1 37–9
Scandinavia 9, 59–60
Schalke 36, 39
Schickeria (Ultra organization, Germany) 44
Scotland 54, 92
Scott, E. 101
Scouse 108–9
Serie A league 42
Shahar, Y. 127
Shankly, W. 100–2, 105, 108–10
Shapira, R. 127
Share Liverpool 11, 100, 103, 107, 109–13
shareholders 72–4, 79, 80n, 85, 92, 101, 104, 111
Sheffield Wednesday 94
Shimshon Tel Aviv FC 125

Signal-Iduna Stadium 44
Six Day War (1967) 126
Sky Sports 56
Slovenia 62
Smith, G. 105, 109
Smith, J. 103–4
social relations 25, 75, 83–4, 88–9
Social Romantics 41
socialism 108–10
socialization 69, 101
society 8, 18, 25, 28, 34, 51, 89, 118–19; capitalist 89–90, 117–19, 126; domination 118–19; Germany 35; Israel 117–31; relative autonomy 118; Spain 66–82
socios *see* Spanish football commodification
South Africa 45, 58, 122, 125
South Bermondsey (London) 58
Spain 3, 10, 29, 54, 60; club member 72, 75, 78; commodification 66–82; fandom 71–5; national team 73
Spanish FA 3
Spanish football's commodification 66–82; club governance 71–5; fans and clubs relationships 68–71; reactions 75–8; study context 67–8
Spanish League *see* La Liga
Spion Kop 101–2, 108, 113
Spirit of Shankly (SOS) 11, 100–2, 105–13
sponsorship 1–3, 8, 12–13n, 36–7, 45–6, 58
Sport La'am 122
Sporting Gijón 3
sports federations 9, 119–30
Sports Law 71–4, 80n
Sportschau (sports coverage) 37
Sportspro (sport marketing agency) 104
SSC Napoli 3
Stabæk 61
stadia 8, 34, 38–40, 44–5, 52–8, 67–8, 72, 130; relocation 15–32
Stanley Park 105
State of Autonomic Regions 69
Stock Exchange 104
Südtribüne (Dortmund stadium) 44
Sugden, J., and Bairner, A. 34
Superior Sport Council 72
supporter discourse 25–8
Supporters Direct 5, 10, 13n, 83–99; background 85–6; context 91–3; political economy 86–91; supporters' trusts 91–4, 8406
supporters' trusts movement 84–6, 91–4, 96n; donations 92–3
Susis Showbar 41
Swingewood, A. 35
Syed, A. 74
symbolic ownership 72–5, 78–9

INDEX

systems world concept 7, 15–16, 25–8; dominance 27; steering structures 26

taxonomy 54
Taylor, I. 52, 88, 102; and Critcher, C. 52
Taylor, R. 103, 107, 110
Taylor Report 56–7
terrace culture 43, 52, 61, 101–2, 107
Tesco PLC 16
The Communist Manifesto (Marx and Engels) 88
The Sandon pub 107–8
thick solidarity 54, 61–3
Tischler, S. 85, 95n
Toffeeweb 18
Tottenham Hotspur 104
Touche 92
traditions 23–4, 27, 73–4, 85, 88, 90
transnational networks 9–10, 51–65
Trondheim 61
Turkey 122
Tynecastle Park 5

UFA agency 37
the Ultras 42–4, 54; political agenda 42–3
Union of European Football Associations (UEFA) 10, 29, 42, 61, 83–6, 128–30
Champions League 1–2, 45–6, 61–2, 90, 102, 106

United States of America (USA) 34, 106–7, 112, 125; National Football League 1–2
upper class 35
use values 88–9

Valencia 67, 73
Valencia FC 3, 10, 67–78
Vålerenga 60–1
VG (newspaper, Norway) 62
Volkswagen 45

Wachovia 106
West Derby Road 107
West Ham United FC 4
What is the Feasibility for a Supporters Direct Europe? (UEFA report) 5
Williams, J. 11, 100–16
Wimbledon FC 53
Wolfenbüttel 36
Wolfsburg 45
working-class 35, 40–1, 52, 56, 85, 88, 101–2, 108–10, 121

Yedioth Hapoel (sport's magazine) 124
Yedlin, A. 124
youth development system 45–6

Zionist parties (Israel) 9

Free Access to Routledge Sport and Leisure Journals

Browse free sample copies across 34 sport, leisure and tourism journals:

www.tandf.co.uk/journals/access/sport.pdf

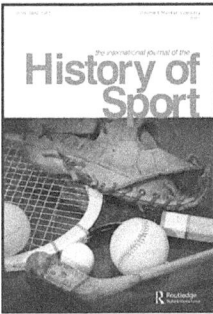   

Do you follow Routledge Sport, Leisure and Tourism on Facebook and Twitter?

By doing so, you can be the first to know when a new issue is released and published online, find out about **exclusive offers** and **special collections** and get **free** access to brand new articles and journal issues.

Like us on Facebook by visiting

www.facebook.com/tandfsport

Follow us on Twitter by visiting

www.twitter.com/tandfsport

For Product Safety Concerns and Information please contact our EU
representative GPSR@taylorandfrancis.com
Taylor & Francis Verlag GmbH, Kaufingerstraße 24, 80331 München, Germany